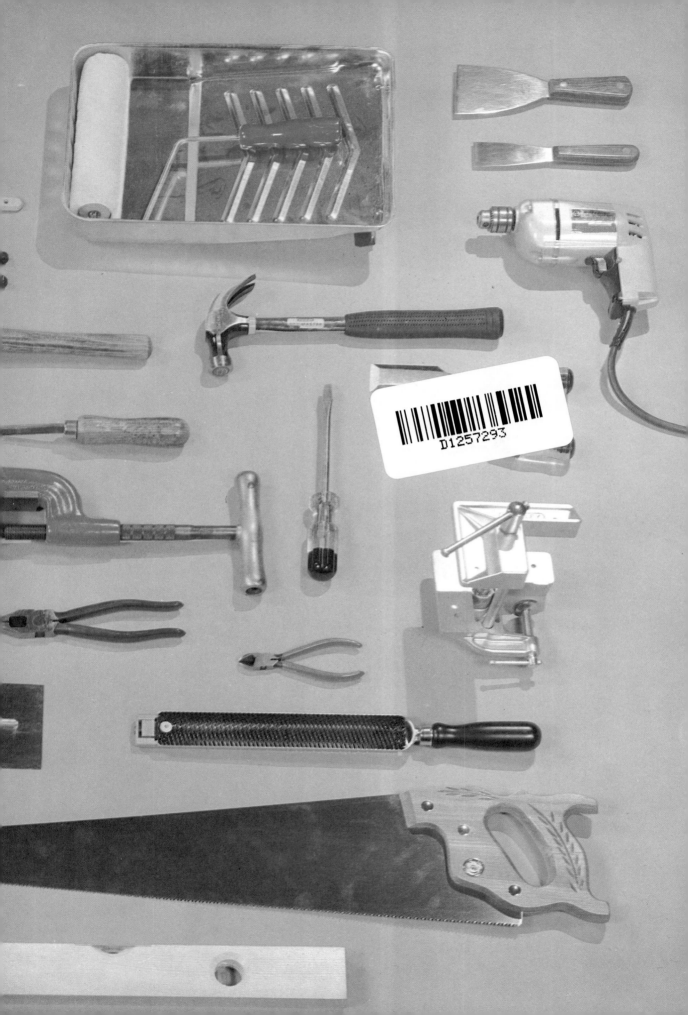

THE
PRACTICAL
HANDYMAN'S
ENCYCLOPEDIA

THE PRACTICAL HANDYMAN'S ENCYCLOPEDIA

THE COMPLETE

ILLUSTRATED

DO IT YOURSELF

LIBRARY FOR HOME & OUTDOORS

VOLUME ONE

GREYSTONE PRESS/NEW YORK · TORONTO · LONDON

YOUR PRACTICAL HANDYMAN'S ENCYCLOPEDIA

OVER 100 expert authors, artists, designers, and photographers and 12 years of painstaking labor were necessary to produce these 4,224 pages of the most massive and comprehensive do-it-yourself encyclopedia ever created for the home handyman.

• All major building projects—including entire homes, cabins, boats, furniture—were actually constructed from the ground up, photographed in step-by-step detail, drawn to exacting dimensions, thoroughly tested by actual use, and proven to save your building dollars before they were accepted for this work.

• Every home repair—including automobile, television, appliance, electrical, heating and plumbing repairs—was performed with tools, parts and materials available to every home craftsman and requiring no special skills or training.

• Each home modernization project—including room and garage additions, new kitchens and bathrooms, attic and basement finishing—was carefully designed to add beauty, practicality and solid financial value to your home.

• Every home maintenance job—including painting, plastering, furniture refinishing, lawn care, masonry work—was expertly planned to save you substantial time and labor yet produce professional results.

• All hobbies and family fun ideas—including photography, gardening, hi-fi, patios and play areas, barbecues, water sports—were created to allow you luxury pleasures at minimum cost.

• In short, in this encyclopedia you will find hundreds of fine projects to bring more fun into your life, to provide more of the good things to make your entire family happy, and to keep you profitably busy for a joyous lifetime!

• The authorities selected to write this encyclopedia have not only acknowledged professional stature in their respective fields, but are best-selling authors whose clear and concise explanations of technical subjects have won them a vast approving audience of Americans who have benefited from their expert advice to enjoy finer homes and a more abundant life. A board of editors with decades of practical experience in do-it-yourself techniques was appointed to organize and edit this practical work—the most useful library of practical how-to-do-it information ever assembled.

THE PUBLISHERS

CONTRIBUTING AUTHORS

JOHN CAPOTOSTO
Home improvement expert. Leading do-it-yourself writer for Mechanix Illustrated, many other national magazines.

T. H. EVERETT
Horticulturist, New York Botanical Garden. World famous lecturer and writer on gardening and landscaping.

JIM MARTENHOFF
Boating columnist, Miami Herald. Winner of Thomas Fleming Award as best boating writer in the U.S.A.

RICHARD DAY
Widely known author of home improvement books covering painting, carpentry,

ROBERT HERTZBERG
Former Editor-In-Chief, Mechanix Illustrated. Electronics authority. Well-known TV and radio author.

PETER GOWLAND
Renowned Hollywood glamour photographer. Author of dozens of best-selling books on all phases of photography.

WALTER IAN FISCHMAN
Articles in Popular Science, Mechanix Illustrated. Author of how-to books.

BILL BAKER
Author of do-it-yourself furniture books. Articles appear in Popular Science, True, Mechanix Illustrated.

SIMON NATHAN
Contributor to U.S. Camera, Popular Photography, Good Photography.

JACK KRAMER
Gardening authority. Articles in House Beautiful, Family Circle, other leading magazines. Author of many best-selling gardening books.

DAVID X. MANNERS
Author of hundreds of articles on do-it-yourself subjects.

ART MARGOLIS
Writer on TV Repairs, Popular Science magazine. Author of television books.

JACKSON HAND
Author of outdoor furniture books. Formerly with Better Homes & Gardens.

LOUIS HOCHMAN
Author of books on refinishing furniture. Contributor to Mechanix Illustrated.

TOM RILEY
Feature writer for Field & Stream, Better Homes & Gardens. Author of top-selling how-to-do-it books.

BILL MOORE
Shopwork Instructor, New York City schools. Furniture building expert.

R. J. DeCHRISTOFORO
Leading author of books on power tools, building, home how-to subjects.

BERNARD GLADSTONE
Home Improvement Editor, New York Times. Well-known how-to-do-it expert.

HAL KELLY
Designer of championship racing boats, family runabouts, cruisers, etc. Writer for major boating magazines.

HI SIBLEY
Long renowned furniture and home repair expert. Writer for Popular Mechanics, Mechanix Illustrated, Popular Science.

HENRY CLARK
How-to artist and designer. Pioneer expert in do-it-yourself diagrams.

RUDOLPH MATERN
Famed architect. His hundreds of home designs are nationally known.

GLEN L. WITT
Naval Architect. Expert designer of all types of family boats.

GRIFF BORGESON
Author and expert on hot rod and automotive subjects.

ARTHUR M. WATKINS
Writer, authority on home heating.

JOSEPH MARSHALL
Author of numerous books, hundreds of articles on stereo and hi-fi subjects.

GROFF CONKLIN
Author of home air conditioning books.

ALFRED MORGAN
Well-known electrical repairs authority.

JOHN L. LACEY
Craftsman and wood carving expert.

We have listed here only a few of the famous authors who have contributed to your Practical Handyman's Encyclopedia.

CONTENTS OF THIS ENCYCLOPEDIA

The following contents lists only major subjects. For a complete,
cross-referenced index of the entire encyclopedia, see last volume.

● CONTENTS

CONTENTS OF VOLUME ONE

Accurate Electrical Repairs

By Robert Hertzberg

EVERY YEAR thousands of electrical appliances are needlessly discarded, either because no repair facilities at all are available in or near the owners' towns or because professional repairs are likely to cost as much as brand-new replacements. Consumers complain a great deal about "built-in obsolescence," but actually many failures are due to ridiculously simple mechanical rather than electrical breakdowns. If you own ordinary hand tools and do the usual maintenance work on a car, a mower or other common machines, you can save many a "defective" appliance from the Monday morning garbage pick-up.

Household appliances fall into two sharply defined groups, "heat" and "motor." Both types contain coils of wire through which electricity passes when the control switches are turned to "on." In the first category are toasters, irons, frying pans, coffee makers, grills, hot plates, etc. In the second are clocks, mixers, can openers, fans, vacuum cleaners, etc.

There is an important difference between the kinds of wire. For heat appliances the wire is deliberately made to impede or resist the passage of the electrical current. Considerable friction develops between the latter and the wire, (as between any two rubbing bodies), and the outward effect is heat. In open appliances having elements exposed to the air, the type, thickness and length of the resist-

Typical heating element of an iron consists of a heavy flat wire on shaped mica form. Wire cannot be repaired; the element must be replaced.

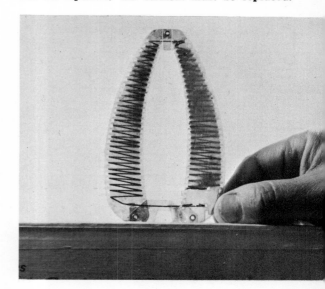

A motor winding consists of many turns of fine copper wire on an iron core or frame. It lasts a very long time because it develops little heat.

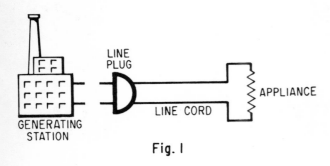

Fig. 1

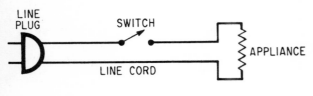

Fig. 2

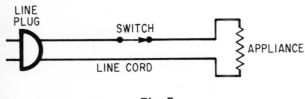

Fig. 3

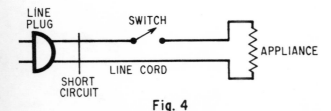

Fig. 4

ance wire, in relation to the line voltage, are chosen so that the coils glow dull red. If they get too hot they simply combine with the oxygen in the air and burn up.

In motors the only function of the wire is to produce magnetism, which in turn is converted into motion. Some heat does develop because of the unavoidable electrical friction of the wire, but this is kept to a minimum through selection of wire type and size.

For any electrical appliance to operate, there must be a complete path or circuit between the source of current and the internal wire and related components. The actual source is a generating station that might be miles away, but for practical purposes it is the nearest wall outlet in a home. A few inexpensive bowl-style reflective heaters do not have control switches, and must be plugged in and unplugged at the outlet when they must be turned on and off. Most other appliances have self-contained switches.

In its basic form a switch consists of a movable metal bar or "pole" and a fixed contact. When the pole is away from the contact the circuit is open and no current can flow; when the pole touches the contact the circuit is closed and current flows. Simple, isn't it? Yet a switch that stays open, or closed, regardless of the position of its handle, is a major cause of appliance "failure."

The basic switch is called "single pole single throw," or more commonly SPST. If the pole can touch either of two contacts it is "single pole double throw," or SPDT, a type widely used for control of a light from either of two positions. Some electric ranges have DPST switches; obviously, this means "double pole single throw." The "dimmer" switch for photo-flood lamps is a DPDT; that is, "double pole double throw," or six connections in all. Some double throw switches have a center "off" position; others are always "on" to one side or the other.

If an open circuit means an appliance is off and a closed circuit means it's on, what's a "short circuit?" This usually de-

Fig. 1: Appliance without on-off switch connects directly to power line through line plug. Fig. 2: Most appliances have a single pole single throw switch in the circuit between it and the line plug. Here switch is open, or "off." Fig. 3: With the switch closed, or "on," circuit is complete and electricity flows through appliance. Fig. 4: A short circuit is an accidental connection across the power line. Fuse blows but does not damage appliance since it cuts off the electricity to it.

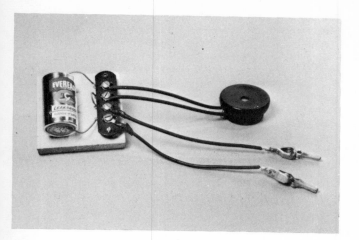

This continuity checker is a simple tester. Phone makes sound when leads are touched to a circuit in which wiring and components are in order.

Is this switch shot, or is it OK? A quick test will give a positive answer. In "on" position the earphone should click; in "off" it should be silent.

scribes an accidental, unwanted connection of extremely low resistance. If a "short" occurs across a house power line, for example, the rush of current through the wires is so great that the fuse or the circuit breaker kicks out almost instantly. If it doesn't, real trouble begins. The wires up to the point of the short circuit start to burn, and if they are exposed and near any combustible material the result is sudden, spreading fire. In many cases, fortunately, the thinnest piece of wire anywhere in the circuit burns up completely before the heavier wires reach incandescence, and the circuit opens.

Simple Circuit Checker

A great deal of productive troubleshooting in electrical circuits can be done with a very simple device called a "continuity checker." As its name implies, its purpose is to determine whether circuits, wires, switches, etc., are unbroken . . . or broken. It consists merely of a single flashlight cell of any size in series with a single or double earphone of any type or kind and a short pair of flexible test leads with bare ends. When you touch the latter together you hear a loud click, and when you separate them you hear another. Tapping the leads together rapidly produces a series of clicks. The sound shows that current from the battery flows through the test leads and the earphone when the leads are short-circuited together.

Suppose you want to determine if a switch is working properly. Simply touch or connect the test leads to its terminals. If you hear a distinct click immediately, you know that the switch is "on" that its

internal contacts are closed. Now snap the handle to the other position, which should be "off," and again tap the leads to the terminals. If you hear nothing, the contacts have opened properly.

Switches that carry the heavy currents of heating appliances tend either to burn permanently open, in which case the continuity checker remains silent whether the handle is on or off; or their contacts weld together, in which case the checker clicks merrily whether the handle is off or on. Sometimes a switch locks on or off because the internal spring that actuates the pole has broken. There is no way of examining most switches without breaking them open and ruining them, so the continuity checker is invaluable.

Similar quick checks can be made on fuses, circuit breakers, most small motors, virtually all types of heat devices, and, even more important, on the flexible line cords that connect all appliances to the power line.

In most homes these cords take a physical beating. They are stepped on, pinched in doors and under furniture, run over by children's toys, etc. Two things can happen to them. More probably, one, both or all three of the individual wires (some cords have 2 wires, others three) break off *inside* the outer covering of insulation, although the latter might remain intact. Less probably, the internal wires rub through the insulation and touch each other, causing a short circuit on the power line that surely blows the fuses.

Internal breaks are a nuisance because they generally are intermittent. The appliance might go on properly, and then die if

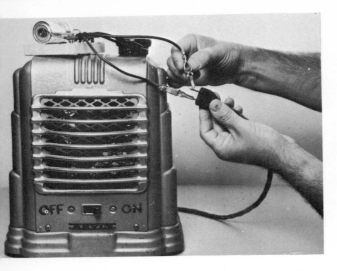

This heater quit one day after working well for twenty years, and was discarded. Retrieved by a boy, it did test open with a continuity checker.

To satisfy boy's curiosity, appliance was disassembled. All fasteners were screws, so only a screwdriver was needed to take appliance apart.

After base plate was removed the entire chassis was pulled out easily. "It's not worth the trouble," said the owner. "It's probably all burned out."

But it wasn't! The heating coil (with white paper behind it to make it photograph better) was completely intact, and all the connections were solid.

Applied to the switch, continuity checker didn't make a sound—line was open! When a new switch was installed, heater came to life.

Before reassembling the heater, the fluff on the blower motor and the surrounding parts, accumulated over the years, was removed with a brush.

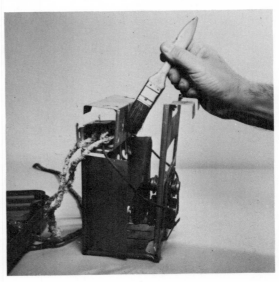

In this table-top coffee heater, exposed element is a spiral of coiled wire set in a molded ceramic form. Current turns off when line is removed.

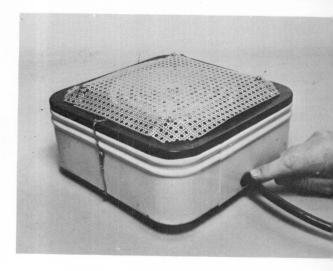

In this type of electric stove the line cord is attached permanently. Point of entry is subject to wear. Should be reinforced to prevent fraying.

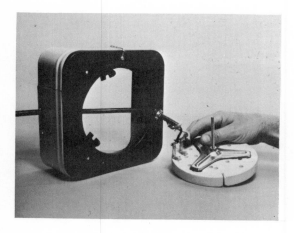

Table-top stoves generally come apart easily for inspection of connections, and also for cleaning and replacement of heating element when broken.

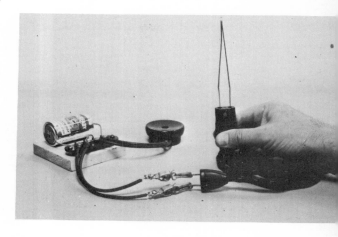

Continuity checker made sounds when connected to line plug and the other end of the cord was shorted, as shown above. It also made sounds when line was left open, shown below. This indicated internal short circuit. Cord was replaced.

the cord is moved slightly. Here again the continuity checker is handy. Disconnect the suspected cord from the appliance, leave the ends well separated, and connect the checker to the prongs of the attachment plug. No sound means no wire-to-wire shorts. Now twist the loose ends together. If the wire is intact there will be one click as the connection is made. Run your hands along the cord, wiggling and twisting it. If it's OK the earphone will remain silent, but if there's a break you'll hear a definite crackling. In fact, with a little experimenting you can locate the break accurately. Usually it doesn't pay to cut the wires open, make new joints, and

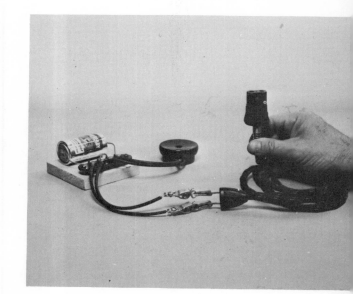

Another reason for replacing cord on tabletop heater was that manufacturer's specially made plug at appliance end was burned and chipped.

Before taking an inoperative appliance apart, be sure that there is juice at wall outlet. A small night light is a handy test light for wall outlets.

At right, also make certain that fuses or circuit breakers are OK. Fuses often become loosened by building vibrations on streets with heavy traffic.

Almost any common tape can be used to repair frayed insulation on a cord: (left to right) masking tape of any color; Scotch tape, preferably the reinforced kind used for strapping packages; adhesive tape from the medicine chest, just the thing for light colored cords; vinyl plastic electrical tape.

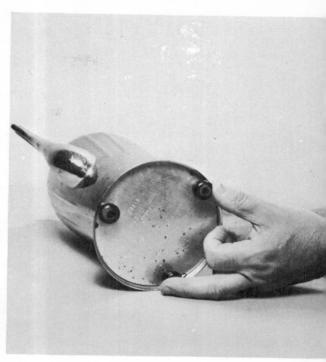

Standard percolator has heating element in base. Since base is sealed to prevent leakage, replacing defective element is difficult; not practical.

There are no screws in sight on bottom of pot except for those attaching leg posts. But, with a slight twisting motion appliance base comes off.

tape them. Replacement cords are cheap and at least give the appliance a fresh start.

Getting Inside

A simple examination of the inside of an ailing appliance often tells you quickly what's wrong with it: a wire broken off at a terminal, a loose screw, a foreign object. Many a toaster is given up for lost when all it needs is removal of encrusted bread from contact points. Many a hair drier gathers dust in the garage because a mere hair pin is jammed in a crucial spot inside.

Taking an appliance apart can be quick, simple and easy, or it can be maddeningly difficult, or it can be just impossible. If the fasteners in sight have slotted heads, go right to work with a screwdriver; if they have smooth heads they are rivets and can only be drilled out or ground off. You may have to face up to it; some appliances are made NOT to be opened. If one goes bad and the fault is not in the external line cord you automatically become a customer for a new model.

The accompanying pictures show how a few typical appliances can be disassembled for inspection, cleaning or repair. •

Heating element has high temperature sealing compound under it. Repair usually requires a factory job. It may be cheaper to buy a new one.

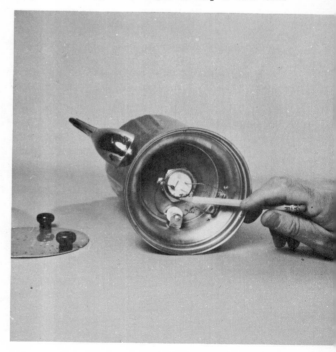

Achieving Efficient Heating

by Richard Day

ANYTHING MECHANICAL—car, corn picker or heating plant—needs periodic checkups to see that it's working right. Most heating experts recommend an annual inspection of the whole heating system. A good time to do this is well before the heating season. Then if any repairs or adjustments are needed, you have time.

Your central heating system consists of five separate systems: fuel burner; furnace or boiler; heat distribution ducts or pipes,

Compactness of furnace design permits utility room or closet installation with sufficient ventilation.

Luxaire Inc. photo

room heating units, such as radiators, registers, convectors, etc.; and controls, such as thermostat, damper, pumps, etc. All must be in good order if you're to get efficient heat.

The house itself may be considered to be an integral part of the heating system, since it governs the rate at which your supplied heat leaves the scene. The subject of tightening up your house is covered elsewhere. Therefore it will not be included here.

Even a small improvement in the efficiency of a heating plant—steam, hydronic (forced hot water), forced air, oil, gas or electric—can bring a substantial saving in fuel bills over a year's time. While no one single thing you do may seem at all big-time, each improvement makes a small difference that adds up to big-time savings.

Heating Plant

An obvious starting point in getting efficient heat is the heating plant. While you are working around the heating plant, clean it inside with a vacuum cleaner. Soot and scale are insulators that can keep combustion heat from getting through to your heater's distribution system. This wastes fuel up the chimney. Remove the access hatch and with the brush attachment of your vacuum clean soot deposits from the inside of the combustion chamber. Boiler scale can be attacked with a stiff-bristle wire brush. The longer the handle the better.

Lubrication—Motor, fan or water pump bearings may need lubrication. Those that aren't self-lubing should have their cups or filling tubes oiled at least twice a year with the lubricant recommended by the manufacturer. Usually this is a good grade 30-weight motor oil. Make sure the furnace switch is turned off when you oil.

Belt adjustment—When you lubricate is the best time to check and adjust tension of the fan belt on a forced-air furnace. Turn off the switch and tighten a loose belt by turning the cradle bolt beneath the blower motor. The belt should have ¾ to 1 inch of play mid-pulley. A belt that's too loose may slip and wear out quickly. At the same time it may not drive the blower as fast as it should. A belt that's too tight wears out belt, motor and fan bearings faster than a properly adjusted belt does.

A belt can cause creaking or squealing noises in the heating system when it reaches the worn out stage. Any belt that is noisy or is cracked or frayed should be replaced.

While you're in this section, vacuum the blower squirrel cage to remove ac-

Owens-Corning Fiberglas Corp. photo

Replace dirty air filters at least twice a year with new ones. Get arrows in the right direction.

cumulated dust.

Clean the filter—Nearly all forced air heating systems use filters to trap dust in the moving air. Most of these are of the replaceable glass fiber type in which the fibers are coated with an oil that reaches out and grabs tiny bits of dust. However, after the fibers have trapped all the dust they can hold, the rest of the dust can go by. An air filter in this condition can only

HOW AN ELECTRONIC AIR CLEANER WORKS

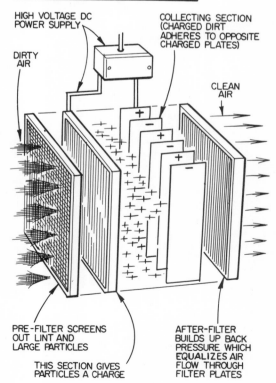

HIGH VOLTAGE DC POWER SUPPLY

COLLECTING SECTION (CHARGED DIRT ADHERES TO OPPOSITE CHARGED PLATES)

DIRTY AIR

CLEAN AIR

PRE-FILTER SCREENS OUT LINT AND LARGE PARTICLES

THIS SECTION GIVES PARTICLES A CHARGE

AFTER-FILTER BUILDS UP BACK PRESSURE WHICH EQUALIZES AIR FLOW THROUGH FILTER PLATES

Blower belt should have ¾″ to 1″ play midway between pulleys. A too-tight belt wears out fast.

Tighten a blower belt with the adjusting screw on motor mounting bracket. Then tighten locknut.

trap larger lint particles. What's more, air movement is restricted, cutting down on the amount of air circulation your heating plant can provide.

Unless you have a means of re-oiling a glass fiber filter, don't try to clean one. Consider it used up and get a new filter element.

You should change filters every month during the heating season in cold climates and twice a year in warmer areas. Install them with the arrows on the frames pointing in the direction of air flow.

Recently a new plastic filter element was introduced. These make use of special plastic fibers that become electrically charged when air passes over them. The static electricity helps to trap dust and even some odors. Since no oil is used on these filters, they can be cleaned with warm, soapy water and put back into service right away. The drawback: plastic filters cost about 10 times what throwaway glass fiber ones do. The cost must be matched against the plastic filter's long life, probably as long as the furnace itself.

Neglected filters cause more complaints of poor heating than any other single factor.

Check breathing—Your furnace or boiler burner must have air, just like you need air to breathe. The biggest danger is that in a tightly sealed home your burner may become oxygen-starved. The possible result is lethal gases released into the house. Whether the heating plant is located in a closet, basement, attic or crawl space, provide some ventilation. Have a screened vent, a door with a grille on it or, in the basement, leave a window open about an inch. The storm sash could be

left off a loose basement window to provide combustion air to a basement burner.

If you smell burning fuel and can't get rid of it by providing ventilation, call your serviceman fast.

Air that gets pushed out by a kitchen or bath vent fan or outside-vented clothes drier must be replaced. The same is true of a fireplace. Keep adequate breathing air for your heating plant by having a window open several inches while these are operating.

One way around the ventilation problem, if you have a forced-air heating system, is to run a return air duct from the outdoors. Then the furnace blower will draw in outside air of its own, presurizing the house slightly. The air drawn in will be run through the furnace to be heated and distributed around the house. The whole house will smell fresher. Drafts will be eliminated. The additional cost in your heating bill won't be great. If you have another type of heating system, you'll have to get your outdoor air by opening a window now and then.

Keep the fireplace damper closed when there's no fire. Otherwise huge amounts of house heat will go up the fireplace chimney.

Pilot light—In spite of what you've heard about turning off the pilot light on a gas heating plant during the off-season, you won't save money by it. Heat from the tiny pilot keeps your furnace dry inside, helping to prevent corrosion.

Oil-fueled firebox—Most old oil burners have fireboxes too large for the capacity of their burners. You can check yours by measuring the area of the firebox in square inches. If the area is more than 75

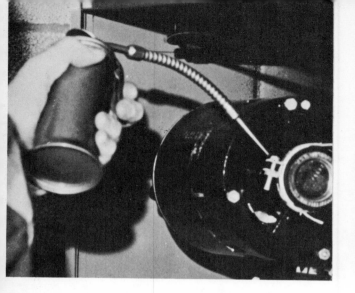

Fill the oil cups on the blower and pump motors with No. 30 oil twice a year unless self-lubricated.

Once a year take apart and clean the fuel filter for a free flow of fuel during the heating season.

square inches for each gallon-per-hour capacity of the burner nozzle, you should have a smaller box. Your present firing box is easily made smaller by installing a liner kit. Johns-Manville makes one called *Cerra Form* out of ceramic-fiber panels. These assemble into a smaller firebox inside your present one.

As part of your annual inspection of an oil burner, have a combustion efficiency check made by your serviceman. The efficiency should read 75 percent or more. Have him check the baffles in the firebox. Are they in place and are there enough of them?

You can inspect the burner nozzle to see that it's the right size for the diameter of your firebox. A 10-inch chamber can accommodate a .50 to .85 gallon-per-hour nozzle; an 11-inch chamber, 1.00 to 1.25 gph; a 12-inch chamber, 1.35 to 1.50 gph; and a 13-inch chamber can take a nozzle with a 1.65 to 1.75 gph capacity. Use the smallest nozzle size that will keep your house heated on the coldest winter day. You can always move to a bigger nozzle.

Flush out the fuel oil strainer to get rid of dirt collected by it. Air leaks into the firebox should be sealed off with calking. Clean out the oil filter. If there isn't one, you'd do well to install one between the fuel tank and burner.

If your oil burner has no draft stabilizer, you are likely losing too much heat up the chimney. Install one.

With any burner, a good chimney is necessary for efficient operation. Your chimney should be clean and free of obstructions. A brick tied to a string and lowered from the top will knock soot accumulations from inside a chimney. After-

During your annual inspection of heating system, drain the expansion tank to replace its air-charge.

Vacuum the air registers to remove accumulated dust and dirt, using special vacuum attachment.

You can find unwanted leaks in firebox of your burner with a candle. The flame follows drafts.

Calk the crack around an oil burner to seal off those efficiency-spoiling air leaks into the firebox.

ward the debris should be removed from the cleanout opening at the bottom of the chimney. Lacking that, you'll have to pull off the vent pipe from your heating unit and remove the soot there.

Some things should be left to the pro's. Don't fool with the pilot flame and safety controls on a gas burner. Never mess with the ignition parts on an oil burner. Leave the oil pump alone too. Your serviceman should do the checking of the safety valve on a steam boiler and the pressure relief valve on a hydronic system. Your family's safety is at stake.

Distribution System

What you can do to the heating distribution system for increased efficiency depends on what type of system it is—air, water, steam or electric. Radiant electric heating components require little maintenance. Electric furnace types, in which air heated by electricity is circulated through ducts, need the same attention any forced-air distribution system needs.

Ducts—Too many ducts and pipes running through unheated spaces aren't insulated. The heat lost into such areas, ups your fuel bill. All supply ducts and pipes should be insulated, except in basements where their heat may be utilized to your advantage. Return runs may not need insulation.

Ducts also should be calked at joints where escaping heat would be wasted. Use calk that sticks tightly to metal and can take heat. Both silicone calks and the new acrylic latex calks will work well.

Drain expansion tank—Every modern hydronic heating system makes use of an expansion tank that's partly filled with water. As the water in a closed system is heated, it expands against a cushion of air. Some of the air is dissolved in water, and the tank becomes waterlogged. The air cushion is depleted. For that reason an expansion tank should be drained every year to restore the air cushion.

Flush your system at the same time. Open the drain valve at the bottom of your boiler and flush until clear water comes out. Then refill to the proper point on the gauge.

Vent radiators—Air collects at the tops of radiators in a hydronic system and should be bled off every year. A radiator that's half filled with air is only half a radiator. Open the vent valve on each unit until all the air escapes. Then close it firmly.

Radiators, convectors, registers—Heating is efficient only when air can freely circulate around and through a radiator or convector. Radiator covers and marble or wood shelves on top of radiators, block air circulation. If you must use a radiator cover be sure the design is correct. Ample space should be provided at the bottom for cold air to enter and at the top for heated air to get out.

Also be sure that draperies, rugs and furniture don't restrict heat from around registers and radiators. Dust or dirt on registers and convectors prevents free movement of heated air. Keep them clean. Most vacuum cleaners have an attachment

With the inlet valve on, to admit fresh water to the system, flush the dirty water from the boiler.

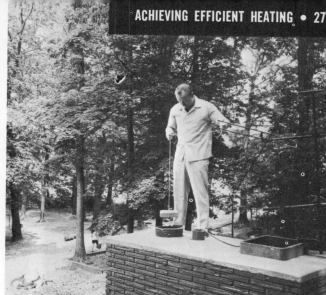

Brick tied to a cord and scuffed up and down the chimney walls knocks off soot that collects there.

for this purpose.

One trick to help a convector pour out more heat is to paint the back of its cover flat black. This will make it transmit heat like a radiator. You can do this easily while you have the cover off. Vacuum the fins too.

Constant Circulation

Whether you have forced-air or hydronic heating, the system should be adjusted to provide the new "constant air/water circulation" deemed best by heating experts. In CAC or CWC, as it's called, the blower or pump should run all the time when the outdoor temperature is below 45 degrees. The purpose is to give you tablespoon quantities of heat continuously, not bucketsful every hour as other adjustments give.

If your system works in the latter method it's the old way: The thermostat calls for heat. The heating system swings into operation and runs perhaps 20 minutes or more. Then it shuts off and stays off, perhaps for another 20 minutes. Your house gets too warm, then too cool. The temperature is only right in between.

With CAC or CWC the heating medium is kept moving through the system continually as long as it's cold outdoors. This keeps your heat evenly distributed from floor to ceiling and maintains constant heat delivery. The cost of running the blower or pump is more than offset by increased heating comfort in both types of systems.

Your blower and pump shouldn't wear out. They're designed for continuous operation. Constant air/water circulation calls for modern adjustable controls. Most heating plants now in use have them.

With CAC and CWC you'll never have cold radiators or cold air blowing from registers. Heating up and cooling off sounds are minimized.

Warm-air systems—To set up a forced-air system for CAC set the blower limit control, if adjustable, to the maximum setting. If the switch has an adjustable differential, set that to the minimum, but not less than 15 degrees. Adjust blower speed by decreasing or increasing the size of the pulley, until the air coming from the furnace plenum is at 165° when the furnace is in continuous operation. The measuring thermometer should be shielded from radiant heat of the firebox. Raise the air temperature by using a smaller motor pulley. Lower it by using a larger motor pulley. Many pulleys are adjustable. You'll probably have to boost the thermostat to keep the furnace burning. Operation of the blower cut-out should be adjusted to the lowest temperature possible without causing discomfort to the occupants. Often this is only about 5 degrees over room temperature.

You can bypass the cut-in and cut-out adjustments by turning your blower manually to *on* and leaving it there.

Return the blower limit control to the furnace manufacturer's recommended setting or that specified by your local code. Usually this is 175 to 200 degrees.

Hydronic systems—To set the hot-water

Flow valves are provided for balancing hydronic heating systems. Screw slot shows angle of valve.

To enjoy continuous circulation comfort, set the blower or pump control to minimum differential.

system for CWC, the pump should be adjusted to run all the time while the heating season is on. Your thermostat will then fire the burner to heat water as needed but to a lower temperature than otherwise, because of the continuous circulation. The one disadvantage is that you cannot heat house water through the boiler. Its water won't be hot enough. You'll need a separate water heater, if you don't already have one.

Heating Balance

Chances are three out of four that your heating system is out of balance. Many are. Unbalance leaves some rooms too warm and others too cool. This is true even of new houses. An unbalanced system wastes heat out of the rooms that are too warm and doesn't provide comfort in the rooms that are too cool.

Whether your system is hydronic or forced-air, balancing it is done in much the same manner. Balancing the system yourself is not complicated, in fact you can probably do as good a job as a professional could. You can spend the necessary time, without call-backs or wasting time waiting for the system to normalize after an adjustment.

Make a balance adjustment during cold weather when the sun is not shining so that the heating system has a good load on it. Balance is achieved by restricting the flow of heat to rooms that need less and providing full flow to rooms that need more. Of course, the room where the thermostat is located will be at proper temperature all the time.

Before making a heat balance adjustment, storm windows should be installed, any filters should be cleaned, expansion tank drained, air bled from radiators and

the blower or water pump should be operating properly. All windows and doors that would normally be closed when maximum comfort is required of the heating system should be closed when balancing it.

Begin balancing by opening all the restrictions in ducts or pipes. In ducts these are in the form of dampers. There is normally a damper in each individual duct run. Sometimes control of heat is at the register. Check these too. Usually each control has a screw slot or other indicator showing the damper's or valve's position. Full flow is when the screw slot is parallel with the flow. In hydronic systems the restrictors are valves located in supply pipe runs where they tee off to a radiator.

Carry an accurate thermometer around to all rooms. Check the temperature of each room about four feet from the floor. Record the readings. Then you'll see which rooms are too warm and which are too cool.

Close the dampers or valves slightly in runs leading to rooms that are too warm. Changing the flow to one room will usually affect the flow to all rooms, so don't over-adjust on the first try. Reducing the flow of heat to warm rooms should provide adequate heat to cool rooms. If they're still too cool, further reduce heat flow to the other rooms or restrict the input of heat to the room containing the thermostat.

Be sure to allow ample time after a change in adjustment for the room to reflect it fully in a temperature change. Forced-air systems react faster to a change than hydronic systems do. In a radiant system make your check the next day.

Mark the damper positions for future reference.

After the system is in balance, recheck the constant air/water flow settings to

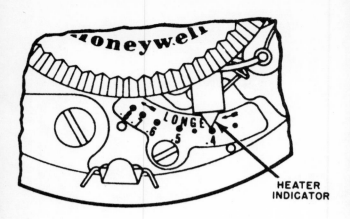

Adjust the heater scale toward smaller numbers to make burner cycle on and off at shorter intervals.

Fiberglass insulation placed on top of the furnace boiler or plenum chamber saves valuable heat.

make sure they're still on the ball.

Your Thermostat

The modern thermostat is a 24-hour servant that automatically controls your heating system for comfort. It is accurate and sensitive enough to control temperatures so you won't even be aware of any change.

If your thermostat is not the modern type that permits the heating plant to cycle on and off in short bursts, for instance, five minutes on, five minutes off, replace it with an up-to-date stat. You'll get more even and comfortable heat.

Don't be a thermostat jiggler. You shouldn't need to move it unless you like different temperatures at different times of the day. Constant running up of the thermostat increases your fuel bills. And when you want heat in a hurry, don't turn the thermostat all the way up. That doesn't help a bit. Think of the thermostat as a light switch not an accelerator pedal. Pushing harder on the light switch won't make the light any brighter. Set your thermostat where you want it and leave it.

You can make temperature adjustments, and even cycle-length adjustments on the inside of a thermostat. You can also sandpaper the contacts on a stat where they're exposed. But that's as far as you should go. For stat adjustments and repairs more than that, call a competent repairman.

There are times when it's advisable to lower a thermostat setting slightly, for instance, when you're airing out the house on a mild day. Set-back will let you avoid heating the out-of-doors. When things are closed up again, return the setting to normal. If you go away for long periods, a slightly lower setting is advisable to economize on heat. Don't cut the heat off en-

tirely, though, because pipes may freeze.

At night, some heating experts recommend a set-back of 6 to 10 degrees with conventional heating systems, 4 degrees with radiant slab systems. There is probably a small saving but the house will be cold while you dress in the morning. Is it worth that?

Residential heating systems are generally designed to keep a room at 70 degrees in the coldest weather expected in a normal heating season. Although a 70-degree indoor climate is comfortable for many people, some want a higher or lower setting. Many specialists recommend a setting of 75 degrees. You should set your thermostat where your family feels most comfortable. Settings above 70 degrees, experts say, will cost you about 3 percent more for every degree.

Several other heating hints may add to the efficiency and comfort of your home's system.

Cool bedroom—if you want a cool bedroom but a warm house, close the bedroom door when the windows are open. Also, turn off the heat to that room or lay a magazine over the register.

Garage door—Keep your garage door closed if the garage is under or attached to the house. Cold air quickly cools off the garage-house walls increasing fuel consumption.

Indoor humidity—Your comfort depends on indoor humidity as well as temperature. If the air is too dry, the house will seem cooler. Install a heavy-duty humidifier on a warm-air furnace or buy a separate humidifier for a hydronically heated house. Many doctors recommend humidifiers. Your family is sure to benefit in having fewer colds when the humidity is kept at desirable levels.

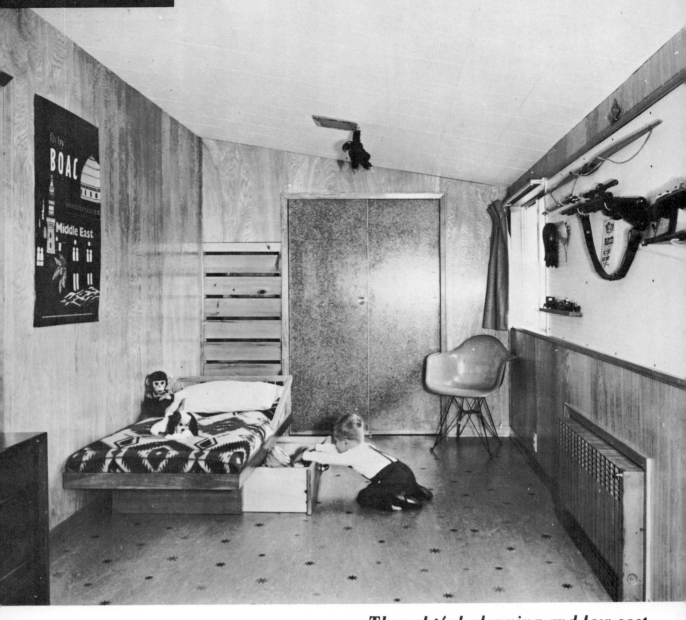

ADDITIONAL BEDROOM

By Harold Kelly

Thoughtful planning and low-cost but good-quality materials helped make this a successful project.

WITH TWO growing boys in the family, we found that we had to add a room to our old house. The structural problems won't be discussed here, except to say that they existed. Every old house and differing local zoning laws present individual problems. As for the finishing, we wanted good-looking and inexpensive materials that could be handled by the average home handy man.

Most of the structural and exterior

Most of framing and exterior work was done by carpenters. Center photo, simple sliding aluminum windows are installed. Right, pump jack proved great time-saver.

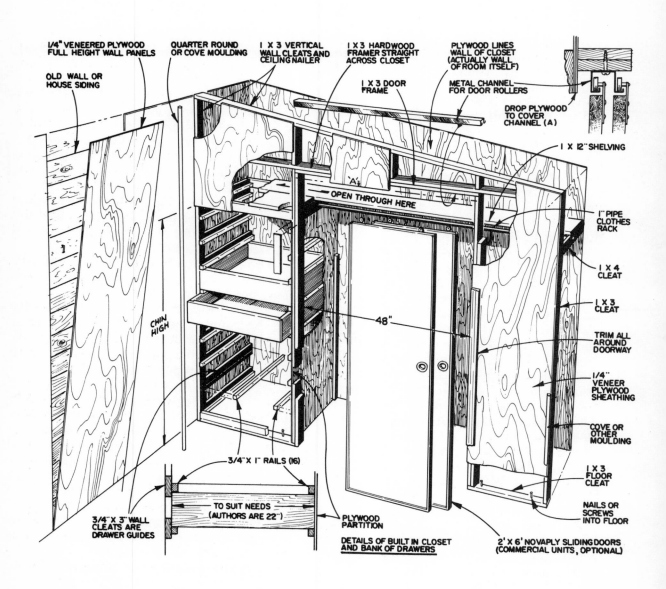

1/4" VENEERED PLYWOOD FULL HEIGHT WALL PANELS

QUARTER ROUND OR COVE MOULDING

1 X 3 VERTICAL WALL CLEATS AND CEILING NAILER

1 X 3 HARDWOOD FRAMER STRAIGHT ACROSS CLOSET

PLYWOOD LINES WALL OF CLOSET (ACTUALLY WALL OF ROOM ITSELF)

OLD WALL OR HOUSE SIDING

1 X 3 DOOR FRAME

METAL CHANNEL FOR DOOR ROLLERS

DROP PLYWOOD TO COVER CHANNEL (A)

1 X 12" SHELVING

'A'

OPEN THROUGH HERE

1" PIPE CLOTHES RACK

1 X 4 CLEAT

1 X 3 CLEAT

CHIN HIGH

48"

TRIM ALL AROUND DOORWAY

1/4" VENEER PLYWOOD SHEATHING

COVE OR OTHER MOULDING

3/4" X 1" RAILS (16)

1 X 3 FLOOR CLEAT

NAILS OR SCREWS INTO FLOOR

3/4" X 3" WALL CLEATS ARE DRAWER GUIDES

TO SUIT NEEDS (AUTHORS ARE 22")

PLYWOOD PARTITION

DETAILS OF BUILT IN CLOSET AND BANK OF DRAWERS

2' X 6' NOVAPLY SLIDING DOORS (COMMERCIAL UNITS, OPTIONAL)

Far window is to become medicine chest in bathroom which can be seen through nearer window: this one will be door into hall.

With all electrical work in, insulation comes next. Be sure to insulate around all windows: they must be well caulked outside.

work was done by professional carpenters who were familiar with the zoning law requirements, and who could get the room under wraps before the rainy season began.

The room addition measured approximately 8x22 feet. Two large aluminum sliding windows were installed, as was a closet at each end of the room. We handled all the electrical work, putting in three wall plugs and two ceiling lights, each on its own switch. Cost of all electrical materials, including the flush lights, was only $35.

All insulating material was put up in about two evenings. For the ceiling we used insulation faced with aluminum on one side, and a low-cost rock lath was nailed to the ceiling beams. All walls were covered with plywood. For this we chose a light-colored wood called Weldwood birch, manufactured by U.S. Plywood; it is tough-wearing and low-cost, and is excellent for almost any type of room and requires a minimum of care.

For wood trim, light Weldwood elm was used. This also is made by U.S. Plywood. Here's a good tip: Before installing plywood and trim, give them about three coats of a good quality, hard-wearing, clear finish such as Satinlac, Fabulon, or brushing lacquer.

Plywood and trim were finished off in the author's shop, brought up to the room, and, there, cut to size and fitted on the spot. The plywood was nailed to the wall studs with 1-in. brads, after the stud locations were carefully marked off.

Next came the floor covering. Linoleum was used.

For the ceiling, acoustical-type square panels were employed to silence the noise that children invariably make. Brand used was Armstrong Cushiontone, which is attractive, inexpensive, and simple to attach. We chose the type that is fastened to the ceiling with an adhesive paste. The ceiling was marked off to locate the panel positions, and the panels requiring it were easily trimmed to size with a matte knife.

The only trick to applying the acoustical panels is to get the paste in four even pats per square. The panels stick easily to the ceiling, and the holding quality of the cement paste is amazing. After the ceiling is in place, you can walk around and push up the squares a bit to make sure you get it nice and even.

Between the windows we attached one sheet of pegboard, painted off-white to match the ceiling. Pegboard is perfect material for a child's room, and my sons use it to display their prize toys, etc. Be sure to space the pegboard at least ½ in. away from the wall so that hangers can be hooked in place.

Where there once was an old bathroom window we installed a large, deep medicine cabinet. Translucent Alsynite was used for sliding doors. A fluorescent bulb inside acts as a night light—a

Ceiling light is in place; notice simple framing for holding light box. Each end of room has a light with its own switch.

Either hand or hammer type of staple gun can be used. However, if you miss with a hammer type, you tear up the insulation.

Low-cost rock lath is nailed into place with large-headed nails after the insulation has been installed. Note how lath is staggered. This material can be cut easily with a matte knife, making the cut on each side and right through the paper backing. After cuts are made it is simple to snap off the excess.

Plywood wall panels are nailed in place with 1-in. brads. Measure off location of wall studs before attaching the plywood.

Brads are then countersunk with nail set and holes are carefully filled, using a natural colored wood dough to match wood.

To cut out holes for the switch boxes, a Porter Cable "Homemaster" was used; it does job well and in a matter of seconds.

After the plywood was in place, switch covers were put on quickly before kids could have a chance to start exploring.

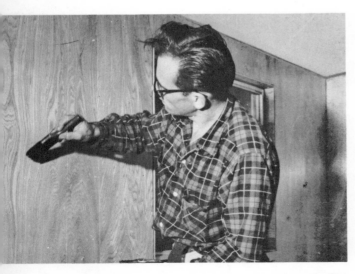

All plywood panels were coated with Satinlac before they were installed; now a touch-up where wood dough covers nails.

Here in author's shop all wood is given three coats of Satinlac before being cut to size; it's quicker and easier this way.

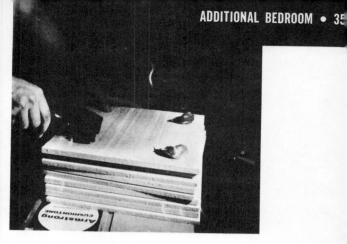

Be sure to use aluminum reflecting material behind radiator; this will reflect the heat out, increase radiator's efficiency.

The trick in putting up Armstrong Cushiontone is to apply the adhesive paste in four neat piles on back of each square.

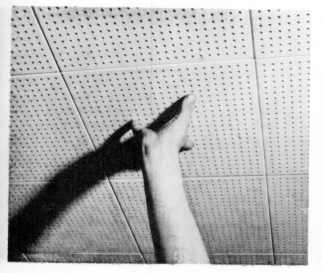

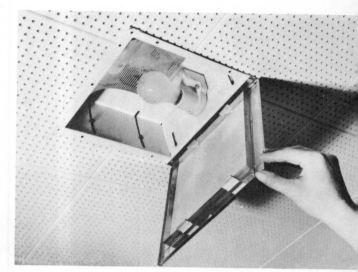

Panels are pushed into place and hold to rock lath quite firmly; when all are in place you should check them for evenness.

Now that ceiling is installed, flush light box is adjusted to fit snugly to ceiling. More photos appear on following pages.

small item, but an important one for any bathroom, we felt. Shelves are glass, and old, heavy plate glass was ideal for these. For complete details on the medicine chest, see the accompanying drawings. Incidentally, an adequate-sized medicine cabinet is a surprisingly expensive item if you go to buy it. It's one item that it definitely pays to make.

At each end of the room, we built a 2-foot deep closet. Both closets are similar in construction, but a row of drawers was built into one of them to hold shirts, other clothing, and for general small item storage.

The sliding closet doors can be purchased in several sizes. Made of Novoply (a water-resistant, laminated wood product for interior furniture and panel use, the doors remain flat and warp-

free through years of use. The doors can easily be cut down in height, and we did so in order to keep them in scale with the rest of the room.

Refer to the drawings and photographs on the next six pages.

The boys have been living in their new room for almost a year now, and the room is standing up very well indeed under the wear and tear they put it to. Everything points to this having been a completely successful project, one well worth the expense and elbow-grease.

Adding room to your house and finishing it properly is like putting money in the bank. You get the principal (and perhaps even more) back if you sell the house, and the interest is in the years of pleasant use you've had from the room. •

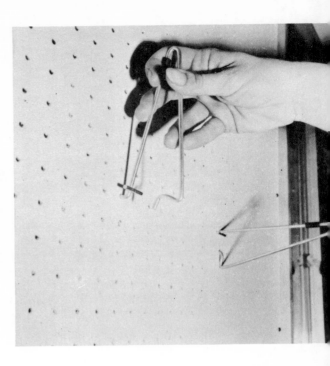

Pegboard is screwed to the wall with roundhead screws. These look unobtrusive and neat, so there's no need to conceal them.

Pegboard hangers come in many styles, shapes, are just slipped in place. Use ½-in. spacer strips in-between board and the wall.

Left, closet at this end of the room is for older boy. Combination dresser, desk and bookcase holds all his other belongings.

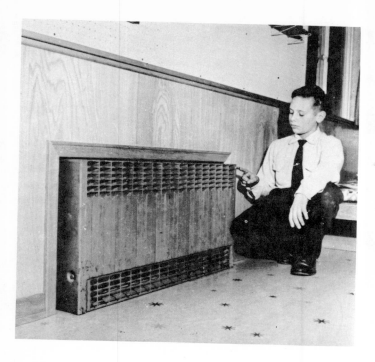

For uniform heat, use same type of heater as in rest of house. This hot-water radiator has air bleeder.

Here's the pegboard in use, with a sampling of some of things the kids will display on it over the years.

See additional photos on following page

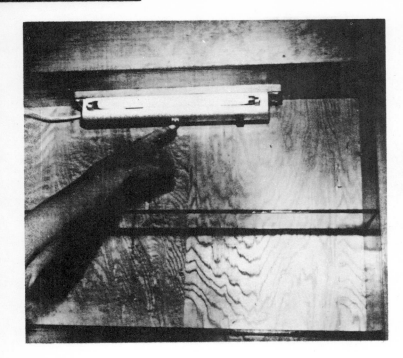

Small fluorescent light in the medicine chest is used for a night light. It's a valuable item; get it in your hardware store.

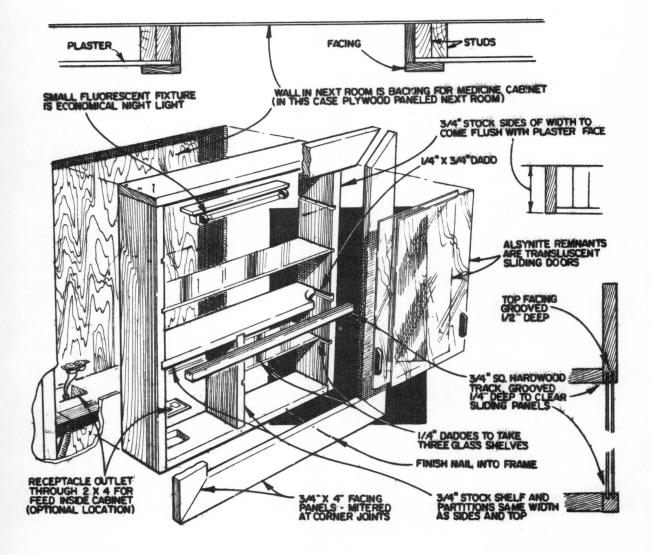

PLASTER

FACING

STUDS

SMALL FLUORESCENT FIXTURE IS ECONOMICAL NIGHT LIGHT

WALL IN NEXT ROOM IS BACKING FOR MEDICINE CABINET (IN THIS CASE PLYWOOD PANELED NEXT ROOM)

3/4" STOCK SIDES OF WIDTH TO COME FLUSH WITH PLASTER FACE

1/4" X 3/4" DADO

ALSYNITE REMNANTS ARE TRANSLUSCENT SLIDING DOORS

TOP FACING GROOVED 1/2" DEEP

3/4" SQ. HARDWOOD TRACK GROOVED 1/4" DEEP TO CLEAR SLIDING PANELS

1/4" DADOES TO TAKE THREE GLASS SHELVES

FINISH NAIL INTO FRAME

RECEPTACLE OUTLET THROUGH 2 X 4 FOR FEED INSIDE CABINET (OPTIONAL LOCATION)

3/4" X 4" FACING PANELS - MITERED AT CORNER JOINTS

3/4" STOCK SHELF AND PARTITIONS SAME WIDTH AS SIDES AND TOP

Sliding doors in medicine cabinet slip right into grooves. Top grooves are deeper than at the bottom for easier installation.

Finished cabinet has modern and attractive appearance in bathroom. Screws on inside of sliding doors hold handle in place. Glass shelves allow the light to illuminate the whole cabinet, and door is translucent to give soft room light throughout night.

Shelves for closet are put in place before the outside trim is nailed on. See drawing on page 31 for closet construction details.

Take your time and be careful when you're nailing the closet sections near ceiling; it's easy to hit and mar ceiling panels.

Note that section used for drawers goes only to eye-level height; space above it is used for the storage of blankets, etc.

After closet walls are in position, trim is nailed on. Trim comes with door unit. Storage space has already been put to use.

Trim is put on with 1-in. brads which are covered with natural wood dough and later touched up with same finish as walls.

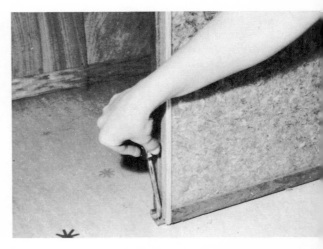

Door guides are fastened down after doors are hung. Note that linoleum floor covering is put down before building closets.

Above, two of the storage drawers are in
place. Check photo and drawing below for
full construction details of the drawers.

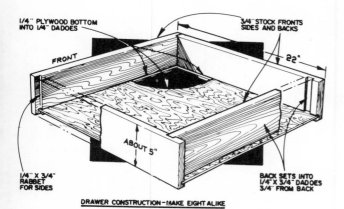

1/4" PLYWOOD BOTTOM
INTO 1/4" DADOES

3/4" STOCK FRONTS
SIDES AND BACKS

FRONT

22"

1/4" X 3/4"
RABBET
FOR SIDES

ABOUT 5"

BACK SETS INTO
1/4" X 3/4" DADOES
3/4" FROM BACK

DRAWER CONSTRUCTION—MAKE EIGHT ALIKE

Right, most of drawers are accessible to youngster. We hope he'll learn to use them.

Below, drapery rod supports
are screwed to window
frames—no window shades!

Right, draw drapes cover the
window, are of same color as
wall, don't "break up" room.

Aerial or Tuner Problem

by Art Margolis

An infallible test for determining which is causing your trouble

SOME discussion of the raster man-ufacturing plant will be of value to us here. The horizontal, high voltage and vertical sections of the TV provide the light source on the phosphor screen just as the lamp in a movie projector provides light on the movie screen.

While the raster is necessary, it is boring to sit and stare at it, unless there is a picture. The picture information in a movie projector comes from the film obstructing the light and producing light spots and dark spots on the screen.

The picture information inserted into the raster comes through the air from the TV studio in the form of electromagnetic pulsing waves. These invisible forces are intercepted by your TV antenna, funneled down your antenna wire and fed into the antenna terminals of your TV set. The TV processes these tiny bits of electronic information and injects it into the electron ray in the picture tube. The ray then produces light spots and dark spots on the TV screen.

Let's examine how a scene at the TV studio can get out into the air.

A TV camera takes a moving picture of the programming at the studio. The photo sensitive plate inside the camera's picture

The first step in isolating confusing front end trouble is to attach a pair of rabbit ears, as shown here.

All of the passengers, picture (P), sync (V, H) and sound (S) are loaded into the carrier wave, as shown.

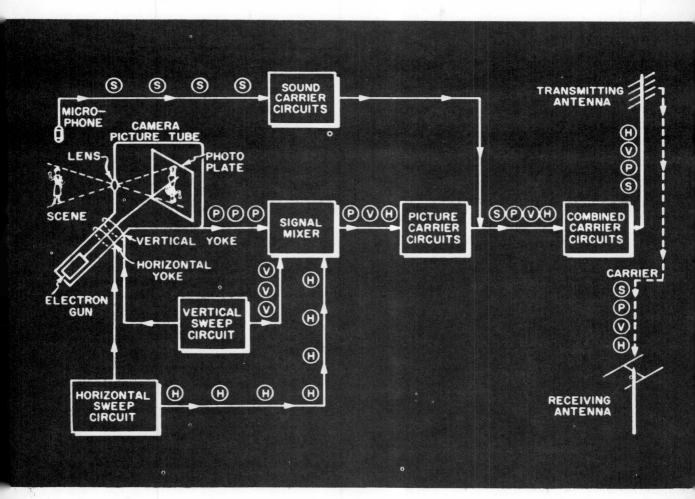

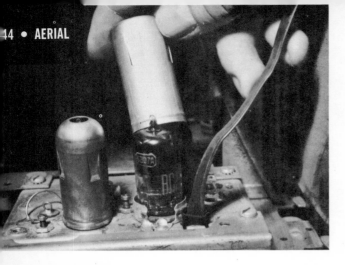

The first circuitry to receive the signal is the tuner. Note the aerial wire going into the tuner unit.

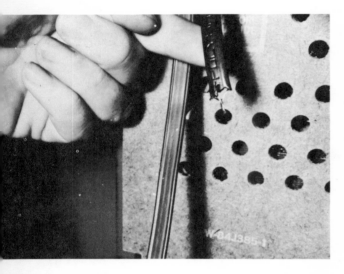

Disconnect your outdoor antenna wire and short leads. Then attach pair of rabbit ears for test.

tube is electrically altered by the light that is focused on it. An electron gun similar to the one in your picture tube, fires a ray through a yoke, scanning the photographic plate with a 15,750 CPS horizontal rate and a 60 cycle vertical rate.

The ray hits either dark spots or light spots according to the scene that is coming through the lens. A wire leads out from the plate. If the ray hits a light spot a small voltage is developed and a small voltage emerges from the wire. If the ray hits a dark spot a heavier voltage is developed.

The signal voltage represents each picture frame in terms of millions of tiny spots ranging from light to dark. The signal voltage at this point is ready to be processed for beaming out on the air waves.

This is where the carrier wave comes in. Each TV station is known by its frequency. Each TV station has a different frequency. As you flip your channel selector you are tuning in a different station each time. The station's designated frequency or carrier is developed by an oscillator set to run at that frequency in the transmitter. It is called the carrier wave because the picture signal is impressed on it for transmission to your set.

The carrier wave is invisible. It exists at the same time as we do but in different dimension. While we have length, breadth and height, a carrier wave has amplitude and frequency, both electromagnetic characteristics. If we graph it, it looks like "A".

In addition to the video we also must have audio. Thus there is a microphone near the camera. It picks up the sound of the scene. The sound is also impressed on the carrier wave, but in slightly different fashion so the sound and picture voltages won't mix. While the picture signal affects

Unmodulated carrier wave is developed at transmitter and runs at assigned frequency, as shown.

The picture signal is impressed on the carrier and modulates the hills and valleys called amplitude.

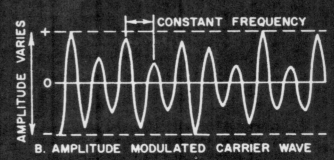

A. UNMODULATED CARRIER WAVE

B. AMPLITUDE MODULATED CARRIER WAVE

the height or amplitude of the carrier the sound affects the frequency. The frequency as we mentioned before is one of the carriers' dimensions and is represented by the distance between the hills and valleys shown on the drawing. Since the audio is varying the frequency, it is said to be frequency modulated (FM).

The video signal, on the other hand, is amplitude modulated (AM) because it affects the other carrier dimensions' amplitude. The fact that the picture and sound are respectively AM and FM helps keep them from interfering with each other.

In addition to transmitting sound and picture, another passenger must be loaded aboard the carrier wave: sync.

In your TV the vertical oscillator runs free and automatically. That's not good enough. For unless your vertical oscillator draws the beam down at precisely the exact time as the camera is doing so at the TV station, your TV picture will roll. So, at the end of every second picture, the studio inserts a vertical locking or sync pulse into the video voltage. This transmitted vertical pulse, upon arrival at your TV is separated from the composite TV signal and sent to the vertical oscillator. At precisely the end of the picture information it is applied, and locks the vertical sweep into step, preventing flopover.

The horizontal sync works in a similar fashion. In order for you to see a picture and not a screenful of horizontal lines, the 525 lines must be drawn and whipped back precisely in time with the picture being scanned at the studio. So, at the end of every line of video information a horizontal sync pulse is placed into the video voltage. This pulse gets into your TV, is separated from the video and is presented to the hori-

zontal oscillator at precisely the end of each line of video. The pulse makes the oscillator fire precisely when it should and the yoke whips the electron beam back for the next line to begin.

This is the way all the passengers, picture, sync and sound, are loaded into the carrier and radiated from the transmitting antenna. Your TV antenna absorbs some of the radiation and funnels it down to your set.

The Infallible "Aerial or Tuner?" Test: The first circuitry the loaded carrier runs into as it leaves your antenna system is the front end or tuner of your TV. Subsequently, antenna troubles and tuner troubles cause similar symptoms of trouble. This can cause you to troubleshoot the antenna system when actually you have tuner trouble or vice versa.

If you have any of the prescribed symptoms there is a test you can perform to steer you correctly.

Disconnect the antenna wire from the antenna terminals and short the leads protruding from the antenna wire together. Sometimes aerial trouble will radiate into the TV even if the aerial is not connected to the TV. With the wires shorted this possibility is reduced.

Attach a substitute indoor antenna onto the TV terminals. Examine the picture you receive with the substitute antenna.

If your trouble ceases at this point and you receive the normal reception you usually get with this substitute antenna, chances are the trouble is in your original, now disconnected, antenna.

However, should the trouble remain even with the substitute aerial, chances are good you have tuner trouble rather than antenna problems.

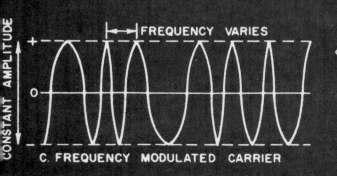

The audio signal in contrast, modulates frequency of the carrier, that is, the distance between the hills.

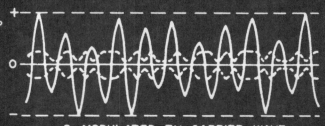

The total transmitted modulated carrier contains AM picture information and FM sound, as shown.

C. FREQUENCY MODULATED CARRIER

D. MODULATED TV CARRIER WAVE

------SOUND—CONSTANT AMPLITUDE, FREQUENCY CHANGES

————PICTURE—CONSTANT FREQUENCY, AMPLITUDE CHANGES

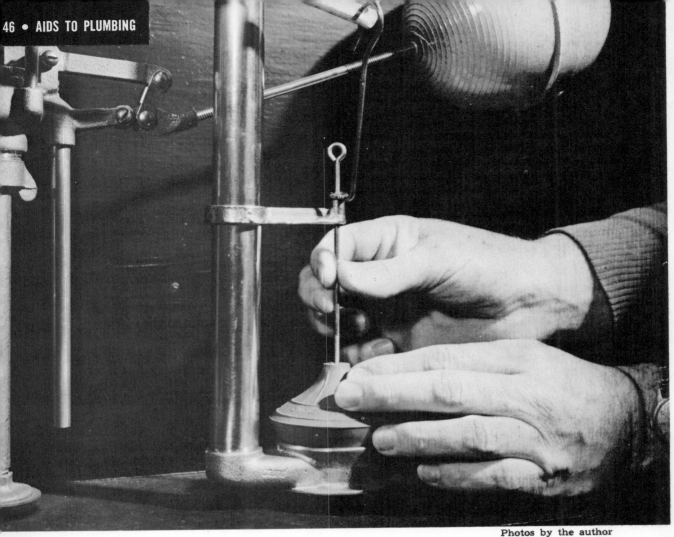

Photos by the author

New lift wires can give new life to your toilet tank. Remove the old ones and fit up the new wires.

Aids To Plumbing

by Richard Day

Your local hardware store can supply a wide variety of handy tools and gadgets.

YOU CAN USE all the help you can get when it comes to doing home plumbing modernization and repairs. The plumbing industry has come to your aid with a number of products. These help you to do an easier and better job. You won't need all of them, but some can benefit you. It depends on what kinds of work you'll be doing.

Fixture Work

The following aids to plumbing are often used in installing and servicing plumbing fixtures, such as sinks, lavatories and tubs:

Slip nut and locknut wrench—One tool does both jobs in installing slip nuts and locknuts to fixtures and fixture drains. Slip nuts are the large usually chrome-plated nuts around a fixture's drain pipe and trap. They draw down on rubber gaskets creating a watertight, gas-tight seal. The nuts are too big to be spanned by an open-end adjustable wrench and they're too big for pliers, even when opened out. While you can use a pipe wrench on a slip nut, you'll likely damage the chrome finish. Instead use a monkey wrench or this specialized tool.

Locknuts are the large threaded rings used to hold drains tightly in the bottom of fixtures. A locknut must be drawn up tight or the fixture may leak water around its drain. Locknuts are not hex nuts. Instead they have toothed projections something like a sprocket. A locknut must be turned with a special tool or by tapping it around with a hammer and chisel. And there's always the danger of missing and ge-bonging the bottom of your fixture. Better to get one of these combination tools for about $2.50. A grooved end on the adjustable jaw hooks over one tooth while you apply turning pressure.

Faucet seat reamer—There are many different seat reamers on the market. The cheaper ones come with only a single cutter. The more costly ones have several cutters for different-sized faucets. A reamer is designed to remove pitting, corrosion and cuts and make a worn household faucet like new again. The seat reamer usually has a T-shaped handle for turning the reamer when you get it in place. To use one follow directions with the tool. Afterwards, the faucet should work like new. Cost of the tool is from 50 cents up, depending on what you buy.

Teflon seal—The wonder material, *teflon,* used as a nonstick coating for pots and pans, is wonderful for stopping water drip. It comes as a white cord-like material. Unaffected by heat or cold, it prevents annoying leaks in shower heads, garden hose fittings, drain and trap slip joints and faucets and valves. It's a big improvement over ordinary valve packing.

To pack a valve or faucet with *Teflon,* remove the old washer or packing and wind a few turns of *Teflon* packing around the stem. Then screw on the bonnet nut or gland follower until the fitting is sealed. That does it.

Teflon's heat-resistant properties make it excellent for use in radiator valves with hot water and steam heating systems. *Teflon* is safe and nontoxic. A ³⁄₃₂ x 24-inch piece costs about 49 cents.

Angle-stop—Is your house equipped with enough valves so that you can work on a fixture without shutting down the entire house water supply? If not, you could benefit from having angle-stop valves on all your fixtures. The best time to install them is when replacing a faucet or fixture.

One end of the angle-stop fits over the water pipe stub-out coming through the

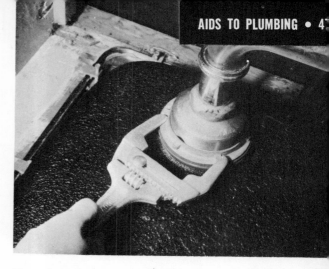

Using a special wrench it's easy to tighten plated sink and lavatory fittings without doing damage.

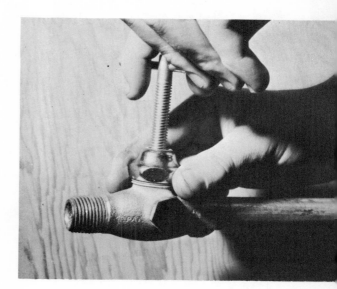

Repairing worn, leaky faucets and valves with a seat reamer is much cheaper than replacing them.

Teflon packing wrapped several times around a valve faucet or stem will keep it from leaking.

An angle-stop helps in connecting fixture supply pipe to house plumbing and provides a shut-off.

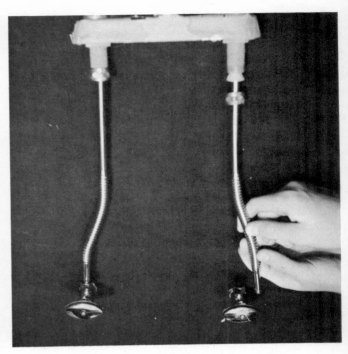

Sample fixture supply hookup shows how flexible copper supply pipes are easily bent to fit needs.

wall behind the fixture. The other end is fitted with a compression nut and collar to take a fixture supply pipe. More about that later.

Angle-stops are useful at toilets, lavatories and sinks where there is easy access below and behind the fixture for emergency shut-off. An angle-stop can cost up to $2.50.

Soft copper fixture supply pipe—Used in combination with an angle-stop, an easily bent fixture supply pipe is a real timesaver for the plumber. These chromed pipes are also useful with straight, non-valved supply fittings. Sometimes called *Speedees*, they are so flexible they bend almost like wet macaroni to reach from the supply fitting to the fixture tailpiece. One end slips into the compression end of the angle-stop or supply fitting. The other end is designed to fit the fixture tailpiece. Order the pipes to suit the fixture. Be sure to get them long enough to reach. They can be cut to length with a saw or tubing cutter. A 12-inch length costs close to $2.

Replacement trap plug—Made of soft rubber, a trap plug saves the day when the threaded plug is damaged or leaking. The rubber end of a replacement plug is inserted into the trap drain opening and the wing nut tightened to expand the plug. A plug costs some 30 cents.

Latex calk—Water-based, it's great stuff for sealing cracks around bathtubs. It can be smoothed with a damp cloth or wet spoon up to about 45 minutes after application. You can even use a wet finger for smoothing. Get it the way you want it. After the stuff sets up—it never hardens—no amount of water will affect it.

Acrylic latex calk also is good for waterproofing under faucets and around drains. It has many other uses around the home too. An 11-ounce cartridge to fit your drop-in calking gun costs $1.50 or less.

Aids to Repairs

As in fixture work there are many products that can help you in making repairs to your plumbing. Here are some of the most useful ones:

Penetrating oil—Penetrating oil is generally useful stuff around the house. As a home plumber, you can apply it to help loosen a corroded pipe joint, fixture screw or slip nut. Squirt some around the stuck threads and wait several minutes for the oil to work. Then apply pressure to unscrew. The oil should have helped. A small can costs around 50 cents

Pipe patch—Usually in a kit, pipe patch parts consist of a metal clamp, rubber gasket and clamping screws. Position the

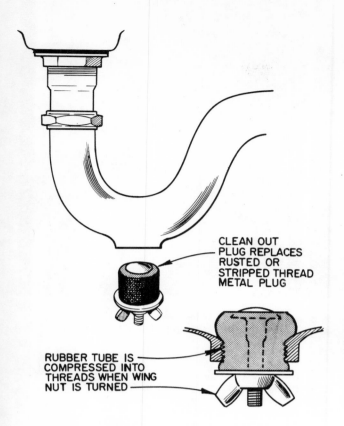

CLEAN OUT PLUG REPLACES RUSTED OR STRIPPED THREAD METAL PLUG

RUBBER TUBE IS COMPRESSED INTO THREADS WHEN WING NUT IS TURNED

Acrylic latex calk around bathtub can be smoothed with a wet spoon handle. It lasts indefinitely.

patch over your leaking pipe and tighten the clamp. Presto, the leak is stopped. One type of patch fits three sizes of pipe: ⅜, ½ and ¾ inch. The approximate cost of this patch is much less than the cost to replace a bad section of pipe.

Pipe repair—More than a patch, this is a rubber-sealed coupling that slips over the remaining ends after a leaking section of pipe has been sawed out. This type must be ordered to fit the diameter of pipe it's used on. Once installed, slip nuts on the ends of the repair sleeve are tightened forcing rubber gaskets to seal around both ends of the sleeve. The gap is effectively bridged. Cost is upwards of $1.

Deep-hub pipe—Replacing a damaged cast iron soil pipe is usually made difficult by immovable pipes on both ends of the damaged one. In such a situation use a deep-hub cast iron pipe. The extra-deep hub lets the new pipe slide in far enough for its spigot end to clear the rim of the next hub. Once it's in, the joints on both ends of the new pipe are sealed. A length of deep-hub costs about twice as much as a regular length of cast iron pipe.

Plastic seal—This single-component product is ideal for small soil pipe jobs. With it you need not bother heating and pouring lead. Plastic seal goes into the joint like putty, sets hard like metal.

To use plastic sealing on a soil pipe joint, spread a thin layer around the inside and shelf of the bell and around the outside rim of the spigot. Join the pipes immediately. Quickly apply a single ring of oakum rammed down well. Spread another thin layer of plastic seal in the joint about ⅛ inch thick and pound in another ring of oakum on top of that. Repeat applying sealer and installing oakum until the joint is filled within ¼ inch of the top of the bell. Tamp and spread plastic seal into the remaining space and smooth it off even with the bell flange.

Plastic seal also can be pressed into cracks in pipes to seal them. A 10-ounce can costs 75 cents.

Self-tapping repair plug—For boilers, water tanks and pipes, the self-tapping repair plug can save a corroded plumbing part. The cost is 20 cents or less. Screw threads on the plug work their way in through the corroded opening. A rubber gasket on the wide-flange head seals off leakage through the hole. Plugs come in various sizes. Sometimes they can be run in without drilling; other times you'll need to drill a pilot hole.

Toilet tank lift wires—When your old toilet tank parts become corroded, scale-encrusted or bent out of shape, they can

Penetrating oil works on plumbing parts too. Use it to help loosen stuck threads wherever found.

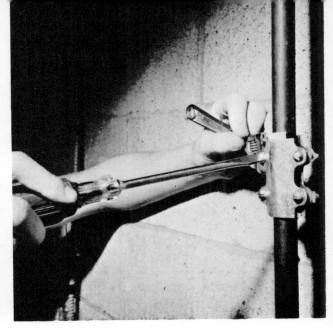

A pipe patch can be a lifesaver. Good idea is to keep one on hand in case you find a leaky pipe.

easily be replaced with new ones. Remove the old lift wires. Insert the longer upper lift wire through the hole in your trip arm and adjust it to the correct length by bending it over. Slide the threaded end of the lower wire through the guide. Screw on the tank ball and you're finished. A pair of new lift wires costs about 75 cents.

Wax flange gasket—The in way to install a floor-mounted toilet bowl—new or old—is with a wax bowl gasket. The better ones cost about 90 cents and are flanges and gaskets in one unit to fit both short-horn and long-horn bowls. Install the gasket at room temperature so it will shape itself to fit. Hold the gasket with the flange in its *down* position and press it firmly over the toilet bowl's horn outlet. Place the bowl in position on the floor. Then push down on the bowl with your body weight to set the gasket firmly into place. Finally fasten the floor bolts or screws.

Toilet bowl caps—These fit over the toilet bowl's floor bolts hiding them. The handiest ones are made of plastic and clip over retainer washers. No putty is needed.

Toilet tank flapper—No it's not something from the Roaring Twenties, but an improvement over the toilet tank flush ball. Flush balls have a tendency to leak. You can buy a flapper conversion for your present tank and install it in a few minutes.

To put one in, remove the old tank ball, guide and lift wires. Slip the flapper down over the overflow pipe and align it above the tank discharge opening. Connect the lift chain to the tank's trip lever and test

out the action. Adjust the chain and height of the flapper, if necessary, to get a proper flush. A new flapper will set you back something like $1.25.

Drain opener—There are many on the market, but one comes highly recommended. Called *Open Zit*, the stuff is for use in sinks, toilets, floor drains, grease traps, etc. It is said to dissolve anything organic that might get in a drain to clog it. Like many of the others, *Open Zit* contains sulfuric acid. Be careful when using it. Follow directions on the package. *Open Zit* in the handy quart size runs close to $3.

De-scaling solution—There are many of these, too. Some are designed for removing lime scale from toilets, sinks, etc. Another type in gallon containers is intended for cleaning scale from water heaters. Instructions vary considerably, so follow the ones for the brand you're using.

Steel Pipe

Get the following to help in working with steel pipe:

Thread cutting oil—If you'll be threading steel pipe, have a can of cutting oil on hand. It helps in making cleaner, sharper threads. Cutting oil not only lubricates the cutters, it cools them. The most useful cutting oils come with handy squirt spout applicators.

Teflon tape—Here's another plumbing use of *Teflon*. *Teflon* tape takes the place of messy pipe dopes. You wind it on the threads of steel, copper, brass or plastic pipe and assemble the joints as usual. The

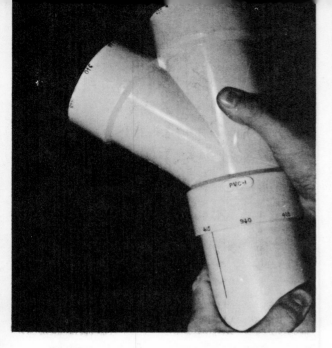

Plastic PVC pipe is excellent for drainage, waste and vent lines. It is easy to handle, cut and join.

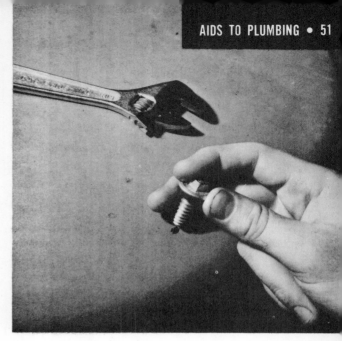

For about 20 cents you can save a leaking tank. Just screw a self-tapping repair plug into the leak.

Teflon withstands extreme pressures and temperatures, will not drip and rustproofs the threads.

Hold the tape with your finger and wrap it around once, stretching tightly so the threads show through the tape. Overlap the starting point about ½ inch and break the tape. Use ¼-inch tape for up to ½-inch pipe; ½-inch tape for ¾- to 1½-inch pipe; and ¾-inch tape for 2- to 4-inch pipe. On 2-inch pipe and larger wrap the joint at least twice.

Copper Pipe

A number of aids can help you in working with copper pipe:

Tubing bender—Made of tightly wound spring steel, a tubing bender is useful in keeping soft copper pipe from collapsing as it is bent. Moreover, you can get smoother, better looking bends. The proper size spring is slipped over the unbent tube. With the spring reinforcing the soft tubing walls, the desired bend is made. You'll need a different size spring for each size pipe. Buy a set if you'll be bending many different sizes of pipe.

Paste solder—The most popular brand of solder in paste form is *Swif Solder*. It comes in cans and tubes. Apply it to the thoroughly cleaned joint, assemble the joint and heat. That's it. The solder contains its own flux and melts to seal the joint. Professional plumbers use lots of paste solder because it's quicker and neater than flux and wire solder. The stuff isn't cheap. A 1¼-ounce tube costs 79 cents.

Pencil-flame torch tip—While a propane torch is almost a must for soldering copper pipe, a pencil-flame tip for your torch can be mighty handy. It concentrates heat to prevent over-heating the fittings being joined. Overheating can make the solder run out of a joint, adjacent ones too. A pencil-flame tip is available as a $1.50 accessory to fit most makes of propane torches.

Leak-stopper—I know of only one brand: *Minit Stop*. It comes in a pressurized can and is especially useful for ensuring that copper soldered joints don't leak. As carefully as you solder them, some are sure to be leakers. And you won't find out which ones until the job is done and the pipes have been filled with water. By then it may be tough to drain the pipes enough to eliminate water and steam which prevent soldering heat from being reached. Leak-stopper makes sure joints are sealed the first time.

To use *Minit Stop* squirt it into the pipe through the long plastic tube that's furnished with the can.

Plastic Pipe

There are three types of solvent-welded plastic pipe: (1) polyvinyl chloride, *PVC*, which is used for DWV piping; (2) chlorinated polyvinyl chloride, *CPVC*, part of the family of rigid PVC materials, which is used for both hot and cold water piping; and (3) acrylomitrile-butadiene-styrene, *ABS*, which is used for DWV and cold water pipes but not hot water piping.

The newest type of toilet bowl flange gasket is wax with a plastic flange for complete sealing.

Be careful using drain-opener. It's also a skin-opener. Pour down drain as directed on the label.

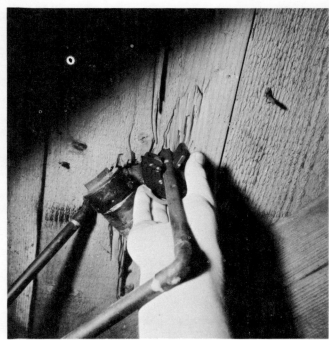

A new kind of tubing cutter is designed to work in close quarters. Its circular body does the job.

Once you use the new Teflon tape, you'll probably never go back to the old methods of pipe joining.

Close-quarter tubing cutter—Something new in a tubing cutter, this one works where there isn't room to swing an ordinary tool. It's made by Chicago Specialty Manufacturing Co., Skokie, Ill., makers of many aids to plumbing. The cutter is placed over the tube in the usual manner. Tighten by turning a curved handle.

The close-quarter cutter has tabs projecting from one side to let you work in impossibly tight spots rotating the cutter with a screwdriver by prying on the tabs.

Other Aids

Automatic air valve—For hot water heating systems, one of these valves can be installed on each radiator to automatically bleed off air in the system. This keeps the radiator from becoming air-locked and saves manual bleeding. Water will not pass through the valve. It lists for 69 cents.

Boiler seal—If you can save a leaky boiler simply by adding a can of boiler seal to the water, it should be well worth risking the price of the can in case it doesn't work. Follow the directions on the can, putting it into the boiler water.

Many aids to plumbing are packaged on cards like this automatic valve for heating systems.

The quick, easy way to tap water out of a pipe is with saddle tee clamped on over a drilled hole.

Saddle tee—Whenever you need to tap water from an existing pipe without going to the trouble of cutting in a tee or wye, you can install a saddle tee. It makes a watertight connection in minutes. There's no pipe cutting, no changing of fittings.

To install a saddle tee, simply peel the backing from the rubber gasket and stick it onto the tee. Position the tee at the proper location and draw the nuts tight. Drill a ¼-inch hole into the pipe. Connect a faucet or pipe into the tee's ½-inch threaded fitting. If a pipe is to be connected, be sure the tee is facing exactly right. Otherwise the pipe may not go where you want it.

A saddle tee doesn't pass as much water as a regular tee or wye fitting. However, if your water pressure is decent, it will pass enough water for most uses. Saddle tees are the easy way of hooking up a washing machine, basement shower, an extra hose outlet, furnace humidifier and the like. Sets cost $1.50 each.

Water hammer arrester — Ordinarily air chambers are provided in plumbing systems to prevent water hammer and damaging pressure build up when a faucet is turned off quickly. If your existing air chambers aren't waterlogged and you're still bothered by banging pipes, you can install a cannister-type air chamber called a water hammer arrester. Screwed into the system at the end of a pipe line, hose bib or pipe drain, the canister provides a needed air cushion.

National Plumbing Code Handbook—Your library no doubt has a copy of this useful book. It tells what the national plumbing code recommends in a plumbing system. Lacking a local plumbing code you may want to follow the national code.

Pipe insulation—Hot or cold water pipes, as well as heating and cooling system piping, may perform better if insulated. There are two types of insulation. One type wraps around the pipe like tape on the handle of a baseball bat. The other type is made in rigid sections. The halves of each section clamp over the pipe like a hot dog bun. Rigid types offer the most protection, but require more fitting than wrap-around types. Use the kind that best suits your piping.

New aids to plumbing are coming out all the time. Visit the plumbing supply dealers in your area and look in mail order catalogs to see what's available.

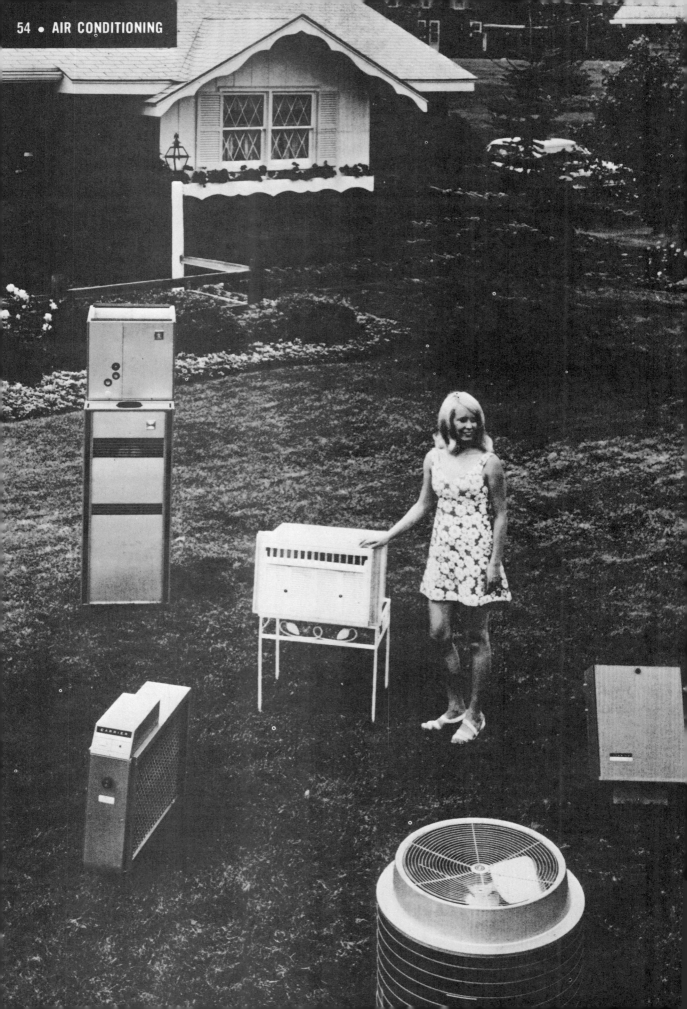

How to Air Condition An Existing House

by Arthur M. Watkins

Salvage as much as possible from your present heating system, check insulation, shade, wiring—then find the most suitable cooling unit.

►*How well is your attic insulated?* Biggest cooling problem is almost always from the huge heat load on the roof that builds up furnace-like temperatures in an attic. Engineers find most attics "inadequately insulated." So your first step should be a thorough attic investigation. As much as six inches of bulk insulation laid over the ceiling or the equivalent in aluminum foil insulation will usually pay for itself. Most houses today have less than three inches of insulation, if any at all. The gable ends of the attic should also be opened up with large ventilating louvers.

►*Are large windows shaded from direct sun rays?* If not, they should be protected by outside shading devices. Remember that ten times as much sun heat invades a house through glass as through an equal area of insulated wall.

►*Are the walls insulated?* Although it may be more costly to insulate the finished walls of an existing house, it will still pay when measured against cooling savings. Walls should get three inches of insulation and this can usually be blown in.

►*Can existing heating ducts be salvaged for cooling?* Because cooling generally calls

Left, basic units for home air conditioning system also include heating and air cleaning equipment. At bottom is outdoor condensing unit supplying refrigerant to cooling coil atop furnace at upper left. Electronic air cleaner is at lower left, central humidifier at lower right, and room air conditioner at center. All products are from Carrier Air Conditioning Co.

Right, individual room cooling units may be as small as this casement window air conditioner by Fedders. It is easily mounted and rarely requires more than removal of a single window pane.

Pre-fabricated ducts are a boon to the home handyman. They include both thermal and acoustical insulation. Lower left, inch-thick duct boards may be formed into varying sizes of rectangular ductwork. Middle, rigid round ducts have inside diameters from 4 to 16 inches. Right, flexible duct is simple to install. Left photo shows 90 degree joint in round duct made by cutting 45 degree angles in two sections and inserting metal elbow. All ductwork shown is from Owens-Corning Fiberglas Corporation.

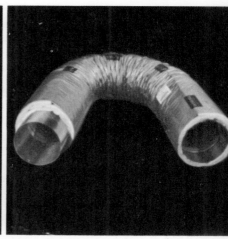

for bigger ducts than those needed just for heating, have a trained dealer measure your existing ducts to see if they are big enough. "Heating ducts almost always work out,". says one top engineer, "but some modifications may be needed." You may need a bigger trunk line in the basement or an extra duct run to a big room facing south. ("The easiest room to heat in winter is often the hardest to cool in summer.")

►*Can you keep the existing warm air outlets?* Proper air diffusion is far more important for cooling than heating. Air conditioning usually calls for a double-deflection type of air outlet—one with both vertical and horizontal louvers that can be opened, closed or slanted so the right amount of air is diffused in the right direction for each room. If your warm air outlets are plain metal grilles with fixed louvers they probably should be replaced.

►*Is the furnace blower big enough for cooling, too?* In about half of the cases, yes.

►*What can you do if your house has hot-water heat or no central heat?* You can put in a chilled-water system, console units or window units. In many houses, however, engineers say that a ductwork system is still your best bet, furring down the ducts in a central hall, for instance, with short ducts branching out to the rooms around. The hot water boiler remains for heating.

►*Is the present wiring adequate?* Most air-conditioning systems need at least a separate 220-volt, 30-ampere circuit wired straight from the main electric board. The board itself should normally have a capacity of at least 60 amperes for the whole house, preferably 100 amperes. The size of the board is usually marked on the cover. Another solution is a gas-operated air conditioner which only needs a relatively small amount of electricity to run its blower.

►*Which is the best cooling system for a particular house?* — There are six principal types, all but one being the same as used in new houses. Here are the advantages and disadvantages of each:

Through-the-wall room unit by Fedders is ideal when blockage of window or view is undesirable.

The Add-On Unit

This was designed especially for adding cooling to an existing forced-air heating system.

The add-on unit is the most inexpensive if you start with a good forced-air heating system. For one thing, you usually save the cost of a cooling fan by using the furnace fan. For another, you use the duct-work already installed. And the remote compressor section can be bought with an air-cooled condenser so no water is needed. Total installation costs start at about $1,200 for a 2-ton size, the more complex the installation the higher the cost.

The Attic Cooler

The horizontal attic cooler is good for existing houses where space is at a premium. Actually the unit not only can go in the attic but can also be suspended from a closet or basement ceiling. If a house has heating ducts the unit can be tied into

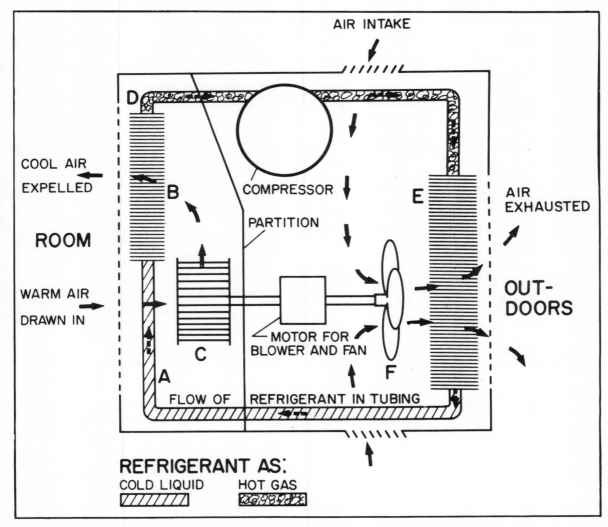

ILLUSTRATION OF THE AIR CONDITIONER IN OPERATION

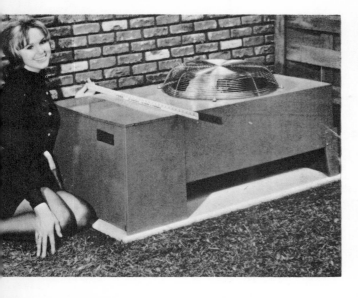

New whole-house cooling systems can be installed as close as 6 inches from house. Unit from York.

Arrangement for a basement installation shows connection between furnace and condensing unit.

Compact unit for apartment and small homes is from Chrysler Air Temp, needs only narrow closet.

Adjustable vanes on this Philco-Ford window air conditioner direct cool air to desired spot in room.

them for distributing cool air. If a house has hot water heat, the unit can be centered in the house and only short supply ducts need be installed to get air to all rooms. Cooling is then independent of the heating.

The Small Duct System

This system gives the advantage in many old houses of using small 3½-inch or four-inch round ducts that can be easily inserted within existing partitions. This eliminates much of the cutting and patching in houses where conventional ductwork would normally mean expensive alterations. Thus the small duct system can be a natural in a house without any heating ducts to start.

The basic cooling equipment used is sim-

Left, room air conditioner from Philco-Ford slides easily into lightweight window housing. At right, electrical and mechanical controls are conveniently serviced without removing chassis from compact cabinet.

New air conditioners do not interfere with room decor. This Westinghouse unit installs flush with window eliminating drape and blind interference. Installation requires only 10 inches taken from window height.

Front panel on Frigidaire unit functions both as a sound baffle and also slides to conceal the controls. Expanding side panels make window installation easy.

Exceptional quiet is achieved in this Westinghouse unit by placing all noise-producing moving parts in an insulated cabinet below the exterior level of the window sill.

Left, air conditioning controls in Lennox system include temperature selector, humidity selector, fan control switch, and the electronic air cleaner lights.

Below, low silhouette and vertical discharge make it much easier to hide this outdoor Lennox condensing installation.

ilar in size and cost to conventional equipment except that the air blower may be somewhat larger to deliver air at higher than normal velocities. This is because the smaller ducts require faster air speeds to handle the same overall cooling load handled by bigger ducts with relatively low air velocities. But the slightly increased fan horsepower used makes very little difference on overall operating costs.

Room Air Conditioners

Room coolers are the easiest way to add air conditioning, especially in doing it piecemeal. But when a whole house is to be air conditioned the total cost can be much higher than the cost of installing a complete central system at one crack. Furthermore, the operating costs of a battery of room coolers will be higher than for a central system because a number of little compressors all running at one time are less efficient than one large compressor. And an odd array of room coolers sticking out of windows will add little to the appearance of any house.

On the plus side, room coolers can save you money if you only want to air condition part of a house and not all the rooms.

Build Your Own Ultrasonic Burglar Alarm

By HERB COHEN

IT'S after midnight. The house is quiet. But trouble is lurking in the shadows. A burglar hiding in the shrubbery approaches a window and starts to open it. He looks carefully for switches, wire strung across the window sill and light beams. Not finding them, he starts to enter. The instant he sticks his hand inside an alarm goes off to alert you of the danger.

Inside a store a shoplifter hides during the day. After the store has closed he leaves his lair and starts for the jewelry counter. As soon as he moves an alarm goes off outside to summon the police.

In your office a prowler intent on cracking the wall safe looks for the usual light beams, switches on the door jamb and wire strung across the room. Not seeing them he heads toward the safe. As he moves towards it an alarm goes off.

What is it that detects the person in each of these situations? It's an invisible spider web of silent sound coming from our ultrasonic burglar alarm system and it fills the room. Our alarm also can be used as a proximity detector or even a fire alarm.

The system consists of a transmitter and a receiver. The transmitter sends out an ultrasonic sound which fills the room. Waves reflected by the walls, ceiling, floor and ob-

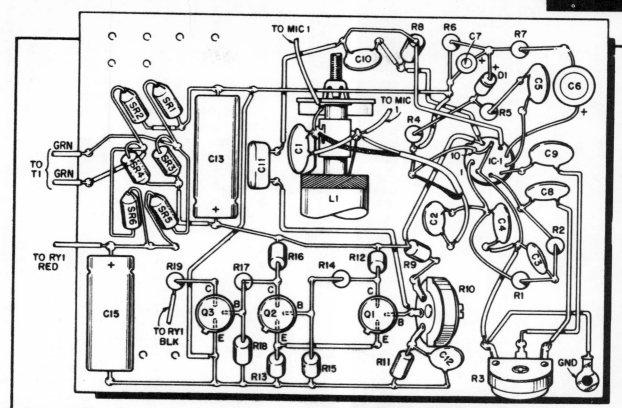

Receiver circuit board is 4 x 5 in. To conserve space, we mounted resistors on end rather than flat. In pictorial we show wiring on top of board; however, as you can see in photo below, wiring in our model is on rear of board.

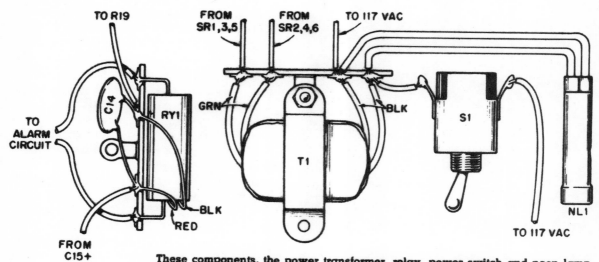

These components, the power transformer, relay, power switch and neon lamp are mounted at the top of the main section of the Minibox as in photo at right.

jects are picked up by the receiver. Any phase or amplitude change in the reflection of the wave appears to the receiver as an amplitude modulation of the signal.

The receiver amplifies the signal and then demodulates it. A Schmitt trigger shapes the demodulated signal and feeds it to a relay driver amplifier, which actuates a small reed relay.

The alarm is sensitive enough to detect the air turbulence that is caused by fire. Connect an oscilloscope to the third-amplifier output (pin 7) of the IC, and you'll be able to see the effect of normal air currents in a perfectly quiet room. The receiver can cover a 120° arc and is sensitive enough to pick up an intruder at a 20-ft. distance.

How the System Works

The transmitter sends out a 17-kc ultrasonic signal which will saturate a small room. The receiver picks up not only the direct signal from the transmitter, but the waves that are reflected by walls, ceiling and other objects in the room. The many waves which have traveled different distances, have different phase relationships at the receiver. The

Rear view of receiver. Note how circuit board is mounted with ¼-in. spacers. Transformer and relay are installed in top of cabinet away from coil L1.

receiver's microphone algebraically adds the amplitude and phase relationships of all the waves and produces a signal which the receiver sees as a single reflected wave.

If an object in the room moves, its reflected wave, as seen by the receiver, will change in amplitude and phase. The amplitude change depends on the position of the object in relation to the receiver and transmitter. The phase change depends on the speed of the object and the wavelength of the transmitted signal.

Since the wavelength of a 17-kc signal is about 0.8 in. an object moving at several feet-per-second toward the receiver, will cause phase reversals in its reflected wave at a rate of 30 to 50 cps. These phase reversals will alternately add to and subtract from the total received signal and appear to modulate the signal at a low audio rate.

Crystal mike MIC1 is tuned to 17 kc by L1 and C1. Capacitor C2 feeds the input signal to the first amplifier of IC1. The signal is amplified and the output at pin 3 goes to *sensitivity* pot R3. This pot determines the level of the signal which is sent to the second amplifier input at pin 4.

The output of the second amplifier is demodulated by D1. It is then filtered by C3, which also attenuates the high frequencies and noise in the modulation envelope. The third amplifier in the integrated circuit is used as a straight amplifier for the demodulated signal. The signal is then fed to the Schmitt trigger (Q1, Q2). Capacitors C4 and C10 are RF bypass capacitors. Potentiometer R10 is a trigger-level pot for the Schmitt trigger.

The Schmitt trigger, which is a regenerative switch, converts the demodulated signal into square waves which feed relay-driver Q3 and relay RY1. Relay RY1 is a reed relay which is used to control an external relay. It has a contact rating of 500 ma. An ordinary relay mounted in the same cabinet as MIC1 will, on closing, cause acoustic feedback and send the system into oscillation. The reed relay's contact closing is almost inaudible.

The transmitter is a standard emitter-coupled oscillator which is powered by a 9-V transistor-radio battery. Crystal microphone MIC2 is connected across the tank circuit. The efficiency of the oscillator and the transducer are so high that the battery drain is only 1.5 ma. This enables the battery to operate the transmitter continuously for one week without replacement.

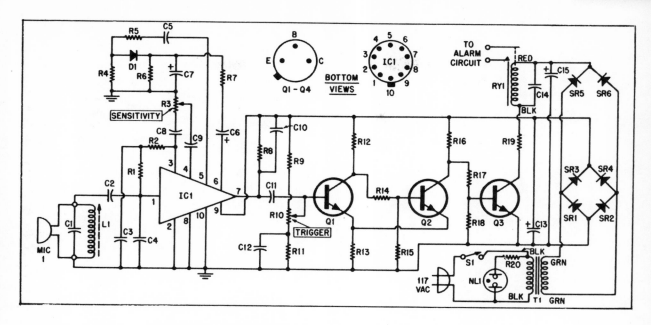

Output of IC1 is fed to Schmitt trigger (Q1,Q2) which converts demodulated signal into square waves that feed relay-driver transistor Q3. Q3 energizes reed relay RY1 which is used to control an external relay.

The transmitter can also be powered from the receiver power supply. Connect two wires across C15 and run them to the transmitter. At the transmitter install a decoupling network consisting of a 200-ohm resistor and a 200-μf capacitor.

Construction

The receiver was constructed on perforated circuit board and eyelets were used for mounting parts. This method proved much cheaper and quicker than using a homebrew printed-circuit board.

The CA3035 integrated circuit should be mounted in a 10-pin socket so you don't have to solder directly to the IC's leads. Transistor leads can be pushed through the eyelets and soldered. However, do not push the transistors flush to the board or the eyelets will short to the transistor case. Let the transistors sit about ⅛ in. above the board.

The circuitry layout is not critical, but try to duplicate ours. However, the position of L1 may be a bit touchy. Inductor L1 should be placed well away from the power transformer or it will pick up hum. Mount the microphones in the cabinets in 1⅜-in. dia. punched holes. Epoxy cement can be used to hold the mikes in place. The power-transformer secondary has a center-tap lead which is not used. It should be cut short and taped so it will not touch the cabinet.

Five-lug terminal strips, with center lug mounting, were used for the AC terminals and the relay connections. The relay itself is mounted by its contact leads. This means they should not be slack or the relay will have a tendency to vibrate when the contacts close and cause acoustic feedback.

Adjustments

To start with, turn on the receiver but disconnect the 9-V battery from the transmitter. Turn R3 counterclockwise for minimum sensitivity. Now turn R10 so that the relay closes. Back off on R10 so that the relay

Transmitter is emitter-coupled oscillator whose ultrasonic frequency is determined by L2. MIC2 is crystal mike. It works well as ultrasonic speaker.

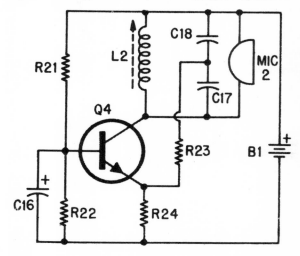

In addition to the ultrasonic burglar system described in this article, conventional electric eye alarms are also available to build from kits or purchased complete and ready for installation. Complete unit above with an effective range of 50 feet costs $22.95. The do-it-yourself kit below sells for $19.95. Both units available from Allied Radio Shack.

PARTS LIST

B1—9 V battery

Capacitors: 50 V or higher unless otherwise indicated

C1,C17—.01 μf, ceramic disc
C2,C3,C5,C8,C9,C10,C14—.04 μf ceramic disc
C4—.005 μf ceramic disc
C6—100 μf, 6-V electrolytic
C7,C16—5 μf, 6-V electrolytic
C11—.25 μf ceramic disc
C12—.002 μf, ceramic disc
C13,C15—1,000 μf, 10-V electrolytic
C18—.1 μf ceramic disc
D1—1N34A diode
IC1—CA3035 integrated circuit (RCA)
L1,L2—1.5-10 mh adjustable width coil (J. W. Miller 6322, Lafayette 34 F 88525)
MIC1, MIC2—Crystal-microphone cartridge (Lafayette 99 F 45908)
NL1—NE-2 neon lamp and holder
Q1,Q2,Q3—2N696 transistor
Q4—2N2270 transistor
Resistors: ½ watt, 10% unless otherwise indicated
R1,R2,R20—100,000 ohms
R3—2,000 ohm linear-taper potentiometer

Mallory Minitrol MTC-23L1, Lafayette 33 F 16452 or equiv.)
R4,R5—5,600 ohms, 5%
R6,R14,R21—10,000 ohms, 5%   R7—680 ohms
R8,R16—3,000 ohms, 5% R9—62,000 ohms, 5%
R10—5,000 ohm, linear-taper potentiometer (Mallory Minitrol MTC-53L1, Lafayette 33 F 16457 or equiv.)
R11—6,800 ohms   R12—5,000 ohms, 5%
R13—330 ohms   R15—2,700 ohms
R17—2,200 ohms, 5%
R18,R22—1,000 ohms, 5%
R19,R24—100 ohms   R23—510 ohms, 5%
RY1—SPST (normally-open contacts) miniature reed relay. Coil: 200 ohms, 6V., Magnecraft W102 MX-2. Available for $2.25 (plus postage) from Allied Radio Corp., 100 N. Western Avenue, Chicago, Ill. 60680. Stock No. 41 D 4554. Not listed in catalogue.
SR1-SR6—Silicon rectifier; minimum ratings: 750 ma, 50 PIV
T1—Filament transformer, secondary 6.3 V @ 0.6A
Misc.—Perforated circuit board, flea clips, 5 x 2¼ x 2¼-in. Minibox, 6 x 5 x 4-in. Minibox, integrated-circuit socket (Cinch-Jones 10-ICS)

opens again. The Schmitt trigger is now set just below its threshold. If RY1 closes unpredictably, back off on R10 a bit until the relay is just into its stable *off* position.

Next, connect a scope from pin 5 of IC1 to ground and slowly turn R3 clockwise toward maximum. If oscillation breaks out connect a 200-ohm resistor across R3. If the 200-ohm resistor does not stop the oscillation, back off on R3 until the oscillation stops. Now connect the scope to the junction of R5/C5 and ground. The transmitter should be about 10 ft. from the receiver. Fire up the transmitter and observe the pattern on the scope. Next, adjust the core of L2 on the transmitter until the pitch of the sound is beyond the range of your hearing. To our ears the frequency was about 17 kc. If the

waveform is saturated (flattened at the top and bottom) back off on R3 until the waveform is clean. Now adjust L1 for maximum signal and back off on R3 if the signal saturates.

A final adjustment should be made with the transmitter in its more-or-less permanent location. If used to detect the opening of a door, the transmitter should face the door and be about 4 ft. from the receiver.

The receiver should also face the door, and all final adjustments should be made from the rear of the receiver, so as not to block the mike. Adjust R3 so that the waveform is saturated. Now back off on R3 until the peak-to-peak signal voltage is half the saturated voltage.

You're now ready for the final test. Stand in front of the receiver about 5-ft. away from it. Now walk toward the receiver. The relay should close. You may have to experiment with the placement of the receiver and the adjustment of R3 and R10 for maximum sensitivity and stability. Relay RY1 should only be used to actuate an external relay, which can operate a bell or any other alarm device.

Keep in mind that spurious responses could be caused by a slowly moving curtain, the movement of a rattling window pane, or the noise of a steam valve.

In any event, you'll get to know the vagaries of the situation, because it's quite clear that whatever can be disturbed by a burglar, an unauthorized person on the premises, can be disturbed by a great many other things.

Layout of transmitter's parts on 2 x 3-in. piece of perforated board is not critical. Bracket holding L2 is made from a piece of scrap aluminum.

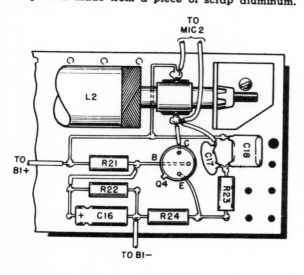

Quality concrete is free from cracks, scaling and other problems plaguing ordinary projects.

All About Concrete

by Richard Day

There's no substitute for quality—and you get it using "6666" principle

IT'S A WONDER that concrete is so popular when you look around at the haphazard ways it's used. You see it scaling, cracking, dusting, spalling, crazing, sinking and even disintegrating. It's a shame. Made right, concrete needn't suffer these failures. *Made right* is another way of saying *quality* concrete.

Quality concrete isn't a brand with a trademark to say, "this is quality." Sometimes it doesn't even look different from ordinary concrete. But it is. The advantages of quality concrete over run-of-the-mill concrete are many. And they all add up to lasting satisfaction with a sidewalk, driveway, patio, porch slab or whatever you make.

You can make good concrete simply by understanding and following a few easy-to-learn facts.

Quality concrete is really a method for making workable, strong, durable, watertight, good-looking concrete that will handle easily in the plastic state. In the hardened state it will not develop any of the common faults.

The Portland Cement Association has done considerable research on quality concrete. Moreover, the entire concrete industry, from those who manufacture portland cement—the backbone of concrete—to the ready mix producers who make and deliver the finished product, is engaged in a nationwide quality concrete program. It has been for some time.

Quality begins with the manufacture of cement. *Cement* is short for *portland cement,* the powdery gray stuff in bags that you put into concrete to make it harden. There are a number of brands of portland

This aggregate sample contains too much silt. Layer in this test should not exceed ⅛ of an inch.

Two-year-old test slabs show that cycles of freezing and thawing have scaled the plain concrete.

But this air-entrained slab was undamaged since it is 100 times more resistant to freeze and thaw.

cement, nearly all of them good.

Concrete, on the other hand, is the mixture of cement, water, sand, stones and perhaps other things. Concrete is used as the building material; cement is an ingredient of concrete. A true cement patio would be so dusty you wouldn't want it around.

Each U.S.-made bag of portland cement holds 1 cubic foot of cement and weighs 94 pounds. You should store cement in as dry a location as possible. When bagged cement is stored for long periods, it sometimes develops what is called a "warehouse pack," a stiffening around the edges. This can usually be corrected by rolling the bag on the floor. To be used, cement should be free-flowing and free of any lumps that can't be broken between your thumb and finger.

Portland cement mixed with water is called *cement paste*. Used as "glue" in concrete, the cement paste sets hard and glues the fine particles of sand and the coarse particles of crushed stones together into a solid mass. Cement comprises from 7 to 14 percent of the volume of a concrete mix. The sand and stone in concrete are called *aggregates*, sand being the *fine aggregate* and crushed stone, gravel or air-cooled slag the *coarse aggregate*. Aggregates make up 66 to 78 percent of the volume of finished concrete.

Concrete made with cement paste but no aggregates would be expensive because it would contain no cheaper materials, like sand and stones, to fill it out. It also would shrink a great deal when it set. While too

Damp sand contains little water and immediately falls apart after being squeezed in your hand.

Wet sand, when squeezed in your hand, forms a ball, yet leaves little moisture on your fingers.

Very wet sand forms a ball when squeezed in your hand, but does leave moisture on fingers.

much cement paste in the mix is not good, there should be enough to surround every particle with paste. A concrete's quality depends largely on the binding qualities of its cement paste. Therefore, nearly every step in making quality concrete is aimed at getting a high quality cement paste.

Because concrete shrinks when it sets, control joints should be made at regular intervals in every large, unreinforced wall or slab so that shrinkage cracks will occur at the joints. There they will not look unsightly. Without control joints the cracks would occur at random. The spacing of control joints is usually a maximum of 10 feet apart. Control joints should be at least one fourth the depth of the wall or slab.

Although making quality concrete may not be as easy as "1, 2, 3," it is as easy as "6666." The four numbers "6666" are the key to concrete quality. They represent cement, water, air (yes, there's air in quality concrete) and curing.

The first "6" is for cement content. Always expressed in bags of cement per cubic yard of concrete, the cement content of good concrete should be 6 bags per cubic yard. This is so that there will be enough cement paste to coat all the particles of aggregate and bind them tightly together. The table of mixes will help you hit the ideal 6-bag mix without sweat.

The second "6" stands for water content. This is expressed in gallons of water per bag of cement. Quality concrete should contain no more than 6 gallons of water for each bag of cement used in the mix. For instance, if you make a half-bag mix in a small mixer, there should be three gallons of water in it. However, because there is nearly always water in the sand added to a mix, you actually would put somewhat less than 3 gallons of water into a half-bag mix. The table shows just how much water to add with each of three wetnesses of sand.

In reality only three gallons of water per full bag of cement is sufficient to hydrate it fully. But such a mix would be so dry and stiff it wouldn't be practical, so an additional three gallons of water is used. This might be called "water of convenience." More water than this, though, is harmful because, as water is added, the cement paste becomes diluted. The extra water doesn't combine chemically with the cement. Instead it evaporates, leaving pores and capillaries throughout the paste. These weaken it, make it porous and less durable.

The third "6" represents air content. Air is an important ingredient in concrete.

Start with these proportions when making your trial mix. The purpose of a trial mix is to adjust these figures to make workable concrete using your aggregates. This table was based on average aggregates. If the ones you use are graded similarly to the average, no adjustments will be necessary. These figures give 6 gallons of water per bag of cement, 6 bags of cement per cubic yard of concrete, 6 percent entrained air. Cure six days and you'll have "6666" quality concrete. The weight of sand used depends upon the amount of water held by it. Decide whether your sand is "damp," "wet" or "very wet". The amount of water added to the trial mix also will depend on the amount of water that gets into the mix via the sand. The wetter the sand, the less water you must add to make the equivalent of 6 gallons per bag.

To use the table, first decide on the size of the batch. This will most likely be limited by the capacity of the mixer you are using. Choose the weights of materials in the column for your batch-size as follows:

1. *Cement*—Use the figure given.
2. *Water*—The amount depends on the wetness of the sand. Select the proper figure.

"6666" CONCRETE TRIAL MIXES

SIZE OF BATCH		1 cu. ft.	2½ cu. ft.	3½ cu. ft.	5 cu. ft.	(Write your trial mix results here.)
CEMENT		21 lb.	52 lb.	73 lb.	105 lb.	
W A T E R	Damp sand	10 lb.	25½ lb.	35½ lb.	51 lb.	
	Wet sand	9 lb.	22 lb.	32½ lb.	46 lb.	
	Very wet sand	7½ lb.	19 lb.	26½ lb.	38 lb.	
S A N D	Damp sand	46 lb.	116 lb.	162 lb.	231 lb.	
	Wet Sand	47 lb.	118 lb.	165 lb.	236 lb.	
	Very wet sand	49 lb.	122 lb.	171 lb.	244 lb.	
STONE		63 lb.	157 lb.	220 lb.	315 lb.	
AIR ENTR. AGENT (Darex)		2 tsp.	1 tb.	1½ tb.	2 tb.	

QUANTITIES TO ORDER
(allows 10 percent for aggregate waste)

CONCRETE NEEDED	CEMENT 1 bag=94 lb.	SAND	STONE	AIR-ENT. AGENT (Darex)
¼ cu. yd.	2 bags	350 lb.	500 lb.	(Get at least a pint and save for future jobs. Need 1 oz. per bag of cement.)
½ cu. yd.	3 bags	700 lb.	1000 lb.	
1 cu. yd.	6 bags	1400 lb.	2000 lb.	

3. *Sand*—The amount depends on its wetness. Select the proper figure.
4. *Coarse Aggregate*—Use the figure given.
5. *Air-entraining Agent*—Use the figure given (*tsp.* is *teaspoon*; *tb.* is *tablespoon*).

Quality concrete should contain 6 percent *entrained air*. Such concrete is called *air-entrained concrete*. Air is incorporated into the mix by adding an oily substance known as an *air-entraining agent*, which causes the formation of billions of microscopic air bubbles throughout the mix. There can be as many as 400-600 billion of these bubbles in a cubic yard of air-entrained concrete.

Air-entrained concrete has far superior resistance to scaling from freezing and thawing and from salt action. All concrete contains water. When this water freezes, it expands up to 9 percent, producing pressures that can rupture the concrete surface and make it scale off. The tiny bubbles of air in air-entrained concrete act as "relief valves" to take up pressures during freezing and thawing cycles without damage to the concrete. Air entrainment is a must for all concrete exposed to freezing and salt action. This includes patios, driveways, garage floors, sidewalks, curbs, walls, planters, etc.

Air-entrained concrete's other benefits make it highly desirable for use in warm climates. The billions of bubbles act like ball bearings in the mix, lubricating it to increase its workability. Air-entrained concrete also is cohesive. It looks and feels "fatty." The disconnected air bubbles buoy up the pieces of coarse aggregate, keeping them from settling to the bottom and weakening the wall or slab.

If you live in a cold climate, your ready mix dealer is sure to have some air-entrained agent. But he buys it by the drum. Take a pint or quart bottle and ask him if he will sell you a little. It isn't expensive. Then ask your dealer what brand his air-entrained agent is. If it's *Darex*, you can use the quantities shown in the

To get accurate proportions, weigh trial batch materials on scale, using P. 67 table as guide.

Measure out all the materials in similar-sized batch cans and dump them into the mixing drum.

Mark batch cans. Then you can fill them to the line each time, assured of the correct proportions.

trial mix table. This is figured at the rate of one ounce per bag of cement. This brand has a self-limiting feature. No matter how much agent you use, it's hard to get much above 6 percent air.

The fourth "6" is for length of curing—at least six days. You can carry quality right up to the last step, but neglect proper curing and you'll end up with weak concrete that lacks durability. Concrete needs six days or more of curing to hold back evaporation of the mixing water until most of its strength has developed. If too much water evaporates, there will not be enough water left to react fully with every particle of cement. Proper curing can develop up to 50 percent more strength in concrete.

While the "6666" principle covers the four most important requirements of quality concrete, a few others are obvious:

Clean Water—Water that you can drink is almost always acceptable for making concrete.

Clean Aggregate—Aggregate should not contain any materials having harmful effects, such as dirt, clay, coal or plant matter. It also should be hard and durable. If you use unwashed aggregate from local pits or creeks, be sure that it has been proved to make good concrete. Most building materials dealers carry aggregates of known performance, but too many don't recognize the difference between concrete sand and mortar sand. The two are not interchangeable. Concrete sand contains particles of ¼ inch and less, while mortar sand has no particles anywhere near as big as ¼ inch. Mortar sand is fine like that you'd want for a sandbox. One good place to get tested aggregates is from your ready mix dealer.

Well-Graded Aggregate—Aggregate particles should have a range of sizes from the largest to the smallest. The big ones fill out the mix; the smaller ones fill in spaces between the big ones; and so on down to dust-size particles. It's like a mixture of watermelons, cantaloupes, tomatoes, radishes, beans, peas, grape seeds and radish seeds all surrounded by glue. Not very taste-tempting, but a good range of sizes.

Now you're ready to mix concrete and get quality. A mixer should not be overloaded. The actual mixing size of a drum is about 60 percent of its stated volume. The identification plate attached to the mixer may give its working capacity. Size your batches to stay within this figure.

Prepackaged concrete mixes are a great convenience for small jobs. They are available in two types: one is a regular concrete mix with gravel; the other, a sand mix without gravel. Sand mix is ideal for thin sections, small precast items, etc. The materials for both are selected and carefully proportioned ready for adding water and mixing. Prepackaged mixes are usually available in 1-cubic-foot bags and smaller.

In hand-mixing, the benefits of air-entrained concrete are lost, for the mixing isn't vigorous enough to help the air-entraining agent create the billions of air bubbles needed. Prepackaged mixes, therefore, don't contain an air-entraining agent. If you use them in a mixer, you still need to add air-entraining agent.

Small batches of concrete may be hand-mixed in a wheelbarrow, on a platform or on a concrete slab. Dump the materials in a pile. Then make a depression in the pile and add some of the water. Mix and add a measured amount of water (at the rate of six gallons per bag of cement) until you get a stiff but workable mix. All the water should be in at this point. If the mix is too dry, reduce the amount of sand and gravel in the next batch. If too wet, add more sand and gravel, but never change the amount of water and cement.

The best way to mix concrete is with a concrete mixer. Any sizable job requires it. Machine-mixing not only saves your energy for placing and finishing, it does a

A "stony mix" is too harsh for easy finishing; too much coarse aggregate and not enough sand.

"Sandy mix" contains too much sand, not enough coarse aggregate; finishes easily but is costly.

"Workable mix" is good. Spaces between particles of the coarse aggregate are all filled with sand.

If the mix is too stiff, add portland cement and water in the same proportions as the trial mix.

This quality concrete is too stiff to be poured into place. However, it is not too stiff to be worked.

better job of combining the aggregates. One man who's in good shape can handle the mixing, placing and finishing of one to two cubic yards of concrete in a day with a good-sized mixer.

The first step in mixing concrete is to make a trial mix. While a table can give you general proportions of sand and coarse aggregate to use in "6666" concrete, it cannot adjust them to the exact materials you will be using. The trial mix enables you to do this. No adjustments are needed in cement or water because these ingredients don't vary from place to place enough to affect the concrete. Sand and coarse aggregate gradations vary, depending upon where the materials were obtained and how they were processed. If you select a good source and get the same materials every time you mix concrete, the proportions arrived at by your trial mix should not change.

A trial mix is one batch of concrete placed into the mixer, mixed, inspected and then adjusted, if necessary, for aggregate gradation. Make your first trial mix using the proportions in the "6666" concrete table on this page. The trial mixes in the table are designed around an average sand and gravel. If the one you are using is graded differently from the average, you may need to change the proportions given. Do this by adjusting the

quantities of *aggregate*. Consider the cement and water proportions shown in the table constant for obtaining "6666" quality concrete.

Sand used in concrete nearly always contains some free water. When the sand is used in concrete, this excess water combines with the cement and thus must be taken into account in the six gallons of water per bag of cement. The "6666" table makes allowance for the free water in three types of sand that might be encountered. Give your sand the hand-squeeze test before you use the table.

The trial mix should be batched by weight. You'll notice that the table gives all proportions in pounds except the air-entraining agent. This allows you to use a bathroom scale to measure materials. It saves making one-cubic-foot boxes, etc. However, don't forget to "zero" the scale with an empty batch-can on it. Once you get the trial mix adjusted to the aggregates you are using, put marks on your batch-cans and you'll no longer need the scale. From then on, batch to the marks. Galvanized pails or five-gallon buckets make handy batch-cans. Always keep one batch-can dry for cement.

A mixer should be batched as follows: Put about 10 percent of the water into the drum before adding the aggregate and cement. Add the rest of the water uniformly

You can rent concrete mixer on wheels. It can be hitched to car, easily maneuvered where needed.

For quantities over 1 cubic yard, ready mixed concrete is the answer. Get plenty of assistance.

along with your dry materials. Leave about 10 percent to be added after all other materials are in the drum. Add air-entraining agent to the water.

All concrete should be thoroughly mixed and the materials uniformly distributed. This means that quality concrete should mix for at least one minute, and preferably for three minutes, *after* all the materials are in the drum.

When thoroughly mixed, dump out a sample of your trial mix into a wheelbarrow or batch-can and examine it for stiffness and workability. If it is not right, here is how to adjust the trial mix for your aggregate:

Too Wet—The mix contains too little aggregate for the amount of cement paste. Weigh out a little more sand and coarse aggregate. Add them to the mixer. Record the amounts it takes to get the mix the way it should be. Add these amounts to your trial mix totals, weigh out a second batch using these totals, mark your batch-cans and you're ready to go ahead with batch after batch of quality concrete.

Too Stiff—The mix contains too much sand and coarse aggregate. Reduce the amounts of these added to subsequent batches until you get a workable mix. Never add more water. Instead, adjust the consistency of the mix by adjusting the sand and coarse aggregate.

Too Sandy—Make a second trial batch. Leave out some of the sand and add more stones. Keep weight records so that when you get the mix right, you'll know just how much sand and stones is enough.

Too Stony—Make a second trial batch. In it leave out some of the stones and add more sand. Write down the weights.

With practice, you may get so expert that you can judge consistency and sand-stone proportion while the concrete is mixing.

As long as the sand and coarse aggregate are the same ones as those used in making the adjusted trial batch, the proportions shouldn't need to be varied. The water content of the sand can vary, though, depending on whether the stockpile has been rained on recently. Check the sand before you start work and use proper water quantities from the trial-mix table to account for water changes in the sand.

All of the steps to getting "6666" concrete will make your project that much surer of lasting success.

Complete curing is last step in making quality concrete. Poly sheeting is the simplest method.

Tub Enclosure

ATTRACTIVE, smart and honestly functional, this bathtub enclosure will give your bathroom that up-to-date look. The basic materials used are aluminum angle and storm sash (or "Y" rails as they are called here). The two sliding door panels are of translucent plastic sheeting. The doors move at the touch of a finger and let in lots of light. It's easy to step in and out of the tub, too, because of the generous width of the doors.

You'll find the unit easy to make if you use the materials and follow the procedure suggested here. The length of your aluminum pieces will of course depend upon the size of your own bathroom and upon your own wishes. Plastic panels such as Resolite which can be worked with woodworking tools are available under several trade names. These panels come in many colors and will transmit up to 90% of the visible light. They can be purchased in either corrugated form or in flat sheets. The flat sheet of course is the proper one for this particular tub enclosure design.

TOP AND BOTTOM TRACKS

Start with your top and bottom tracks. After looking at the detail drawings shown here, cut these aluminum angles (⅛ x ¾ x ¾ inches) to the proper size on your table saw. Rivet the two angles together solidly.

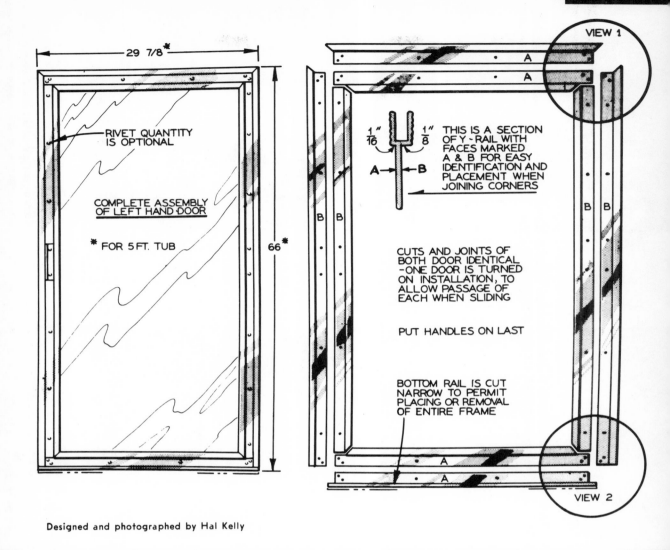

RIVET QUANTITY IS OPTIONAL

COMPLETE ASSEMBLY OF LEFT HAND DOOR

* FOR 5 FT. TUB

29 7/8 *

66 *

VIEW 1

THIS IS A SECTION OF Y - RAIL WITH FACES MARKED A & B FOR EASY IDENTIFICATION AND PLACEMENT WHEN JOINING CORNERS

1/16"   1/8"

A → ← B

CUTS AND JOINTS OF BOTH DOOR IDENTICAL —ONE DOOR IS TURNED ON INSTALLATION, TO ALLOW PASSAGE OF EACH WHEN SLIDING

PUT HANDLES ON LAST

BOTTOM RAIL IS CUT NARROW TO PERMIT PLACING OR REMOVAL OF ENTIRE FRAME

VIEW 2

Designed and photographed by Hal Kelly

For water-tight bathing comfort, build yourself this bathtub enclosure. It's attractive, smart, and honestly functional.

Remember that the end of the rivet is peened into a countersunk hole so that the rivet is flush with the surface of the aluminum angle. This will enable you to cement the track to the tub edge. Drill your weep holes in the bottom track next. Then use your file, sandpaper, and steel wool on all rough or sharp edges.

Cementing the bottom track to the tub is a simple job. Just use two lines of masking, Scotch, or some similar tape spaced ¾ inch apart along the edge of the tub. Cover the area between tapes with tile cement. Place the bottom rail in position with a little pressure so that the cement is pushed into the pores of both surfaces. Do not

To make bottom tracks, fit two lengths of angle together as shown in drawings; join by riveting.

Drill holes for riveting; centerpunch, then add rivets as you go to keep tracks properly aligned.

Top and tub side of tracks can be trimmed to the desired width on table saw after being riveted.

Saw your storm sash members or "Y" rails to correct over-all length with handsaw or table saw.

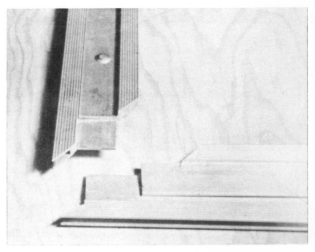

If you have a planer-jointer, run your tracks and "Y" rails through it to secure a true edge.

Cut miters as shown in detail drawing and join storm sash members to form sliding door frame.

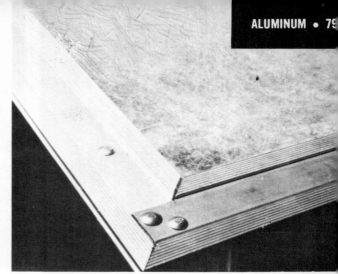

Cut translucent plastic panel to required size; form frame around it and rivet corners to secure.

Upset rivets on inside of door frame, leaving clean, rounded rivet heads on outside of frame.

install the top rail until the doors are finished.

THE SLIDING DOOR

At this point a careful study of the detail drawings of the door corners will save you time, energy, and even money. Saw your storm sash or "Y" rails to the correct over-all length first. Note that the chan-

nel section of the "Y" rail which slides over the bottom track has been reduced to ¼ inch and that there is a $\frac{3}{16}$-inch space left between the top of the upper "Y" channel and the upper track. This will enable you to remove and install the doors whenever you wish by simply lifting the doors up and pulling them out at the bottom.

This bottom "Y" rail can be sawed to

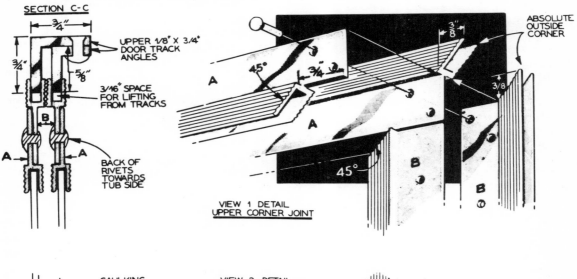

SECTION C-C

VIEW 1 DETAIL UPPER CORNER JOINT

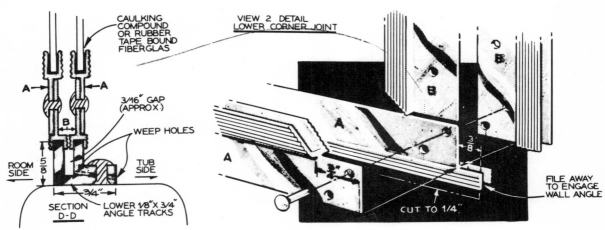

VIEW 2 DETAIL LOWER CORNER JOINT

SECTION D-D

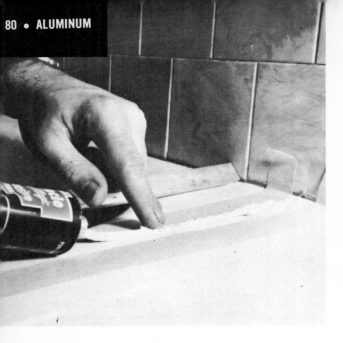

To cement bottom tracks to tub edge, first apply tile cement between two strips of masking tape.

Place bottom tracks in position, seating firmly; let dry, then strip off tape with excess cement.

the correct width on a table saw and then sanded. It can also be run through a planer-jointer a few times (if such a machine is available to you) to secure a true or straight edge. If necessary, of course, a hand saw and a plane can be used similarly for this purpose.

Mark and saw your corner miters next. These corners can be sawed on a table saw or with a hacksaw. Once the corners are sawed and fitted together they can be marked for drilling.

The pair of rails lettered "A" in the drawing can be marked, centerpunched, drilled, and riveted together before the corner joints are drilled and riveted. The same procedure can be followed with the pair of rails marked "B" in the detail drawing. You can use a C-clamp or wood screw to hold the rails in position for drilling. Any vise will do the job, too.

RIVETING THE DOOR FRAMES

It's a good idea to buy rivets which are the correct length. Add to the thickness of the materials to be riveted together a distance equal to about two times the thickness of the rivet. This will give you, under any circumstances, the over-all length of the rivet to be used. If your aluminum rivets are too long you can easily cut them down with a pair of pliers or saw them shorter in a vise. A quick method of getting the right size rivet hole is to check the shank of your twist drill against the body of your rivet. They should be the same size.

Place your rivet in the hole with the rivet head on a solid steel surface. This can be the head of a hammer held in a vise, or a steel stake as shown here.

INSTALLING SIDE ANGLES

Measure these for length carefully. Remember that the top angle track must be $\frac{3}{16}$ inch above the bottom of the top "Y" channel (see section c-c of detail drawing). If your walls are of plastic tile just drill pilot holes through both the aluminum angle and the tile. Then insert self-tapping screws. You can secure a tighter bond with some tile cement applied to the aluminum angle also.

The aluminum corner braces ($\frac{1}{16}$ x ⅜ x 2 inches) can be riveted or screwed into place with self-tapping screws; the protruding ends can be nipped off, filed, and sanded.

THE TOP TRACK

The top track is installed last. Mark and cut it carefully. Then mark the location of holes for the corner braces and fasten them into place.

DOOR HANDLES

Since the position of the door handles is important, mark their location with the doors in place. Then remove the doors, mark and drill, and rivet the handles to the doors.

FINISHING NOTES

Use a file first on any edges which are rough or need to be rounded. Follow the filing with sandpaper and fine steel wool. Light rubbing with fine steel wool will leave a bright, uniform finish on the aluminum. •

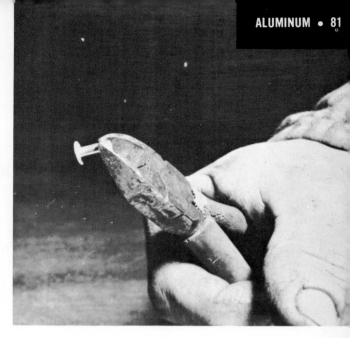

Use head of a nail punch to get at rivets when securing angle inserts in corners of door frame.

If the aluminum rivets you have are too long, you can easily cut them down with a pair of pliers.

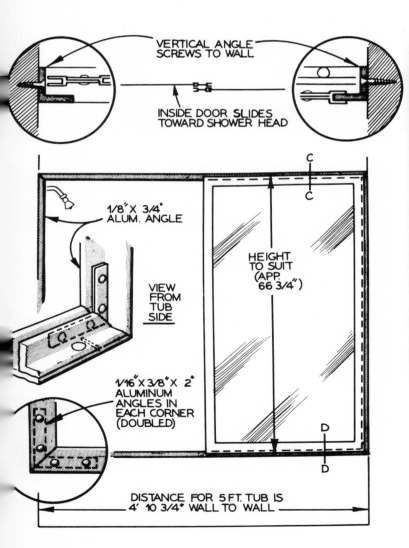

VERTICAL ANGLE
SCREWS TO WALL

INSIDE DOOR SLIDES
TOWARD SHOWER HEAD

1/8" X 3/4"
ALUM. ANGLE

VIEW
FROM
TUB
SIDE

HEIGHT
TO SUIT
(APP.
66 3/4")

1/16" X 3/8" X 2"
ALUMINUM
ANGLES IN
EACH CORNER
(DOUBLED)

C
C

D
D

DISTANCE FOR 5 FT. TUB IS
4' 10 3/4" WALL TO WALL

Mark the positions of the door handles with the doors in place, then remove doors and attach handles by riveting.

How to Anchor and Use Lines

"A ROPE is to tie things with." That's an oft-quoted youngster's definition, and it should be good enough for any pleasure boatman, provided he knows how "to tie things," what rope is needed and how to care for it.

A boat left to its own devices is a restless thing. Without rope you can't moor or anchor, tow a water skier, haul a bucket of water aboard, or toss a line to a man overboard.

Another saying applies to the mariner: "It takes a fluke to stay put." Anchors, like fire extinguishers, all too often are not given much thought until they are needed in an emergency.

The vital link between your boat and the bottom is rope. Rope, when cut into specified lengths and used aboard a boat, is generally called line. The pleasure boatman has a choice of four basic varieties of rope from which to make up lines. These are Manila, nylon, dacron and polyethylene. The choice of the lines should depend on the job each is expected to perform.

All rope is cordage whether constructed of natural or synthetic fibers or, in some instances, wire.

Manila, which is made from natural plant fibers, is a general all-purpose rope and can be used wherever line is required. Typical good-quality, three-strand Manila of ¼-inch diameter has a breaking strength of approximately 600 pounds; $\frac{5}{16}$-inch, 1000 pounds; ⅜-inch, 1350 pounds; $\frac{7}{16}$-inch, 1750 pounds; ½-inch, 2650 pounds; ⅝-inch, 4400 pounds, and ¾-inch, 5400 pounds.

Working strength of any rope should be figured at 20 per cent of its breaking strength. Therefore, the working strength of $\frac{5}{16}$-inch Manila is approximately 200 pounds. Since Manila generally costs less than half as much as nylon and approximately one quarter as much as dacron, pleasure boatmen frequently select Manila for reasons of economy. If Manila is kept clean and dried before storing, it will offer a long and satisfactory life. It is lightweight, flexible, easy to handle, doesn't kink and coils readily.

Nylon is a synthetic yarn rope with breaking and working strength approximately three times that of Manila. It offers a number of advantages over Manila, but also has disadvantages. Nylon has high

This boating clown is heaving the anchor out as though he were doing the hammer throw. The line easily could tangle around his ankles and pull him overboard or, at best, it will snarl up into a bird's nest.

Left: The proper way to put down your anchor is shown here. Lower it gently over the side, keeping the line free of your legs while you pay it out from a neat coil on the deck to prevent tangling.

In this case, the sailorette has made use of three lines in tying up between two finger piers. The bow is secured by one line which runs port and starboard from the cleat; two lines, one each side, hold the stern.

elasticity. Stretched, it quickly recovers its original length and will recover repeatedly within short time intervals. This ability to stretch and absorb shock makes nylon desirable as mooring or anchor line, for moored or anchored boats are often kept in motion by wave action. Nylon resists rot, decay and fungus growth and is superior in abrasion resistance to Manila. It may be stored wet and can be washed with a detergent solution without damage.

In contrast to Manila, nylon is difficult to splice and its fresh-cut ends will fray unless they are seized (wrapped with small line) or fused by applying heat. One common method to prevent nylon from losing its lay (that is, untwisting into a fluffy mass of hard-to-handle filaments) is to hold the end in a match flame until the filaments melt. They fuse together as they cool.

Dacron has approximately twice the breaking and working strength of Manila, has far greater stability than nylon. It is silky smooth to the touch, making it desirable to handle. However, since it offers a minimum of stretch, it is not recommended for use as anchor or mooring lines. It is favored for running rigging on sailing craft where stretch is not wanted. On racing yachts, linen lines are most highly regarded for halyards and sheets.

Polyethylene has approximately the same strength as nylon and no more elasticity than Manila. It is recommended for use wherever floating rope is desirable. Polyethylene is lightweight, soft and very flexible. This, combined with its flotation characteristic, makes it a top choice for water ski towlines, dinghy painters, and ring buoy or throwing lines.

As a generality, boats of under 20 feet should carry a 100-foot length of anchor line in ½-inch Manila or ⅜-inch nylon. Boats 20 to 25 feet in length should be equipped with both a lightweight service anchor and a heavy storm anchor. For the light anchor, 100 feet of ½-inch Manila or ⅜-inch nylon will be satisfactory. The heavy anchor calls for 150 feet of ⅝-inch Manila or ½-inch nylon. Boats of 25 to 30 feet should carry 100 feet of line for the light anchor, either in ⅝-inch Manila or ½-inch nylon. The heavy anchor should be fitted with 175 feet of ¾-inch Manila or $\frac{9}{16}$-inch nylon. Boats of 30 to 45 feet in length should carry 150 feet of light anchor line of ¾-inch Manila or $\frac{9}{16}$-inch nylon. The storm anchor should have 200 feet of 1-inch Manila or ¾-inch nylon.

Small power craft up to about 18 feet in length may be satisfactorily moored with two lines, each approximately equal in length to the boat's overall length. These

When someone falls overboard, a life preserver should be thrown to him—but don't secure life preservers to your boat with lines. A separate line should be used for pulling in the person.

If the sailor who has gone overboard knows his lines, he can tie a line athwartships, make up a foot stirrup in an end and pull himself over the gunwale without fear of capsizing the boat.

are secured to the bow and stern cleats, run off at about a 45° angle to the center line of the boat, and made fast to the dock. However, if your boating is done in waters where there is a considerable range in tide, a pair of spring lines are often required in addition to bow and stern lines. Spring lines prevent the boat from moving forward or astern and yet allow freedom for rise and fall.

Boats over 25 feet in length should carry a minimum of four mooring lines. This permits two-directional tie-ups at bow and stern in finger piers or provides for spring lines when mooring only to one side of a dock.

It's nearly impossible to take an active part in any form of pleasure boating without being required to know your ropes, how and where to use them and how to take care of them.

Someone once said, "Give a man enough rope and he'll hang himself." He obviously wasn't thinking of a boatman. Though there have been hangings at sea, mutiny on pleasure boats is a rarity and capital punishment for a mutinous crew of passengers is frowned upon.

Give a seaman enough rope of the right kind and if it's used properly it will add to pleasure and safety of crew and craft. A competent boatman is quickly distinguished from a landlubber by a knowledge of marlinspike seamanship, which entails a knowledge of ropes and skill in working with them.

Several times each year you should inspect all of your lines. Rope is deteriorated by mechanical action, surface wear, internal friction, biological action, bacteria and mold, or boring marine organisms. Don't check only for exterior wear; look below the surface, for the exterior appearance of lines may be deceptive. Twist open sections of the line and check for broken inner

fibers due to mechanical or biological action. Manila lines will wear out from the inside. Synthetic fiber rope surface filaments, when abraded, form a protective fuzz that shields the inner fibers. You are often dependent for your own or your craft's safety on the soundness of your lines. A weak line is often worse than none at all, so replace all damaged and worn lines as soon as they are detected and be sure that your supply of lines is sufficient.

Here are some hints on the care of your lines:

Whenever you beach a boat and put out a line to secure it from drifting, the line should be rinsed carefully before further use. Otherwise, grit, dirt or sand may work between the strands and cut the line's fibers.

Care should be taken not to store lines near storage batteries, for acid from the electrolyte or acid fumes can damage the fibers.

Chafing gear (sections of old sheeting, canvas, burlap or any acid- or alkaline-free rags) should be wrapped around lines where they pass over the sheer rail or through chocks. Sections of split garden or fire hose make excellent chafing gear.

Pulley sheaves and chocks that are too small for the diameter of lines increase wear and friction. When in doubt, it is better to use oversize rather than undersize sheaves and chocks.

Knots and kinks tend to shear rope fibers when lines are under strain. Remember that when using rope as a sling, for lashing or turning sharp corners, an excessively heavy strain is placed on the outer fibers of the rope and you should never exceed working loads of more than one fifth the breaking strength of line, giving additional safety allowance for rope that is worn or weakened.

Whenever possible, always use a splice

This craft is being tied up at a place where considerable tide variation is expected. Note spring lines which run fore and aft; others at bow and stern.

instead of a knot, for the shearing tendency of knots may weaken a rope by as much as 50 per cent, while splices will often offer as much as 90 per cent of the breaking strength of the rope.

Manufacturers always coil rope in the same manner. Right-laid rope is always uncoiled in a counterclockwise direction. In uncoiling rope, lay the coil flat with the inside end at the bottom. Then draw the inside end up through the coil. New lines often are difficult to handle as they have a tendency to kink. I recommend securing the end of a new line to the stern of your boat (once under way so the line won't tangle in your prop) and allow the line to trail behind your boat for 10 or 15 minutes. Stop your engine before pulling in the rope, again to prevent prop snagging. You'll find that the permanent wave set into the line when it was coiled will be freed and the line will be pliable for use.

Care in mooring will save you embarrassment and may often prevent extensive damage. I learned how not to moor a boat by goofing badly. My lesson occurred during a fishing junket on the Gulf Coast of Florida.

The Everglades coastline just north of Cape Sable is broken by dozens of rivers and inlets that reach back into the mangrove jungles where tarpon and snook are often as commonplace as goldfish in 5 and 10¢ store aquariums. The fishing party I was with selected one of these narrow inlets, Graveyard Creek, as our headquarters. Our campsite's only claim to fame was that it was the breeding area for the hungriest mosquitoes east of New Guinea. The fish, by contrast, were apparently better fed than pet cats at a creamery.

We had planned to stay at Graveyard Creek for three days. My lack of attention to proper mooring techniques nearly made our stay permanent. We had arrived in two outboard runabouts. When we killed the motors, we heard mosquitoes singing like banshees and there was no question that they were out for blood. To preserve as much fuel as possible, we tossed all of our fishing gear into the boat and shifted food, spare fuel and camping equipment into the other. I hastily tethered our supply boat to a branch overhanging the creek bank. Thoughtlessly, I allowed only three feet of slack in the line.

Shortly after dawn the next morning we returned hungry, tired, bitten and fishless.

When making fast to a dock cleat, take the half hitch with the free part of the line as shown. By doing so, you may then release the line even with a considerable strain on the standing part.

When you tow another craft, you will find that there is less tendency for it to yaw and cause steering difficulties with the towing craft if you rig up a bridle across the stern as shown here.

Two half hitches are useful in making the end of a rope fast around its own standing part. End B is passed under the ring and under and over the line's standing part twice.

Below: One of the most useful and widely-known sailor knots is the bowline. It is used if you require a loop that will not slip, jam or fail and is easily untied, even if soaked.

STEP 1   STEP 2   FINISHED KNOT

The tide had fallen and risen during our absence. The sight that greeted us was a shocker. Our moored outboard hull, once laden with supplies, was upside down. The motor was hopelessly soaked. Tools had been dumped along with food, spare fuel, clothing and practically everything we owned other than rods, reels and tackle.

I had taken the precaution to tilt up and secure the outboard motor, expecting the boat to be supported on the creek bottom at low tide. It had, but I hadn't figured on the steep angle of a bank that sloped at about a 45° angle. When the tide had run out, the boat simply dangled at the end of its short mooring line. As the tide turned and ran in again, the boat had filled with water almost to the steering wheel before it became buoyant. Then, as its artificial flotation gradually gave it lift, the sweep of the incoming current rocked the nearly foundered hull, causing it to become unbalanced. Finally, it simply rolled. Through sheer luck, we located two spare fuel tanks with closed vents about a quarter of a mile upstream.

The lesson is obvious. Though I hadn't, every boatman should carefully check water conditions where he plans to moor or anchor, know what tide may be expected, and sound the bottom.

Care and thoughtfulness in properly securing a boat can save the embarrassment of having a boat stray off on its own or suffer damage due to banging or chafing.

When beaching a boat, it is always tempting to run the bow up onto the shore. This technique begs for wear and tear. Where no waves and tide are present, drop an anchor astern and secure a bowline to an object ashore. This will prevent the boat from turning broadside and drifting onto the beach. Where waves prevail, moor the boat with a bow anchor to prevent shipping water over the stern.

Five basic knots will serve for most mooring situations: the square or reef knot, used to secure two ropes of the same size; the sheet, weaver's knot or becket bend, three names for the same means of tying two lines of different diameter; the bowline, used to create a nonslipping loop at one end of a line; the clove hitch, used to tie temporarily to a bollard or piling; and two half hitches, used for the same purpose.

The half hitch method is commonly used to secure lines to cleats. The free end of the line should be passed around the front of the cleat; that is, that part of a cleat farthest from the secured part of the line. The standing or free part should then continue around the rear of the cleat, passing over the secured line. A half hitch is placed over the forward end of the cleat, then another half hitch over the rear of the cleat. The important feature is to see that the section of line leading to the free or standing end of the rope is always on the bottom of the loop.

At some time you may be called on to take another craft in tow. Rather than pull the entire load from a single stern cleat on your boat, I recommend rigging a bridle with the line secured to both stern quarters. In heavy going, you may find that the weight of the tow limits the maneuverability of your hull. If it is possible to rig the lines farther forward, you will improve your boat's maneuvering ability.

If you take an outboard boat in tow, have the towed boat's operator tilt his motor or motors free from the water so as to reduce drag. Should the towed boat yaw back and forth, have its operator shift movable weight aft as far as possible.

In following seas, be sure the towline is sufficiently long so that the craft under tow doesn't override the crest of a wave while you are in its trough. In such a case, the towed craft may surfboard down the slope and strike your boat, broach or capsize. Adjust the length of towlines in conformance with the distance between one or more waves. Since the distance between wave crests and wave troughs will remain quite constant, strain on the towline will be at a minimum with both the towed and the towing boat ascending and descending the waves simultaneously.

Pay close attention to the freeboard of the boat being towed. If it has shipped water, it will be unstable and, should you tow at a high rate of speed, you may pull the towed boat's bow under. You must also pay close attention to the safety of your own boat, so that the stern is not dragged under. This is of particular importance if you are towing with an outboard with a shallow, 15-inch rather than a 20-inch transom—or with an outboard not fitted with a self-draining well.

You may find that in extremely rough weather it is better to delay returning to the nearest mooring. Instead, it may be more prudent to head directly into the sea, maintaining only enough headway to keep excessive slack out of the towline and to prevent your boat and the towed craft from pounding.

An additional line dragged aft of the towed craft will reduce its tendency to yaw. In extreme cases, add a sea anchor to the end of the line dragging behind the boat in distress.

Don't tow a disabled craft into a crowded anchorage where wind, tide or current may cause the towed boat to collide with others.

SQUARE KNOT

Figure 1

Figure 2

The square knot, as pictured here, is useful to reef or furl sails, and it can be shaken apart. (1) End A is passed over and under B. (2) B is passed over and under A and ends are tightened.

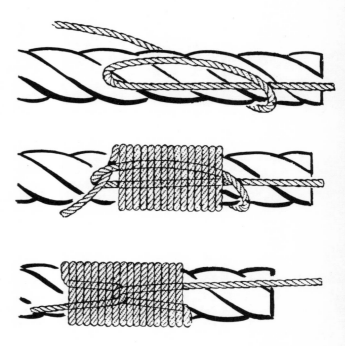

Raveled lines are unsightly. To whip them, use heavy linen fish line. Wind the line tightly as shown for a distance at least equal to the diameter of the rope; then pull the ends and cut.

STEP 1 STEP 2

Right: A fisherman's bend is used to join two light lines. It consists of two overhand knots, each tied in one line and tightened down on the adjacent one.

Left: The carrick bend is useful if two heavy lines must be joined. To finish it, each end is seized to the standing part. Use it to lengthen anchor lines.

Left: The clove hitch is used in fastening a line around an object. If used at the end of a line, adding a half hitch or two is a good idea.

Instead, have the disabled boat drop anchor. Then remove its passengers if necessary.

Hardware on some production boats is made up of cheap castings which may snap under stress. If you have any reason to be doubtful as to the strength of towing bits or eyes, or if you do not feel that the fittings are sufficiently secured, exercise extreme caution. Move all of your passengers to a protected area in a cabin or up on a foredeck. With smaller, open craft, have them get down on the floorboards. A broken towing line—or worse yet, a line with a piece of broken hardware secured to it—may under certain conditions be as lethal as a bullwhip or a missile.

A heavy stone tied to a crude rope was the anchor used by the earliest boatmen, but it took a heap of muscle to handle stone anchors large enough to keep even a dugout canoe from straying. Today, the dead-weight anchor has been replaced by far more efficient and lighter types with a hooking action.

One major anchor manufacturer claims that if a lightweight anchor had been designed centuries ago, the entire history of the world might have been changed! This sounds like an extravagant statement, but it's true that the Greeks, Romans, Spanish and English might all have handled their ships differently in exploration, trade and battle if they could have made their rigs stay still when they wished it. The technique of island jumping and amphibious landings used during World War II was made possible only by the modern anchor. Our Navy was able to put and hold ships in any desired location.

The size of the anchor you need for your boat will depend on many factors: the type of bottom on which the anchor will be dropped; wind velocity; exposure of the mooring location; the hull form, size and weight; and the scope (length of the anchor line in relation to water depth). The riding anchor line, incidentally, is called the anchor rode by the salty set.

Since only the hull size, weight and form can be securely determined in advance, the following generalities should serve as a guide in selecting an anchor:

Weight alone has little to do with an anchor's efficiency. That the design is important is apparent when it's realized that a concrete block will hold little more than its own weight. A mushroom-type anchor will hold only about twice its weight, while the modern lightweight patent anchor with pivoting flukes can hold up to 1000 times its weight.

A small outboard utility of under 15 feet can be anchored safely under most circumstances with a four-pound patent anchor. A 15- to 20-foot outboard will require an 8- to 12-pounder. The heavier the boat the heavier the anchor.

A lightweight 25-foot cruiser, either outboard or inboard, should be safe from straying with a 12- to 15-pound anchor, while a 30- to 35-footer will ride out a heavy blow with a patent hook of 20 to 25 pounds.

The anchor line should be long enough and heavy enough so that it will cushion sudden shock loads due to wave action. It should lead nearly horizontally away from the anchor, that is, parallel to the bottom, even when it is under strain.

As a general rule of thumb, the anchor line should be about seven times as long as the depth of the water.

If you've ever had a power failure in bad weather, and had nothing to hold you off a lee shore but your ground tackle, you'll

MAKING FAST TO A CLEAT

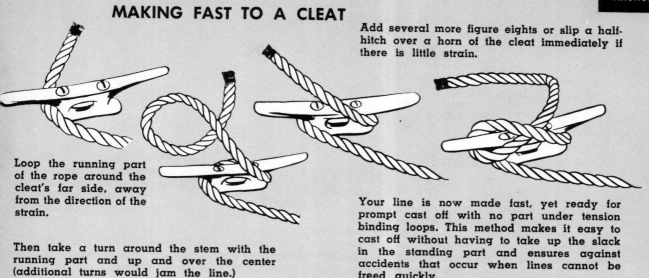

Add several more figure eights or slip a half-hitch over a horn of the cleat immediately if there is little strain.

Loop the running part of the rope around the cleat's far side, away from the direction of the strain.

Then take a turn around the stem with the running part and up and over the center (additional turns would jam the line.)

Your line is now made fast, yet ready for prompt cast off with no part under tension binding loops. This method makes it easy to cast off without having to take up the slack in the standing part and ensures against accidents that occur when lines cannot be freed quickly.

appreciate the importance of a good anchor and line. It's at such a time that you're most likely to remember the boatman's prayer, "Oh, Lord, Thy sea is so great and my boat is so small." Aside from choosing a seaworthy boat, one of the most effective ways to assure your safety and that of your equipment in the event of a breakdown is to be certain that you carry suitable anchors and enough good line so that your boat will hold and ride out any blow.

Every boat should carry two anchors. One, the lighter, should be stowed in such a way that it can be broken out and dropped at an instant's notice in an emergency and be readily available at all times for anchoring under normal conditions. The other will serve as a spare and may come in handy if you are forced to anchor where there is danger of yawing and swinging about under varying wind conditions where such a shift may endanger your boat.

Anchors, like engines, should be matched to the boat they will be expected to hold to the bottom, the scope, current drag and wave and wind action. The design of the anchor used will also provide a variance.

Odd as it may seem, wind on a cold, dry day will exert more drag or force against an anchored boat than will wind of the same velocity on a warm, humid day. This accounts in part for the greater severity of winter seas and also should serve as a warning that boats left at anchor in the winter may require more scope than they do at the same anchorage in summer.

Your marine dealer can help you choose an anchor of recommended size and type for the design and length of the boat you have, as well as for the operating conditions you will meet locally.

There are a number of tips that will help

simplify your anchoring problems and develop your anchoring technique. Keep in mind that the design of your boat will affect its action at anchor. A shallow draft, planing-type hull will react more quickly to shifts in wind and is more prone to swing at anchor than a deep-draft powerboat or a deep-keel sailboat. A deep-keel boat will react faster to changes in current.

In a crowded anchorage, make allowance for the variance of different hulls to wind and current shifts. You may find, for example, that you cannot use the recommended average scope of 7 to 1 and may have to shorten to as much as 4 to 1. The shorter scope will naturally greatly lessen your anchor's holding power. One trick you may use is to secure a weight approximately halfway down the anchor rode. This, in essence, will reduce the angle of line pull in reference to the bottom and reduce the chance of dragging anchor in the event it starts to blow. The weight is called a sentinel.

Don't overlook the effect of tide. If you're in an area, for example, with a six-foot tide and anchor in ten feet of water with 80 feet of line, your scope is 8 to 1. However, if the tide rises six feet, the scope is shortened to 5 to 1, which may be dangerous under certain conditions.

A helpful indication of whether you have sufficient scope is to watch the reaction of waves on the rode. If an upward pull appears to be exerted as the bow rises, you have insufficient line out and should be wary of dragging anchor.

Always select two ranges (landmarks or navigational aids) to fix your position. Watch these ranges for signs of dragging. The bearings also may serve to aid you in recovering your anchor if the line should part. •

Be Your Own
Antenna Specialist

Most antenna problems can be solved with everyday tools
by Art Margolis

Antenna problems in suburbia are minimized by the wide open spaces; metropolitan troubles are complex.

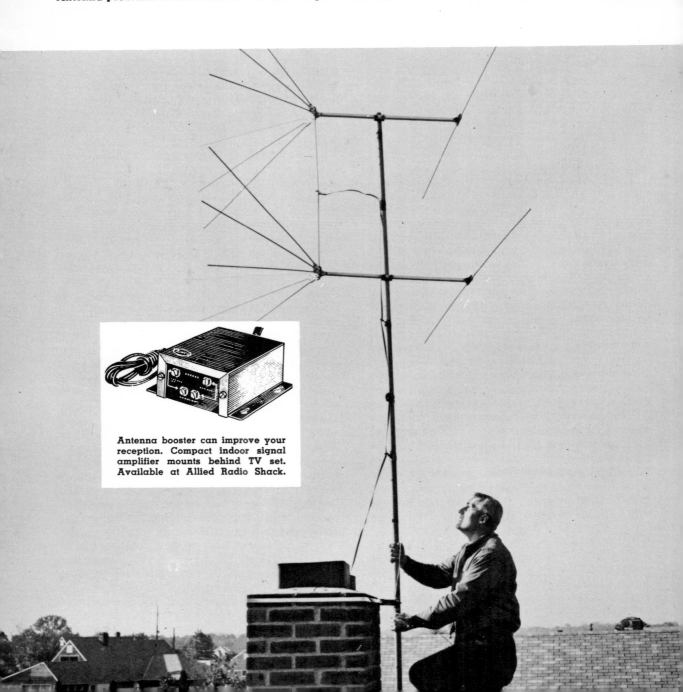

Antenna booster can improve your reception. Compact indoor signal amplifier mounts behind TV set. Available at Allied Radio Shack.

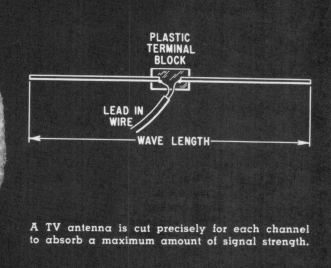

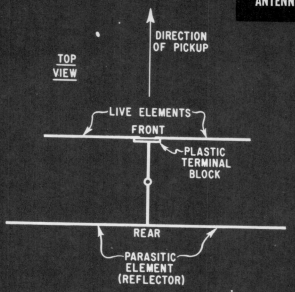

A TV antenna is cut precisely for each channel to absorb a maximum amount of signal strength.

TV antennas stand with the live elements broadside in a horizontal plane to the TV transmitter.

I WOULD say the only requirements anyone needs to handle 95 per cent of home antenna problems are normal handyman house tools, ability and a drop or two of steeplejack blood.

One word of caution at this point. Working on a roof can be dangerous. You must observe strict safety first. Falls are the largest form of home accidents. When you are on a roof, and I don't mean to be facetious, take every precaution so you won't fall off.

A second danger on roofs is the wires. Some carry lethal electricity, others might trip you. If you do go on your roof be sure it is in bright daylight so you can see and steer clear of all wires.

A third danger to watch out for is dilapidated masonry. Before you attach any mounts to any masonry be sure it is strong enough to hold it. I hope I came across on these very important points.

Once you have the roof situation under control, the rest is purely mechanical. Antenna considerations break down into three categories. Installation, maintenance, and troubleshooting. To handle these three antenna areas of endeavor, it would be wise to understand the answers to the . . .

Ten Most Asked Antenna Questions:

Question 1. Why do we need TV antennas when we do not need radio antennas?

Answer 1. Nobody ever said we do not need radio antennas. In every radio there is an antenna or else it couldn't operate. However, due to the long experience of radio, developments have been able to squeeze the antenna down to a tiny size. TV on the other hand is comparatively new and while tremendous strides have been made in antenna developments, little shrinking of the antenna has taken place.

The reason is the high frequencies that TV operates at in comparison to radio. These high frequencies are much more susceptible to losses of strength. They won't travel easily through structures and have a limited "line of sight" range. In order for you to grab yourself a workable portion of these electromagnetic energies it is advantageous to have an antenna cut to absorb the wave lengths, outdoors and up high.

Question 2. How does a TV antenna work?

Answer 2. A TV antenna with its stick appearance is in reality a complete tuned circuit just like a combination of coils, resistors and condensers. The right TV antenna is tuned to the TV frequencies.

The tuning is performed by cutting the metallic sticks to match a particular half wave length. Channel two's wave length is 200.2 inches while channel thirteen's is 54 inches with the in between channels being in between. (See Antenna Length Chart.)

The line or driven element (the one that is attached to the lead in wire) is thus cut at half wave lengths.

Practically speaking, in a good signal area the actual length is not really critical. So antennas are cut on or around the channel three length requirement. (The lower channel is picked because smaller wave lengths can be absorbed easily by a larger length, while larger wave lengths cannot be absorbed as easily by the smaller piece of metal.)

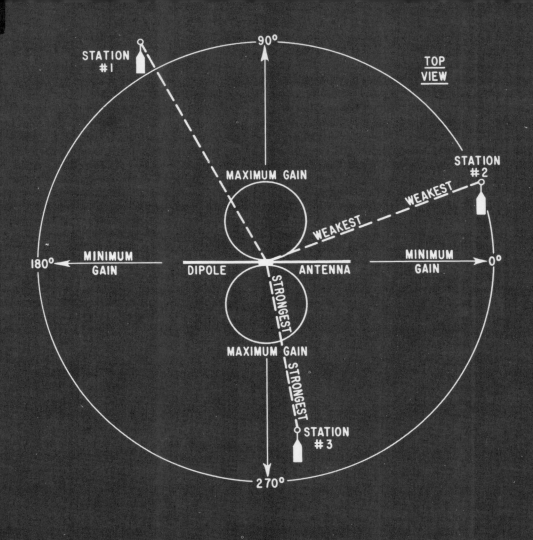

Question 3. How can one tell which way a TV antenna is pointing?

Answer 3. There are two considerations in determining the direction an antenna is looking just as there are two considerations in determining the direction you are looking while you are wearing your polarized sun glasses.

You know that light travels in all planes 360° around. When you don the glasses they obliterate all glare from above and below and the only light that passes through them is on a horizontal plane. If you should lie on your side you would be rotating the polarized glass and then the only light that passed through the glasses would be on a vertical plane.

In addition to the polarization the other consideration is actual nautical direction, north, south, east or west.

Since TV waves are of the same nature as light waves the antenna direction is considered in both polarized and nautical terms.

Radio waves are propagated in a vertical polarized fashion—TV waves in a horizontal fashion. Radio antennas are straight up and down. TV antennas stand arms outstretched, the line elements broadside to the transmitter.

Question 4. Why are there so many different kinds of antennas?

Answer 4. Because there are so many different reception situations. An antenna is chosen for a particular situation according to its basic reception "pattern".

The pattern shows the way the antenna absorbs the signal. Let's examine the four basic TV antennas.

1. The Single Dipole—A single driven element, a dipole produces this pattern. A dipole is two metal sticks that are physically held together by a plastic terminal block that insulates each arm from the other. The lead in wire is attached to the block, one side of the wire touching right element and the other side of the

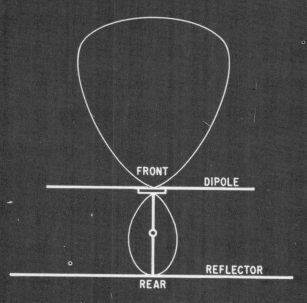

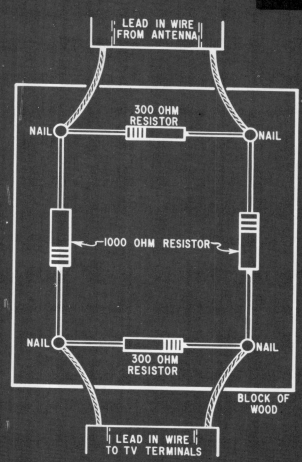

Dipole and reflector pattern. Addition of reflector reduces the rear entrance pickup, narrows pattern.

Dipole pattern. The more area in the figure eight the signal path can cover, the stronger a signal.

Attenuator pad is constructed with four resistors, wood and nails. Signal is reduced through it.

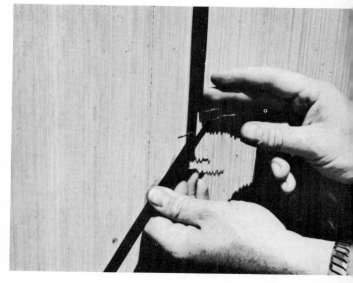

Cut lead-in wire. Spacing must be preserved and staggered to avoid losses. The two ends should fit.

Wind the bare wires together tightly; let them stick out from insulation. Solder them if possible.

wire touching the other element involved.

If the TV transmitter is spewing waves anywhere between 120° to 60° or 240° to 300° the antenna will absorb to its maximum. If the TV rays lob in anywhere else in the circumference the antenna will absorb less and less till it responds at an absolute minimum at 0° and 180°, the ends of the antenna.

Obviously then, for best reception you must aim the dipoles broadside at the transmitter. If there is more than one station you must compromise your aiming of the fixed antenna for best reception from the multiple stations.

2. Dipole and Reflector—a single driven element plus one parasitic element, a parasitic element being one that is not attached to the lead in wire. The driven element could be a single dipole, a folded dipole, a conical or one of a few other variations.

The addition of the parasite called a re-flector, makes the antenna higher in gain and more directional. The reflector sits broadside behind the dipole as they look at the transmitter. The pattern is narrowed and rear entrance pickup is reduced drastically. For all practical purposes you can consider the reflector like a mirror. It bounces back signal to the dipole and bounces off any signal trying to come in the rear entrance. The best reception is obtained by carefully aiming the antenna's front door, the dipole, at the transmitters.

3. Dipole, Reflector and Director—a single driven element plus two parasitic elements. In addition to the reflector behind the dipole, a director is in front of dipole. With this additional parasite the gain is increased even more and the directivity of the antenna is made more critical. You must be a sharp-shooter aiming this type antenna.

4. Multiple Dipoles and Multiple Para-

Trim off excess but be sure to leave enough windings to insure a very strong windproof connection.

Wind electrical tape in overlapping layers over the joint for weatherproofing and extra strength.

A good splice is hardly noticeable. If done properly, it will cure snow and related TV troubles.

Super antenna installed has 28 elements. Follow the lead in. You'll count 9 dipoles, 19 parasites.

sitic Elements, Super Antennas. There are many antennas on the market that have many reflectors, directors, and driven elements. They are listed by their mileage: 100 mile, 150 mile, etc. They are expensive. Their advantage: highest gain possible plus extraordinary directivity. With the right setup you can pick up stations from far away.

Question 5. What good is a motorized antenna?

Answer 5. In some cases no good. In other situations invaluable. In my area between New York and Philadelphia a careful selection of motor and high gain antenna results in receiving every channel from 2 through 13.

The motor is for use with an antenna such as described in type number four. With the motor you can aim the antenna bull's-eye at a transmitter. Then when you change channel aim the aerial at your new selection. This is the worth of the motor.

Question 6. Why is the lead in wire flat?

Answer 6. Just as the antenna is a tuned circuit, so the lead in wire must also possess the same characteristics. The main characteristic is called "impedance". The impedance of an antenna ideally is 300 ohms. The input of the TV set also is 300 ohms. To match the antenna into the TV, the lead in wire must also be 300 ohms. If it's not some of the hard gained signal strength is lost.

If you think of the antenna as a funnel on the roof and the TV set as a rain barrel, the lead in wire can be thought of as the hose connecting the two. It's obvious if the hose fittings are not correct you'll lose rain water. Similarly you'll lose signal if you do not match impedance.

To obtain a 300 ohm impedance in the wire, the copper must be separated by exactly the distance 300 ohm wire is spaced

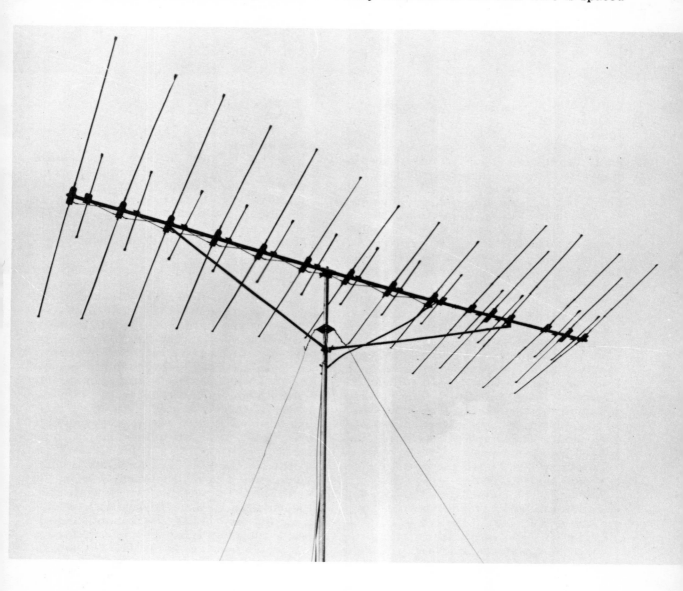

Arrester is best mounted close to antenna. Mount
on the mast, wall, window sill or the water pipes.

A mast standoff is attached, and the lightning
arrester wire is drawn through it and tightened.

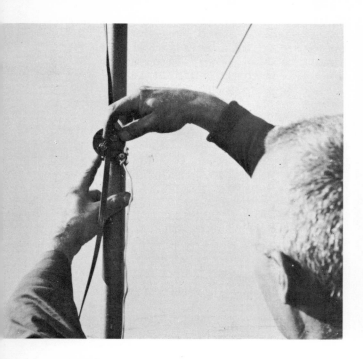

by flat plastic insulation. Remember this.

Question 7. Why use the standoff insulators?

Answer 7. In order to maintain the 300 ohms throughout the length of transmission wire it must receive special care. The wire can't touch or come close to any metal. If it does the impedance will change at this point. At an "impedance bump" some of the waves are bounced back like a mirror reflection. These reflections cancel out some of the signal strength and also enter the TV at the wrong time causing ghost images.

Question 8. Why are some antennas stacked one on top of another?

Answer 8. Two advantages are obtained by stacking one antenna head above another. One, there is increased gain for there are two heads working instead of one. Two, while there is increased gain in the horizontal plane effectively, there is less pickup in the vertical plane. Airplane flutter and most interference travel in the vertical plane. Stacking reduces these unwanted interferences.

Question 9. What are the prime factors to obtain best reception?

Answer 9. The factors are all in a mathematical formula but they are simple. There are seven of them.

1. The HEIGHT of the transmitter.
2. The geographical ELEVATION of the transmitter.
3. The DISTANCE between the transmitter and your TV antenna.
4. The WATTS of power the transmitter is permitted to radiate.
5. The heights of any geographical shadows between the transmitter and your antenna. This includes hills, forests, and buildings.
6. The distances of these shadows in respect to your antenna and the transmitter.
7. The HEIGHT that you install your antenna.

Question 10. What is this thing called signal strength?

Answer 10. Nobody really knows! It can be described somewhat. It can be produced, charted, used and its results felt strongly. It is the same thing as light only it has a lower frequency. We can't see it because our eyes are tuned only for light frequencies. It travels at 186,000 miles per second, which from the transmitter to your antenna means instantly. Anyway, don't worry about it. You can install, maintain, and repair your antenna system without knowing.

Antenna Troubles and Repairs: Antenna troubles are usually the result of wear and tear due to the weather. The wire breaks, the antenna breaks, the connections corrode, the mast bends, the standoffs deteriorate, the mounts weaken, etc. However, the trouble shows up on your TV screen by means of a visual symptom just as in-

Heavy duty lightning arrester wire is drawn to ground through standoff insulators; twin lead also.

Special copper ground rod is taken to out of way place and pounded into ground, leaving 3 inches.

ternal TV troubles indicate their presence.

Once you have ascertained that the trouble is in the antenna system via the rabbit ears test you are ready to trouble-shoot. There are nine general types of symptoms.

Snowy Picture: The picture becomes snowy when you lose signal strength. The snow is static that you see. Usual troubles are breaks in the lead in wire. The break can occur at the antenna head connection anywhere along the lead in wires length, at TV input connection and on rare occasions on the piece of lead in wire that connects the antenna TV terminals and the tuner. The job, find the break and splice it. Or if the wire is old and worn replace the entire length.

Weaves and Ghosts: The picture will become distorted in this fashion if your antenna is not pointed correctly at the transmitter. This can happen if it blows around a bit or even if a new building is erected between you and the transmitter. To correct you must reorient your antenna. The best procedure for orientation is one person on the roof and one by the TV.

The one on the roof slowly rotates the antenna. The person by the set yells up the quality of the picture. At best picture setting the antenna should be tightened up permanently.

Flashing: Your picture will flash and break up into all forms of wild disturb-

Final touches on installation are made by connecting ground wire tightly to copper ground rod.

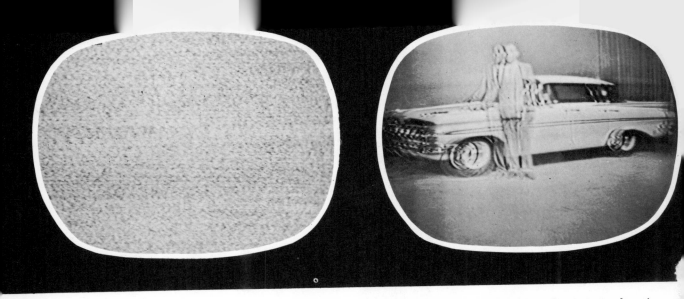

A snowy picture with or without a program happens if the lead-in breaks. Find break and splice it.

Ghosts appear in picture when the antenna is not pointed correctly. Reorientation should be big help.

When lead-in wire flaps in the wind, your picture can bob up and down. Snug wire to remedy.

There is always increasing interference. A new type antenna will do much to exclude the trouble.

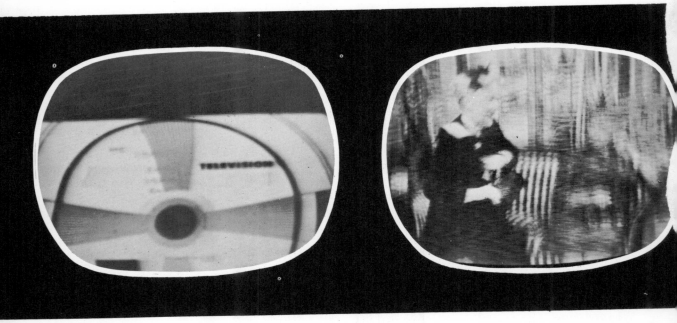

ances if you develop a loose length of lead in wire and the wind causes it to fray or break. Then as the wind continues to buffet the wire the screen symptoms will appear. The cure for this trouble is, replace or splice the lead in wire and snug it down so it won't move in the wind.

Bouncing Pic: The picture will bob up and down seasickwise if your lead in wire gets loose and flaps against some metal such as the TV mast or rain guttering. The cure, snug down with new standoffs till the wire is tight and won't move in the wind.

Excessive Interference: The TV screen will receive excessive interference if you have a simple type antenna in a bad signal area. The weak aerial permits all of the unwanted signal to enter the TV along with the desired signal. The best way to reduce interference is install a stacked, motorized, high gain, highly directional antenna, in place of the simpler types.

Loss of Fine Detail: Loss of fine detail is actually ghost images almost but not quite correctly on top of normal signal. You lose the picture detail because of incorrect lead in wire installation. The lead in wire is too near or mounted right on top of some metal causing impedance bumps or standing waves. The cure, reroute such lead in wire and liberally use standoffs at

Closeup photo shows ghost on top of normal picture. More standoffs will bring back the fine detail.

A signal that is too strong causes excess contrast and bends. A pad will cut down strength.

If your picture should wash out or turn negative due to your neighbor's TV, reorient it or relocate.

This antenna length chart should give you an accurate notion of how long dipole should be cut.

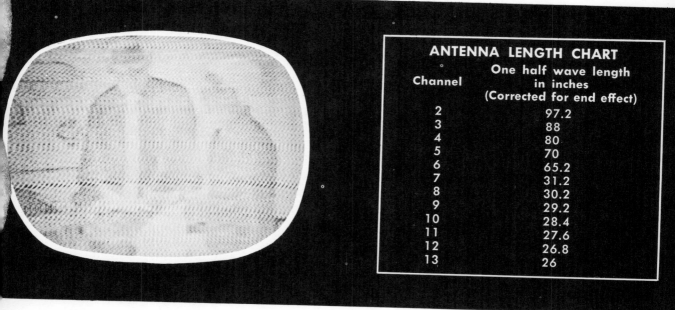

ANTENNA LENGTH CHART

Channel	One half wave length in inches (Corrected for end effect)
2	97.2
3	88
4	80
5	70
6	65.2
7	31.2
8	30.2
9	29.2
10	28.4
11	27.6
12	26.8
13	26

any possible impedance bump or area.

Overloading: There is such a thing as the TV signal being too strong. That occurs by use of high gain antenna systems in strong signal areas. For instance, the far-away stations come in excellently but the nearby stations are too contrasty and have the bends. The cure is to reduce or attenuate the local stations' strength. This is done by means of a "pad" as illustrated. The pad is switched in for the local stations and switched out for distant TV viewing.

Interaction Between Two TV's: If you discover when your neighbor turns on his TV, you are picking up radiation from his TV, there is only way to attempt

a cure. You must get your antenna as far away from his antenna as possible. In addition to relocation, reorientation might also be necessary. As a last resort try relocating or reorienting your neighbor's antenna.

Perfect Picture: It is very possible that you have antenna trouble but it doesn't show up on the screen. You usually find out about it when your neighbor calls. "Your aerial fell down!" The way to circumvent trouble is to examine your antenna system after major storms or at least every six months. At this time exercise normal maintenance as indicated by worn or broken materials in your installation. •

It's easy to disassemble fractional horsepower motors for inspection, cleaning or repair. In most cases you just remove nuts from the ends of the long screws through frame, pull out the screws themselves.

The Important Motors

What goes on inside a motor? Here's how they work and what usually goes wrong

MOST of the fractional horsepower motors found in household appliances, ranging from about ⅛ to ½ H.P., are of the "split-phase" type. A variation is the "capacitor-start" type generally found in refrigerators and ironers, but the same physical construction is used as in the split-phase variety.

Inside the case of the motor are two interwoven "stator" coils of enameled wire of different diameters. The thinner wire is on the starting winding; the heavier on the running winding. When the motor is at rest, the windings are connected in parallel. One end of one winding is connected permanently to one end of the other winding, and this junction represents one terminal of the motor. The other two ends are connected by a simple single-pole spring switch mounted in one of the end bells; this juncture is the other terminal.

The rotor has no outside connections of any kind. On the end of the shaft nearest the stator switch, however, is a pair of spring-loaded weights. These are collapsed when the motor is at rest. When the line switch is turned on, alternating current flows through both windings causing twisting magnetic fields to be set up around them and through the rotor which is in close proximity. The rotor is dragged around by the magnetic fields and builds up speed rapidly, provided it is not overloaded by the mechanism it is supposed to spin. In a second or two the centrifugal force of the rotation pushes the weights outward against the fixed switch causing it to open and to remove the starting winding from the power line. The motor now operates only with the single running winding.

In the capacitor motor, a large fixed capacitor (or "condenser"), very much like the ones found in radio and television sets, is connected between the free ends of the two windings. This improves the initial

End bells pull off readily and rotor (1) slips out. Stator windings are inside center frame (2). Switch for starting winding (4) is on inner side of one end bell (3). At left, pencil points to centrifugal throw-out that opens the starting switch.

Terminals are usually screw-type binding posts behind small cover plate in same end bell that has starting switch mounted on it. With some motors, direction of rotation can be changed by switching position of one lead on terminal block.

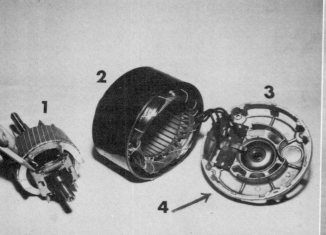

starting twist or torque without increasing the starting current. Otherwise, the throw-out action is the same as with the split-phase type.

The starting winding is alive only momentarily and does not have a chance to heat up. For this reason it can safely be wound of thinner wire than that used for long periods of running. However (and this is a *big* however), if the switch contacts should fuse together or if too big a load on the motor should keep the rotor from attaining normal speed, the starting winding remains on the line and starts to heat up very rapidly within 15 or 20 seconds. Several things may happen. If the motor has an integral thermal overload protector of the automatic resetting type, it will simply stop before the burn-out point is reached. If the power is still on, the motor will attempt to restart after the overload device has cooled off and re-established the circuit. At this point the heating

cycle will begin again and the motor will kick off again. This sort of spasmodic action is a sure sign of a defective throw-out switch, or, more likely, of a simple overload.

If the machine of which the motor is a part uses an external overload breaker, it will usually be found to be of the manual resetting type. The first overload will snap it open, and it will stay open until you press the reset button down. The machine may struggle to start but, if the trouble persists, it will be turned off again by the breaker.

Some motor-driven machines have no built-in protective devices. If a rotor locks, only the line fuse can save the windings. If the fuse is oversized for the momentarily high starting current of a particular motor, it may not blow at all, and your nose will tell you quickly that insulation and copper are overheating. If you don't get to the switch quickly you can be sure that the winding will pop. •

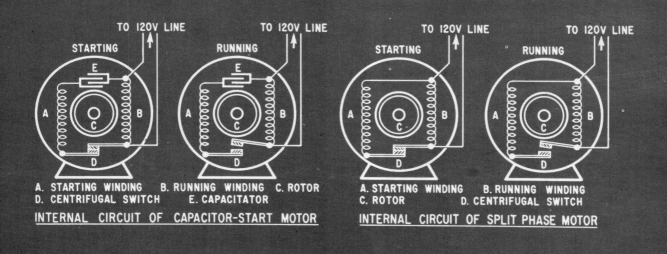

TO 120V LINE   TO 120V LINE   TO 120V LINE   TO 120V LINE

STARTING   RUNNING   STARTING   RUNNING

A. STARTING WINDING   B. RUNNING WINDING   C. ROTOR
D. CENTRIFUGAL SWITCH   E. CAPACITOR

INTERNAL CIRCUIT OF CAPACITOR-START MOTOR

A. STARTING WINDING   B. RUNNING WINDING
C. ROTOR   D. CENTRIFUGAL SWITCH

INTERNAL CIRCUIT OF SPLIT PHASE MOTOR

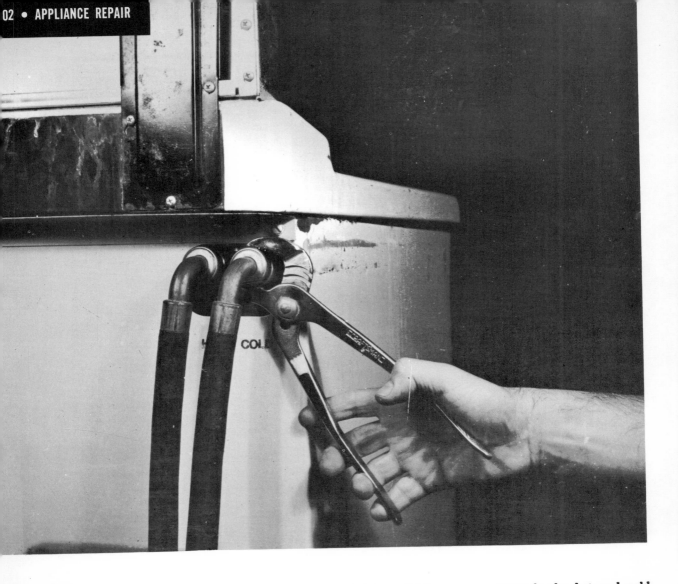

The first step, of course, is to remove the line cord, after which you can uncouple the hot and cold water hoses (for washer). A slip-jaw wrench is the best tool for the job, but gas pliers can be used. There will be some water in the hoses, so have a pail handy into which they can first be drained.

Disassembly

Disassembly is half the job. Find out how to get at the mechanism and take a look

HALF THE TRICK in finding and fixing faults in an appliance is knowing how to take the machine apart so you can get at its innards. With the top cover or back plate off, you can usually spot loose wires, broken belts, leaking valves, etc., in short order.

If you've ever replaced spark plugs, rotated tires or drained the radiator of the family car, you should have little difficulty applying the same wrenches to washers, dryers, broilers, fans and other appliances. You may have to poke around a bit at first to learn which screws hold what parts together, but you can be sure of one thing: Anything that was put together with nuts and bolts can be taken apart. In many cases the fasteners are not even nuts and bolts,

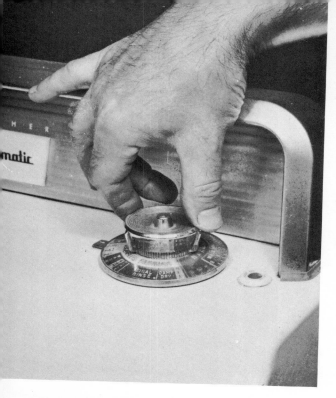

The timer control is turned clockwise for proper cycling of various kinds of clothes, then pulled out slightly to start action. Puzzle: How to remove it? No set screws are in sight. Answer: Twist the knob sharply counterclockwise. It will unscrew readily and separate from dial assembly.

With the knob off, the dial can be removed. It fits over a flattened shaft, and can be simply slipped off. A husky hex-head screw, invisible with the dial in place, now appears in front of the shaft. This is one of the two fasteners that hold the entire top of the washing machine in place.

On the left side of the washing machine is a decorative name plate similar in design to the control dial. This has no mechanical function, but does serve to hide the other hex-head screw that holds the top to the machine. In disassembly, it is simply pried up with a screw driver as shown.

The hex-head screws can now be removed in order to take the top off the washer. The top can be simply lifted free. Caution should be observed here, however. Lift it carefully and watch for wiring along the back side of the machine. Instructions sheet, if it's available, will be helpful.

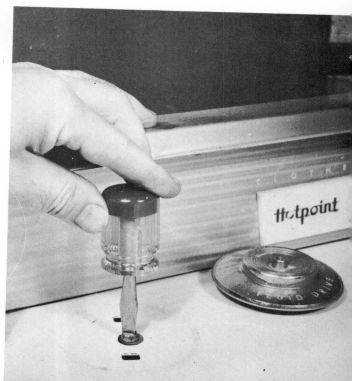

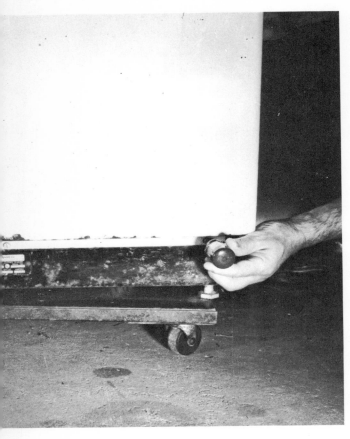

This washer has removable panel in front (some have three-sided cabinet with removable back). Look for self-tapping screws along bottom edge. Machine is resting on a dolly (a square of wood shelving with plate casters in corners) to ease job of moving heavy washer around for inspection.

Damp atmosphere that naturally attends a clothes washer raises havoc with screws and exposed metal surfaces. A few drops of "liquid wrench" penetrating oil will help to loosen stubborn fasteners, making it easy to remove them. Machine has been turned on side to make screws accessible.

With the bottom screws removed, the front panel of washer lifts off spring hooks at the top. Entire inside "works" of machine are now accessible.

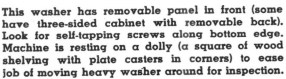

but merely self-tapping screws which form their own "nuts" in the bottom layer of a sandwich of two or more pieces of sheet metal.

Actually, the best time to acquaint yourself with the anatomy of an appliance is when it is in normal working order. Then, if something should happen to it, you can attack it with assurance and save a lot of time and fumbling.

It is helpful, of course, to have an instruction sheet or service manual for a machine but, since these are generally not easy to obtain, you often have to proceed by inspection and touch. Almost immediately you may encounter a puzzle in the form of knobs or dials that have no set screws or other visible means of attachment. If a knob appears to be of solid, one-piece construction, grasp it firmly with your fingers and merely *pull* straight out, and to your surprise it will probably come off readily. Examine its center hole and the

Not a television receiver, but the top of a washer stood on end. Look for pull-apart connectors on various leads and make a careful note of color markings on the latter. Soldered connections are almost never found in modern day appliances.

An unexpected but welcome bonus! Removal of the front panel of the washer reveals a clear and highly valuable schematic diagram of the wiring. With this and a volt-ohm-meter, it becomes easy to trace all connections, locate possible troubles.

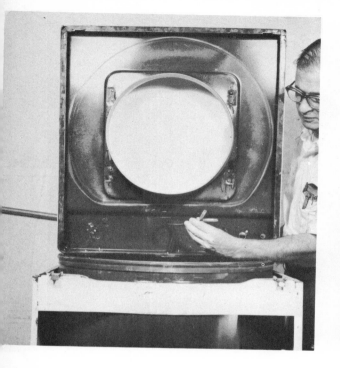

Solderless plug-in connections save manufacturing time, but they are vulnerable to vibration. Machine once failed to operate on spin cycle because this lead had jogged loose from controlling solenoid. All the connector receptacles were squeezed slightly with a pliers to grip more firmly.

This is the timer, the heart of an automatic washer with seven connections to the panel and two more to the timer motor (underneath). Once the tube filled properly with water and then refused to agitate. When the top was pulled off to free the timer, one lead was found to have separated completely from its end plug! Evidently the wire had been pinched a little too much in assembly, and the shaking of the machine finally broke off the few strands that remained.

A very simple reason why this washer stopped working after about six years—the drive belt had finally separated. This is a "normal" failure, and must be expected sooner or later with most machines. Replacement is just a matter of minutes.

shaft from which it came and you will observe that a flattened area on the latter permits the knob to fit only one way while a spring in the hole tightens the assembly. Removal of the controls is the first step in most disassembly operations.

To give you an idea of what to expect, the series of photographs shown here illustrate a typical take-down job on a typical clothes washer. This machine performed honorable service on everything from handkerchiefs to bed sheets, quit a number of times for typical reasons, was repaired each time by the owner and was finally retired after nine years because it was just plain worn out. Since the useful life of most heavy-duty machines is conservatively figured at five years, this washer could be considered a good investment. •

Preventive Maintenance

Routine maintenance is important—get the habit of checking appliances regularly

YOU'VE UNDOUBTEDLY gotten into the habit of checking your tire pressure, the water in the radiator and the oil in the crankcase, and you know that regular attention of this kind assures you trouble-free driving and maximum car life. Extend this same habit of preventive maintenance to your household appliances.

The accompanying photos illustrate just a few of the important points that need emphasis as suggested by the service department of Sears, Roebuck & Co. In poking around your machines you will probably find other elements that can stand occasional cleaning, lubrication or adjustment —simple jobs all. •

Maximum capacity of common clothes washers is between 7 and 9 pounds, but how many home laundries boast a scale of any sort for actually measuring daily piles like this one? Overloads not only strain the machine dangerously but defeat its purpose: crowded clothes do not wash clean. When in doubt as to how much of a load is too much, play safe and divide it. Two washes are cheaper than headache of stalled drive mechanism.

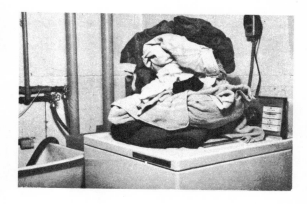

A surprisingly small quantity of most detergents, like this mere handful, does a thorough washing job even on very dirty clothes despite the fact that it creates little or no suds. Solution flushes out readily without clogging machine. If any bleaching is needed, use a bleach—not more soap.

Opening a machine may reveal the existence of unexpected lubrication points such as this one on the drain pump of a washer. Go easy on the oil; three or four drops every three or four months is enough. Some fittings require application of auto-type grease guns. Motor bearings are generally of the "permanently" lubricated type and need no attention during normal life of appliance.

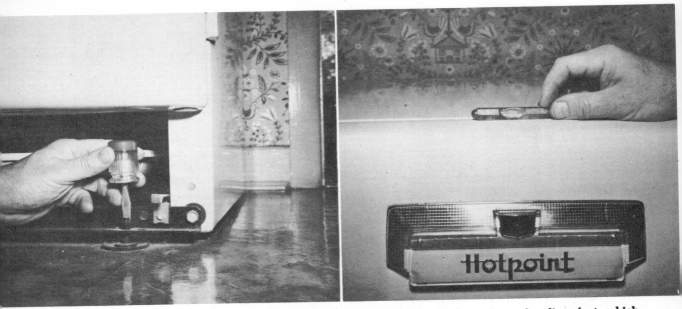

Practically all large machines such as refrigerators, freezers and washers have leveling feet which are adjustable by means of a screwdriver or a wrench. A small spirit level is necessary, and should be used to check both the front and the rear. A properly leveled machine runs smoothly without a shake. This adjustment is also important with refrigerators to make the door swing shut by itself.

Slightest leakage around door gasket of a refrigerator or freezer will cause the cooling unit to run for longer periods than normal. Look for signs of hardening or cracking, the result of frequent slamming of the door. Installing new sealing material around a door is relatively simple.

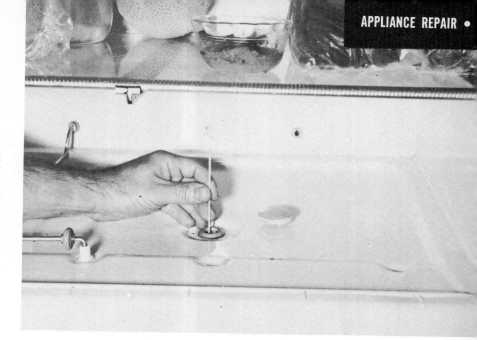

Look for a drain plug on the bottom shelf of a refrigerator. This often becomes clogged with bits of food, and a puddle of water may form around it. Poke the hole clean with a toothpick or a length of wire.

The drain plug has to empty into a receptacle of some sort, usually a shallow pan out of sight behind a panel at the floor line. This lifts or slides off to reveal the drip catcher. The water that accumulates here normally evaporates by itself. However, the pan should be washed now and then to remove any food particles that attract insects.

Thomas Industries photo

For some jobs, spraying is the only way. Do it outdoors with protection for the driveway or lawn.

Applying Paint

by **Richard Day**

A knowledge of paints and how to use them can make painting a pleasure.

BEAUTY IS truly only skin deep when it comes to painting. And skin deep is deep enough. A coat of paint only a few thousandths of an inch thick can transform the inside or outside of a run-down house into a palace. What's more, painting is so easy these days that if you simply follow the directions on the can, you can't go far wrong. Knowing a bit more about paint can help you do an easier, better job.

Those who really swing with a paint brush or roller usually use one kind of paint—latex—for most purposes around the house. It goes on easily and you can clean up with tap water. Latex paints last as well or better than most harder-to-use paints. Latex paints are quick-drying. With some you can paint your way down the ladder, then climb right back up again for a second coat. You can take a break any time you want when using a latex paint. It won't show lap marks. Clean-up is with water. Latex house paints usually produce cleaner, brighter colors than oil-

To mix paint, pour off most of the vehicle before stirring. Finish by pouring mix back and forth.

You save time by rolling paint onto most surfaces. The smoother the surface—the shorter the nap.

base house paints. Their sheen is low and the uniformity of sheen is often better than with oil paints.

Damp surfaces? Latex paint goes on right over them. When you wash a wall before painting it, there's no need to wait while it dries. Outdoor painting can start right after a rain.

Latex paints are so easy to brush and roll on, there's a tendency to spread them out too thin. There's hardly any brush drag. The recommended rate of application—usually 450 to 500 square feet per gallon—should be followed.

Mildew can affect an oil-base paint but it does not attack a latex, although it will go after an oil-base paint underneath the latex. The mildewcide in most latexes will take care of this problem, however.

Nothing is all good. There are a few drawbacks to latex paints. But they're minor. For instance you dare not paint with a latex at temperatures below 50° F. If you live in a cold climate, this restricts the days when you can paint. On the other hand, an oil-base paint can be applied in any temperature that you can stand to work.

Whether your home is built of bricks, blocks, or siding, painting it is almost fun. Before applying any paint put a little time in on surface preparation. On the exterior this should start with an inspection tour. Look at some of the areas where painting problems usually show up. These trouble spots include window and door frames and the areas around them; bases of columns on porches and entryways; steps; siding;

around downspouts; and under-eave areas. Look especially at spots where moisture can collect.

If there's any excessive cracking or peeling in these spots or if the troubles have spread into other larger areas, you are in for a nasty job of paint removal. When excessive cracking or peeling is found, you had better remove all paint in the areas involved if you want a lasting paint job.

Spot-paint-removal is best done with a paint scraper. Reduce the chipped paint down to bare wood and then feather out the raw edges with coarse No. 80 production sandpaper on a wood block or in a power sander. If you have a power sander, use that along with the scraper to take down the old damaged finish. Whenever sanding, work with the grain of the wood.

Wherever the old paint has been removed, a pre-painting prime is in order. Be sure to prime with a paint that is suited to both the old surface and the finish paint you'll be using.

Scratches or cracks found during your inspection tour should be filled with compounds formulated for this. Most paint dealers have these. Application can be with a putty knife, kitchen knife or even your thumb. Let the compound dry and sand the area smooth before priming and painting.

Calking

Countersink all nails and prime over them with metal primer. See that calking at butt joints, around doors and windows and at other through-the-wall openings is in good shape. If not, rake it out and re-calk. The easiest, most economical calk to use under paint is one of the new latex calks. Water-based, they extrude from the gun easily, smooth out by rubbing with a wet finger. They clean up with just water if they haven't set. After setting they're waterproof.

After cleanup, brush any loose dust and dirt away and remove any oil or grease that might be on the old surface. Replace crumbly putty around window panes.

Outside metal that has rusted should have the loose rust scraped away and be primed before painting. It can then be painted with the same coating as the rest of the house.

Under-eave areas and other parts of your house exterior that don't catch sunlight for full weathering of the old paint may need special attention. If they're glossy, dull them with sandpaper or with a chemical gloss remover.

If the existing paint is still in decent condition but has weathered, and it is strong and clean, pre-painting preparations will be minor. In this case a thorough going over with a wire brush will put down surface dirt sufficiently. If the old paint is very dirty, it may be easier just

WHAT OUTDOOR PAINT TO USE AND WHERE

Surface	House Paint (Oil-Base)	Transparent Sealer	Cement-Base Paint	Exterior Clear Finish*	Aluminum Paint	Wood Stain	Roof Coating	Roof Cement	Asphalt Emulsion	Trim-and-Trellis Paint	Awning Paint	Spar Varnish	Porch-and-Deck Paint	Primer or Undercoater	Metal Primer	Latex Paint	Water-Repellent Preservatives	Epoxy, Urethane, Polyester
CLAPBOARD SIDING	✓•				✓									✓		✓•		
BRICKS	✓•	✓	✓		✓									✓		✓		✓
CONCRETE AND CINDER BLOCKS	✓•	✓	✓		✓									✓		✓		✓
ASBESTOS-CEMENT	✓•													✓		✓		
STUCCO	✓•	✓	✓		✓									✓		✓		
NATURAL WOOD SIDING AND TRIM				✓		✓								✓				
METAL SIDING	✓•				✓•										✓	✓•		
WOOD FRAME WINDOWS	✓•									✓•				✓		✓•		
STEEL WINDOWS	✓•									✓•					✓	✓•		
ALUMINUM WINDOWS	✓•									✓•					✓	✓•		
SHUTTERS AND OTHER TRIM	✓•									✓•				✓		✓•		
CANVAS AWNINGS											✓							
WOOD SHINGLE ROOF						✓											✓	
METAL ROOF	✓•														✓	✓•		
COAL TAR FELT ROOF							✓	✓	✓									
WOOD PORCH FLOOR													✓			✓**		
CONCRETE PORCH FLOOR													✓			✓**		✓
COPPER SURFACES												✓						
GALVANIZED SURFACES	✓•									✓•					✓	✓•		
IRON SURFACES	✓•									✓•					✓	✓•		

Bullet indicates that a primer or sealer may be necessary before the finishing coat (unless surface has been previously finished).

*To be avoided if possible
**Floor type

to wash with trisodium phosphate and water. After scrubbing down, rinse well with clear water.

Mildew should be removed before painting. To get rid of it make a witch's brew of the following: 3 ounces tri-sodium phosphate, 1 ounce household detergent, 1 quart household chlorine bleach (sodium hypochlorite) and 3 quarts warm water. Wearing rubber gloves, apply the solution with a scrub brush, let stand for a few minutes and rinse off.

If there is a tendency toward mildew in your climate, re-paint with mildew-resistant paint.

Spots of resin around knots should be removed and the knots covered with knot sealer or aluminum paint. Don't use shellac outdoors.

Masonry with powdery efflorescence needs the powder brushed away before you paint, especially with a latex paint. Sometimes, if the masonry is too powdery, a surface conditioner is needed before painting. Cracks, of course, should be calked to keep moisture out.

Indoor Painting

Indoor preparation is simpler. It follows two key points—cleaning and repairing. Clean walls to remove grease, oil and loose

WHAT INDOOR PAINT TO USE AND WHERE

	FLAT PAINT	SEMI-GLOSS PAINT	ENAMEL	INTERIOR VARNISH	SHELLAC	WAX (LIQUID OR PASTE)	WAX EMULSION	STAIN	WOOD SEALER	FLOOR VARNISH	FLOOR PAINT OR ENAMEL	POLYURETHANE	ALUMINUM PAINT	SEALER OR UNDERCOATER	METAL PRIMER	LATEX PAINTS	CATALYTIC COATINGS
PLASTER WALLS AND CEILINGS	✓•	✓•												✓		✓	
WALLBOARD	✓•	✓•												✓		✓	
WOOD PANELING	✓•	✓•		✓	✓	✓		✓	✓					✓		✓•	
KITCHEN AND BATH WALLS		✓•	✓•											✓			✓
WOOD FLOORS								✓	✓	✓•	✓•	✓	✓•	✓•			✓
CONCRETE FLOORS										✓•	✓•	✓		✓		✓*	✓
VINYL AND RUBBER TILE FLOORS										✓	✓						
ASPHALT TILE FLOORS										✓							
LINOLEUM							✓	✓	✓				✓	✓			
STAIR TREADS										✓		✓	✓	✓	✓		✓
STAIR RISERS	✓•	✓•		✓	✓							✓	✓	✓			
WOOD TRIM	✓•	✓•		✓	✓	✓		✓				✓		✓		✓	✓•
STEEL WINDOWS	✓•	✓•													✓	✓	✓•
ALUMINUM WINDOWS	✓•	✓•													✓	✓	✓•
WINDOW SILLS					✓									✓			
STEEL CABINETS	✓•	✓•													✓		
HEATING DUCTS	✓•	✓•													✓	✓	✓•
RADIATORS AND HEAT PIPES	✓•	✓•													✓	✓	✓•
OLD MASONRY	✓	✓												✓	✓	✓	✓
NEW MASONRY	✓•	✓•												✓		✓	✓

Black dot indicates that a primer or sealer may be necessary before the finishing coat (unless surface has been previously finished).

*Floor type

When painting with brush or roller, paint into already-painted wet areas, not out from them.

Painting neat, clean lines at the ceiling line is a snap with an edge applicator dipped in paint.

dirt that keep paint from sticking to the wall. This *may* be as simple as wiping them with a damp cloth. Tight dirt can be painted over easier than it can be cleaned off. Examine plaster walls for small cracks and mars. Carefully fill small hairline cracks with spackling material using a putty knife, kitchen utensil or even your thumb and finger. Larger cracks should be filled with special patching plaster.

To ensure adhesion of plaster fillers, it is sometimes best to chisel out a triangular channel in the wall, narrow on the surface and wider inside. Feed patching plaster into the channel through the narrow opening. When the patch has thoroughly dried, simply sand the surface smooth and you're ready to apply undercoating or primer. Hole- and crack-filling creates a firm, intact surface for the finish. See that wallboard panels are well nailed to the wall framing and that nails do not stick out of the surface.

Glossy enamels should be dulled with fine sandpaper or gloss remover to aid adhesion of the new paint. Prime any bare metal with metal primer.

Nail holes, joints and cracks in woodwork should be filled with spackle, wood putty or plastic patching material. Sand smooth when dry.

Tools

Assemble what tools you'll need for painting before you open the can. If brushes are used, you'll need two, one large brush for flat expanses such as siding and a narrow brush for edging and trim. If you're planning a roller-painted job, you'll need a roller cover of the proper material and nap length, a roller handle

and tray. You'll also need a brush or special applicator for cutting in round corners where a roller cannot reach.

Roller application is best for large wall and ceiling areas. It has less going for it when used on chopped-up areas that are full of trim, windows, doors, cabinets and fixtures. Even so, rollers can often save you time.

A good paint brush will last for years. You would do well to spend a good deal in getting a set of quality brushes and then keep them clean and useful for a lifetime. A good brush picks up more paint than a cheap brush. This means less effort, faster results. A good brush applies paint smoothly without excessive dripping and splattering. The bristles are held tightly by the ferrule so they won't come out in your paint. A good brush has bristles that are flagged at the ends for spreading paint smoother.

No matter what brush you use, clean it as soon as you're through painting. Don't wait. Waiting's what makes messed up paint brushes.

Bristle brushes should not be used with water-thinned paints. The water affects them. For latex paints use synthetic-bristle brushes, such as nylon.

Paint rollers should be matched to the paint to an even greater extent than brushes. Lambswool rollers are great for most paints, but not for latex. You know what water does to wool. Rollers with synthetic fibers should be used for latex paints. Mohair works well with latexes too.

Use rollers with short nap lengths for walls, smooth ceilings, woodwork and smooth masonry. Long-napped rollers are for use on bricks, blocks, stucco, wire fencing and other such rough surfaces. In

Using brush, wipe excess paint off flat against back of container—and on one side of brush only.

NEVER wipe a brush off sideways like this. Brush will be ruined in short order with such handling.

general, the smoother the surface you're painting, the shorter the nap of the roller should be. The opposite is true too.

Use a 7-inch or 9-inch roller for walls and ceilings, a 3-inch one for doors and trim. You can get even smaller ones for cutting in. A donut-shaped roller will paint both sides of an inside corner at one time, eliminating a brush for this use.

Short-nap rollers make smoother finished surfaces. They do, however, require more dipping than rollers with longer naps.

Exterior Paints

House paints for outside use should be designed for protection from the weather as well as for beauty. Always buy reputable brands of paint. The material cost of the paint is so small compared to the labor you expend in applying it, that saving money by buying cheap paint seems silly. It makes more sense to buy the best paint you can get. In the long run it will save you money.

House paints are made in latex formulations. If you want something else, you can select from exterior gloss, self-cleaning white, chalk-resistant, tints and dark body colors, one-coat paints and tinting bases to which you add tinting colors. There are also blister-resistant flat finish and linseed oil emulsion paints for exterior use. For special applications you can use fume- or mildew-resistant paints. Floor paints are designed specifically for that use. For masonry walls, portland cement paint can be used.

Trim paint, which is used for window sashes, doors and shutters, dries to a glossier surface than house paints. These paints are available in water- or oil-base formulations and in a variety of sheens. The smoothest-surfaced ones are called *high-gloss* enamels while others are classified as *semi-gloss* coatings.

A home-made protective stain can be made by mixing oil-base house paint with up to an equal part of turpentine or paint thinner. A coat or two stains bare wood the color of the paint, but doesn't completely hide the wood's grain.

Painting the Exterior

Before starting to work with paints, rub protective cream onto your hands and arms. A film of this cream makes it easy to remove all paint from your skin when your job is done.

A 4½- to 5-inch brush is recommended for painting the larger surfaces outside your house. Trim and such is best painted with a 1½- to 2-inch sash brush. Apply paint with the tips of the bristles, not with the sides. They last much longer with proper use. Work the paint into the surface with smooth, even strokes whether you're painting the first coat or the second.

Paint during a relatively dry time of day when the temperature is above 40° and after any morning dew has evaporated. Some latex paints can be put on under imperfect conditions. For instance, the surface needn't always be bone dry for painting with latex.

To avoid between-coat peeling of paint, apply top coats within 2 weeks after priming. Do not prime in fall and delay top coats until spring. It's better to treat outside wood with a water-repellent preservative and delay all painting until spring.

Always paint the side of the house that

will be shaded while drying. Start in the morning on the east side of the house and finish up on the west side. This will help prevent blistering of the fresh paint caused by sun shining on it before it dries.

Start painting a house at an upper corner, usually the lefthand one as you face the wall, and work downward. While professionals start at one corner and paint straight across to the other, you will have less ladder handling if you paint down. On an all-wood house, do the siding first, then the trim and window sash. When you're working up at the peak of the roof, it may pay you to make an exception and paint both the siding and trim and avoid moving the ladder back there again.

When rolling paint on lap siding, buy a small roller to paint the undersides of siding boards.

For outdoor painting, get the type of roller tray that fastens to a ladder. This will save you going up and down the ladder to reload the roller with paint.

Special Surfaces

The best finish for shingles and siding that are to be left natural is either a clear water-repellent preservative or a high-quality pigmented stain. Avoid clear finishes outdoors. They just don't last.

Masonry may be painted with one of the colorful rubber-based coatings. Latex and alkyd paints may also be used on most types of masonry. Almost all exterior house paints may be used on masonry if surface preparations are done properly. Consult the label.

Galvanized iron, tin or steel building materials may corrode if not properly protected. While copper and aluminum do not rust, they corrode unless protected. The corrosion washing off of them stains materials below, so protection is in order for these materials too. Although conventional house paints can be put on these metals, some of the rust inhibitive coatings are better suited. Ask your paint dealer which primer and paint is best for your outdoor metal.

Porch floors and steps are usually built of wood or concrete. The paint chosen for them must not only be compatible with the material but must be able to withstand heavy wear from foot traffic. Most paint stores stock special porch and deck paints that wear well under such use. The primer selected should suit the material being painted. For example, when painting wood steps, you can prime with a thinned version of the top coat. Concrete areas may

call for an alkali-resistant primer.

Chlorinated rubber paint produces the best results in painting concrete porches and steps. Roughening the surface with a wash of 1 part muriatic acid in 10 parts water gives the surface additional "tooth" to hold the paint tightly to the surface. In any case, follow the label instructions closely.

The catalytic coatings are good for areas where foot traffic would wear out ordinary paints. They outdo everything in the wear department.

Paints for Inside

Inside paints must have different properties than outside paints. For one, they shouldn't chalk away with age and exposure. If they did, you'd have a dusty house. Desirable interior paint properties are quick drying, lack of spatter, ease of application, lack of a powerful odor, washability and covering power. Not all paints have all of these qualities. Latex paints come the closest to being ideal. Other possibilities for interior use are oil-base paints, alkyds, enamels, texture paints, epoxies, calcimine, casein paint and floor enamel. Interior latexes come in flat wall paints, dripless types and semigloss enamels for trim, and even texture paints. Casein paints and calcimine are outmoded products. You won't want to use them.

A great primer-sealer for indoor use is pigmented shellac. It dries so quickly you don't have to wait to paint over it.

For interior clear finishing, you'll want to consider shellac, varnish, clear enamels, clear lacquer and polyurethane. Polyurethane is ideally suited for refinishing wood flooring. Get the moisture-curing type if you can. It wears best.

Roll Paint on Walls

For painting walls and ceilings, rollers win all bets. Get a roller extension handle for floor and ceiling painting and you won't need to move a ladder around to paint ceilings. Floors are easily painted too with a roller and extension handle.

For corners use a 2- or 2½-inch brush to paint strips at the wall and ceiling corners and around woodwork. Unless you're using a latex paint, don't cut in the whole room at once. Instead do each area as you come to it. Roll paint onto the larger wall areas working into the cut-in strips. This procedure will keep you from getting ugly lap marks when the cut-in area dries before the rest of the wall.

Thorough preparation is the key to a long-lasting paint job. Peeling paint should be scraped off.

Pour the roller tray one-third full of paint and run the roller roll back and forth until it is evenly covered with paint. Remove the excess paint by rolling on the ramp of the tray. To apply an even film of paint, roll with uniform pressure in up-and-down strokes. On a vertical surface the first stroke should be upward even if you're painting downward. Follow the up with a down, then roll crosswise. Always roll first in a dry area and then work into a freshly painted one blending the laps.

Resist the temptation to roll too fast. Hot rod rolling causes spattering, even in dripless paints. Fast rolling also may give uneven coverage.

When you paint walls, start at an upper lefthand corner and work down toward the floor. Follow this same procedure whether using a brush, roller or both. If you're a southpaw, work from right to left.

When painting a ceiling, work across the width, rather than the length, of the room. This enables you to begin a second lap before the first has completely dried. Never try to paint a strip more than two feet wide, both for lapping and safety purposes. Don't try to move ladders or scaffolds with paint, brush or roller aboard or you'll end up painting the floor too.

You can paint acoustical tile on ceilings with a roller, brush or spray gun. If any of the cells become clogged with paint, poke them open with a pin. Flat paint, somewhat thinned, should be used for painting acoustical tile ceilings, but be sure to check with your dealer on thinning instructions.

When painting woodwork use a round 1-inch brush for window sash and a 2- or 3-inch one for the balance of the trim.

Wipe up spills and spatters immediately with a cloth dampened with the correct solvent for the paint—water, turpentine or paint thinner. Do this right away if you're painting with a latex paint. It dries quickly.

When you roll paint onto a ceiling, work across the width of the room.

One "no-no" about painting. Because young children are liable to chew on anything they come in contact with, it's important to use paints indoors that contain no harmful ingredients. Sometimes well meaning home painters use the wrong type of paint when refinishing toys, furniture or walls. Outdoor paints, for instance, sometimes contain lead and should not be used where children can get at them. They should be used only outdoors. Finishes designed for indoor surfaces seldom contain anything really harmful; however, it's a good idea to check with your paint dealer if at all in doubt about the type of paint to use. This is good advice any time.

Expand Your Attic

By Henry Clark

HAS your family grown beyond the limits of your house? A simple solution to this dilemma is to look to your attic for space to add those extra bedrooms and bath. As it stands, your attic area may strike you as a puny space for such growth. If so, just visualize a full rear shed dormer, complete with two or three brand new windows. It can give you about 50% more cubic content and make a second floor living area a reality.

Don't be dazed by the terrifying prospect of ripping open your roof to the elements and flooding your home with rain water as you struggle to complete what seems a Herculean task. Exposing your attic interior isn't necessary with the unique method described here, and the job itself can be completed by you alone over relatively few weekends of work.

The secret is to build the dormer roof right over your existing roof and rip out the present roof only when the dormer is completely boxed in. Thus you may extend the period of work indefinitely and never subject your home interior to weather damage.

Before plunging into this money-saving project, save yourself the stray chance of a headache by checking your local building codes to see if a building permit is required (the cost is insignificant). Also there may be a few minimum requirements as to spacing between studs, rafters and joists.

Now do a little preliminary common-

Typical dormer structure begins with erection of studs. Remove or chop hole through eave boards to expose the wall plate upon which studs will bear.

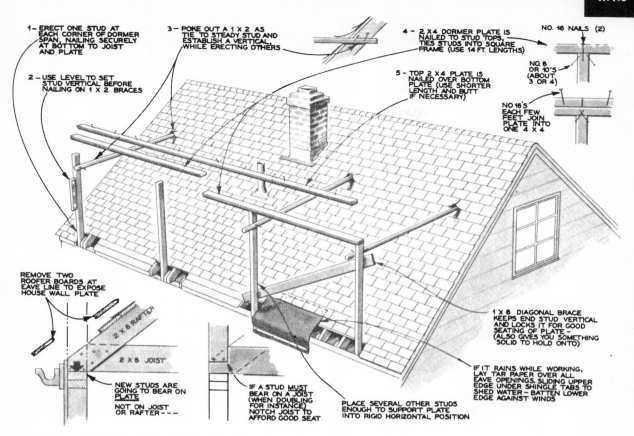

1 – ERECT ONE STUD AT EACH CORNER OF DORMER SPAN, NAILING SECURELY AT BOTTOM TO JOIST AND PLATE

2 – USE LEVEL TO SET STUD VERTICAL BEFORE NAILING ON 1 X 2 BRACES

3 – POKE OUT A 1 X 2 AS TIE TO STEADY STUD AND ESTABLISH A VERTICAL WHILE ERECTING OTHERS

4 – 2 X 4 DORMER PLATE IS NAILED TO STUD TOPS, TIES STUDS INTO SQUARE FRAME (USE 14 FT. LENGTHS)

5 – TOP 2 X 4 PLATE IS NAILED OVER BOTTOM PLATE (USE SHORTER LENGTH AND BUTT IF NECESSARY)

NO. 16 NAILS (2)

NO. 8 OR 10'S (ABOUT 3 OR 4)

NO 16'S EACH FEW FEET JOIN PLATE INTO ONE 4 X 4

REMOVE TWO ROOFER BOARDS AT EAVE LINE TO EXPOSE HOUSE WALL PLATE

2 X 6 RAFTER

2 X 8 JOIST

NEW STUDS ARE GOING TO BEAR ON PLATE

NOT ON JOIST OR RAFTER – – –

IF A STUD MUST BEAR ON A JOIST (WHEN DOUBLING FOR INSTANCE) NOTCH JOIST TO AFFORD GOOD SEAT

PLACE SEVERAL OTHER STUDS ENOUGH TO SUPPORT PLATE INTO RIGID HORIZONTAL POSITION

1 X 6 DIAGONAL BRACE KEEPS END STUD VERTICAL AND LOCKS IT FOR GOOD SEATING OF PLATE – (ALSO GIVES YOU SOMETHING SOLID TO HOLD ONTO)

IF IT RAINS WHILE WORKING, LAY TAR PAPER OVER ALL EAVE OPENINGS, SLIDING UPPER EDGE UNDER SHINGLE TABS TO SHED WATER – BATTEN LOWER EDGE AGAINST WINDS

STEP 1   OPENING EAVE BOARDS FOR LOCATING STUDS TO FORM DORMER GENERAL FRAME

Create a second floor living area by building a full shed dormer on your roof with this unique method.

sense paper work. The photographs and sketches in this article illustrate every basic building step you need to know. But exact dimensions for height, width, depth and styling must necessarily depend on the individual home. A number of actual houses are used in the photos to show varieties of procedure and finishing techniques. Plan the size of your dormer, the number of windows you want, the type of finishing to match the present exterior and a dormer roof pitch that will blend architecturally with the house.

To start actual work, remove the first and second eave boards, which will reveal the plate bearing on the wall studs below. At each intersection of a joist and this plate

A single 2x4-in. plate is nailed to initial studs. Double plate later. Use 1x2-in. braces to hold studs in true vertical. Check each with a level.

End rafters and gable plates follow erection of initial studs and stud plate. See details below.

Gable plate is attached at interior end to an existing rafter and beveled to match roof pitch.

Make opening through ridge boards to expose the ridge pole to which the end rafters are attached.

you will spike your new 2x4 dormer studs. At this point be careful to avoid an important pitfall. Do not nail your new studs to existing rafters as these will eventually be torn out from inside. Nail only to the plate and joists. Examine the top lefthand photograph on page 113 for correct procedure.

Put up just a few studs at first to form a support for your new dormer plate. Use 1x2-in. ties to support the studs and establish a vertical. Install the plate atop the studs as illustrated. We might presumably erect all studs at once, but this would form a dangerously heavy structure without adequate support. At this point we merely want to form a basic frame of studs, rafters and gable plates.

With stud plates placed, measure, cut and nail in place the two gable plates that form a horizontal directly beneath the end rafters. One end of each gable plate rests on the front dormer plate, while the other end is secured to an existing inside rafter of the house. Note that this is the only instance we will attach a dormer member to an existing rafter, since these particular bearing rafters for the two gable plates will not eventually be removed. See the second photo from the top on this page to note inside attachment of the gable plate.

When the gable plates have been spiked in place, remove the two top ridge boards and install the two end rafters to the ridge pole and dormer plate. First measure properly for span and cut accurate angles at the rafter ends for secure seating on the plate and ridge pole. These will form patterns for all your rafters so cut them carefully. We presume, of course, that the house ridge pole is straight. If not, it will necessitate shortening or lengthening the new rafters accordingly.

You now have a basic frame upon which you may install all remaining studs and rafters. It is perhaps best to cut and place all rafters first since it is desirable to close in a shelter for the old roof as soon as possible. Note that all rafters placed between the two end rafters must be nailed to the plate and ridge pole only. Do *not* nail to existing rafters, as these will be ripped out later. See the bottom photo on this page to see rafter attachment to the ridge pole.

So far we have our old roof intact but considerably punctured in a number of places. Let us suppose storm clouds are gathering and you don't plan to work on your new dormer for a few days. Merely

Left, close-up of end rafter spiked to the ridge pole. Bevel ends to seat accurately against pole.

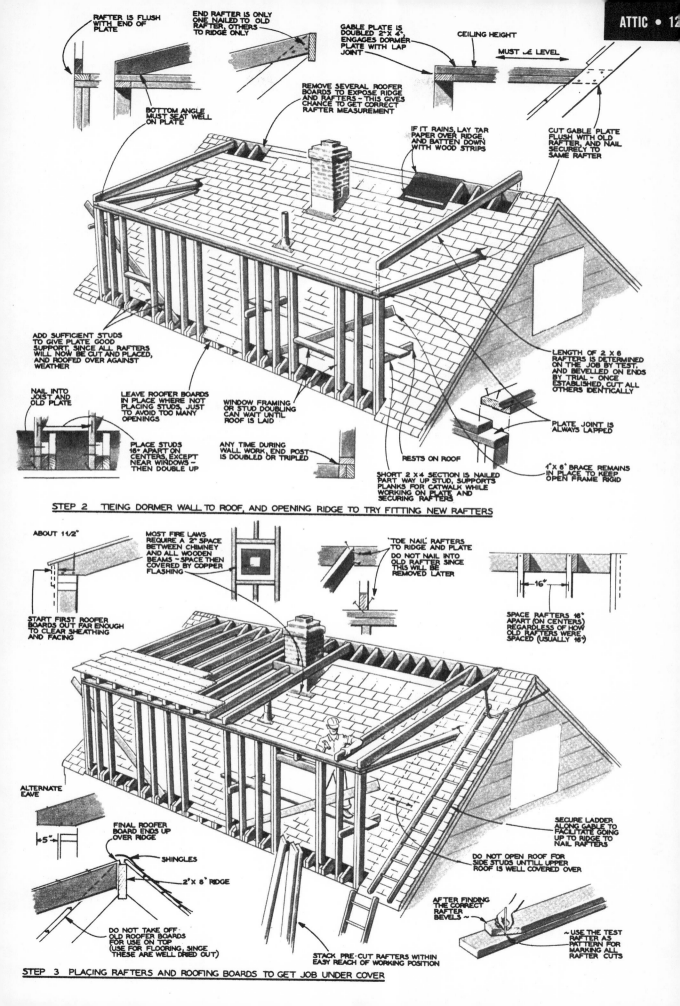

RAFTER IS FLUSH WITH END OF PLATE

END RAFTER IS ONLY ONE NAILED TO OLD RAFTER, OTHERS TO RIDGE ONLY

GABLE PLATE IS DOUBLED 2" X 4", ENGAGES DORMER PLATE WITH LAP JOINT

CEILING HEIGHT

MUST BE LEVEL

BOTTOM ANGLE MUST SEAT WELL ON PLATE

REMOVE SEVERAL ROOFER BOARDS TO EXPOSE RIDGE AND RAFTERS – THIS GIVES CHANCE TO GET CORRECT RAFTER MEASUREMENT

IF IT RAINS, LAY TAR PAPER OVER RIDGE, AND BATTEN DOWN WITH WOOD STRIPS

CUT GABLE PLATE FLUSH WITH OLD RAFTER, AND NAIL SECURELY TO SAME RAFTER

ADD SUFFICIENT STUDS TO GIVE PLATE GOOD SUPPORT, SINCE ALL RAFTERS WILL NOW BE CUT AND PLACED, AND ROOFED OVER AGAINST WEATHER

NAIL INTO JOIST AND OLD PLATE

LEAVE ROOFER BOARDS IN PLACE WHERE NOT PLACING STUDS, JUST TO AVOID TOO MANY OPENINGS

WINDOW FRAMING OR STUD DOUBLING CAN WAIT UNTIL ROOF IS LAID

LENGTH OF 2 X 6 RAFTERS IS DETERMINED ON THE JOB BY TEST, AND BEVELLED ON ENDS BY TRIAL – ONCE ESTABLISHED, CUT ALL OTHERS IDENTICALLY

PLATE JOINT IS ALWAYS LAPPED

PLACE STUDS 16" APART ON CENTERS, EXCEPT NEAR WINDOWS – THEN DOUBLE UP

ANY TIME DURING WALL WORK, END POST IS DOUBLED OR TRIPLED

RESTS ON ROOF

1" X 6" BRACE REMAINS IN PLACE TO KEEP OPEN FRAME RIGID

SHORT 2 X 4 SECTION IS NAILED PART WAY UP STUD, SUPPORTS PLANKS FOR CATWALK WHILE WORKING ON PLATE AND SECURING RAFTERS

STEP 2   TIEING DORMER WALL TO ROOF, AND OPENING RIDGE TO TRY FITTING NEW RAFTERS

ABOUT 1 1/2"

MOST FIRE LAWS REQUIRE A 2" SPACE BETWEEN CHIMNEY AND ALL WOODEN BEAMS – SPACE THEN COVERED BY COPPER FLASHING

'TOE NAIL' RAFTERS TO RIDGE AND PLATE

DO NOT NAIL INTO OLD RAFTER SINCE THIS WILL BE REMOVED LATER

START FIRST ROOFER BOARDS OUT FAR ENOUGH TO CLEAR SHEATHING AND FACING

SPACE RAFTERS 16" APART (ON CENTERS) REGARDLESS OF HOW OLD RAFTERS WERE SPACED (USUALLY 16")

16"

ALTERNATE EAVE

FINAL ROOFER BOARD ENDS UP OVER RIDGE

SHINGLES

2" X 8" RIDGE

5"

SECURE LADDER ALONG GABLE TO FACILITATE GOING UP TO RIDGE TO NAIL RAFTERS

DO NOT OPEN ROOF FOR SIDE STUDS UNTILL UPPER ROOF IS WELL COVERED OVER

DO NOT TAKE OFF OLD ROOFER BOARDS FOR USE ON TOP (USE FOR FLOORING, SINCE THESE ARE WELL DRIED OUT)

STACK PRE-CUT RAFTERS WITHIN EASY REACH OF WORKING POSITION

AFTER FINDING THE CORRECT RAFTER BEVELS ~

~ USE THE TEST RAFTER AS PATTERN FOR MARKING ALL RAFTER CUTS

STEP 3   PLACING RAFTERS AND ROOFING BOARDS TO GET JOB UNDER COVER

Installed end rafter and gable plate. Fit end rafters with care as they form pattern for others.

Complete installation of remaining studs by removing eave boards to reveal wall plate, joists.

take some sheets of tar paper and a few battening strips and cover the rafter gaps you've made near the ridge pole and the stud holes made near the eave. See the top photos on page 113 for examples of stormy weather precautions.

When all rafters are installed, place and nail the roofer boards. These are cut from 1x6-in. tongue-and-groove or shiplap stock. The amount of overhang you want on the dormer eave will dictate the placement of the first roofer board. It must overhang rafter ends enough to clear sheathing and the facing board. Let the roofer boards lie at odd lengths beyond the end rafters and then trim evenly when all are in place. Secure each board with two No. 8 nails in every rafter. Continue to place and nail boards clear to the ridge.

Upon completion, immediately apply asphalt felt of 15-lb. weight (tar paper) over the entire dormer roof, overlapping generously. It is excellent insurance against wood rot and a well rewarded investment.

Shingling can wait till the remainder of the dormer structure is completely sheathed. Also, we do not want too much roof weight until all bearing studs are in place.

Cut and place the rest of the front dormer wall studs, securing as previously mentioned. Double all studs that will bear window assemblies. Be sure you have accurate measurements of proposed window installations at this point and then proceed to place headers and sills. If openings are to be long for large picture windows, use 2x6-in. or 2x8-in. headers to support the rafters bearing on the plate directly above such headers.

Studding for the dormer sides is the next step. Saw away the old roof directly between two rafters where the dormer side wall will enter the attic. Then erect the vertical side studs between the gable plate and a plate installed along a double joist in the floor of the attic. These studs will butt against the existing rafter holding the gable plate and will be nailed to it. As pointed out previously, this rafter remains permanently in place and forms an untouched natural gable at each end of the house. This completes framing of the dormer "cheeks."

Now sheath the face and sides with 1x6-in. tongue-and-groove boards, shiplap stock or composition panels, as you choose. Whatever you use, work from the bottom up and secure firmly with No. 8 nails. As

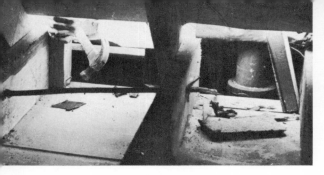

Detail of stud attachment seen from inside. Nail stud to plate and joists, not to existing rafters.

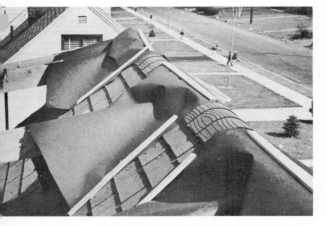

Prepare for rain at any time during construction by battening down tar paper over roof openings.

Stormy weather precautions include covering eave openings well as they receive the most watershed.

Below, framing nears completion. For large window openings use 2x6-in. or 2x8-in. stock for headers to give rigid support to dormer rafters bearing on plate above them.

with the dormer roof, apply tar paper over all sheathing.

Shingle the roof and sides to taste. Butt asphalt rectangles are as durable as anything but slate. Work from the eave up, doubling the first course to hide open slits. Flashing around the chimney and extended vents is usually copper.

With the exterior complete or nearly so, you may plan a period of inside work and get your first glimpse of the added area you have created. Start knocking out the old roof and you can begin to see the space you've wanted for new bedrooms.

You may have some use for this old lumber, so work carefully in removing the old rafters. Saw as close to the eave as you can and try prying the remainder away from the ridge pole.

However, before doing so, note a vitally important precautionary measure. Do *not* remove any rafters until you have erected a group of 4x4-in. temporary supporting studs to hold up the ridge pole in the center of the attic. Space each about ten feet apart. Leave these in place until you have placed attic ceiling joists between the dormer plate and the opposing rafters on the untouched side of the roof. These joists will act as ties or trusses. Still further, leave the supports in place until you have erected one or more bearing partitions inside the attic area to form separate rooms. Be sure these bearing partitions rest on or near a bearing wall on the first floor of the house. Only then is it really safe to remove these temporary studs from beneath the ridge pole.

If you want a wall parallel to the floor joists, double the joist it rests on. Double the top and bottom plates of all bearing wall studs. Try to place a bearing wall as near to the center of the attic as possible to more surely guarantee support for the ridge pole. If you have some spare pieces of 2x4-in. lumber, give the dormer roof added support by installing short lengths of studding between the dormer ceiling joists and the dormer rafters. The pitch of the dormer roof will naturally be shallower than that of the regular house roof and this will be added support against the weight of snow if you are situated in a northern area.

Your dormer is now virtually finished. The installation of electrical outlets, plumbing, etc., is another project and you had best consult your local building codes

Note doubled 2x6s for long span window frame. A 1x6 tops plate in this case for special ceiling.

Fire codes usually require 2-in. gap between a chimney and wood. Cover the gap with flashing.

Securing remaining rafters which have been precut to match end rafters. Spike firmly to plate.

Roofer boards are cut from 1x6-in. tongue-and-groove or shiplap stock. Secure with No. 8 nails.

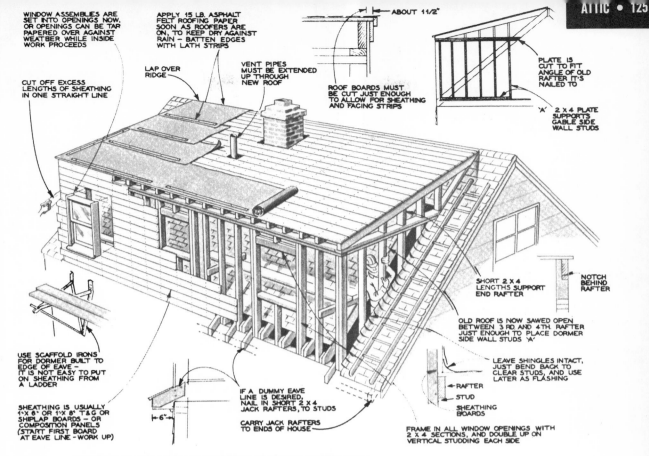

CUT OFF EXCESS LENGTHS OF SHEATHING IN ONE STRAIGHT LINE

WINDOW ASSEMBLIES ARE SET INTO OPENINGS NOW, OR OPENINGS CAN BE TAR PAPERED OVER AGAINST WEATHER WHILE INSIDE WORK PROCEEDS

LAP OVER RIDGE

APPLY 15 LB. ASPHALT FELT ROOFING PAPER SOON AS ROOFERS ARE ON, TO KEEP DRY AGAINST RAIN — BATTEN EDGES WITH LATH STRIPS

VENT PIPES MUST BE EXTENDED UP THROUGH NEW ROOF

ABOUT 1 1/2"

ROOF BOARDS MUST BE CUT JUST ENOUGH TO ALLOW FOR SHEATHING AND FACING STRIPS

PLATE IS CUT TO FIT ANGLE OF OLD RAFTER IT'S NAILED TO

'A' 2 X 4 PLATE SUPPORTS GABLE SIDE WALL STUDS

SHORT 2 X 4 LENGTHS SUPPORT END RAFTER

NOTCH BEHIND RAFTER

OLD ROOF IS NOW SAWED OPEN BETWEEN 3 RD. AND 4 TH. RAFTER JUST ENOUGH TO PLACE DORMER SIDE WALL STUDS 'A'

LEAVE SHINGLES INTACT, JUST BEND BACK TO CLEAR STUDS, AND USE LATER AS FLASHING

RAFTER

STUD

SHEATHING BOARDS

USE SCAFFOLD IRONS FOR DORMER BUILT TO EDGE OF EAVE — IT IS NOT EASY TO PUT ON SHEATHING FROM A LADDER

SHEATHING IS USUALLY 1"X 6" OR 1"X 8" T&G OR SHIPLAP BOARDS — OR COMPOSITION PANELS (START FIRST BOARD AT EAVE LINE - WORK UP)

6"

IF A DUMMY EAVE LINE IS DESIRED, NAIL IN SHORT 2 X 4 JACK RAFTERS, TO STUDS

CARRY JACK RAFTERS TO ENDS OF HOUSE

FRAME IN ALL WINDOW OPENINGS WITH 2 X 4 SECTIONS, AND DOUBLE UP ON VERTICAL STUDDING EACH SIDE

STEP 4 WEATHERPROOF ROOF, APPLY SHEATHING, FRAME IN DORMER SIDES

Close-up of new roofer boards nearing ridge pole. Note old roofers beneath plus old and new rafters.

View from on top of old roof and under new roof shows gable plate and side studding of dormer.

With roofer boards on, cover entire roof with asphalt felt of 15-lb. weight to avoid wood rot.

Photo taken during an actual blizzard shows how method described here protects the home interior.

Cover sheathing completely with asphalt felt paper. Note flashing where dormer wall joins roof.

Sheathing material is optional. Use 1x6-in. tongue-and-groove, shiplap stock or a composition panel.

Interior view clearly shows enormous space gain. Note old rafters stripped of shingles, sheathing.

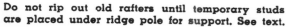

Do not rip out old rafters until temporary studs are placed under ridge pole for support. See text.

Basic dormer is completed when new dormer joists and bearing wall are installed to suit new layout.

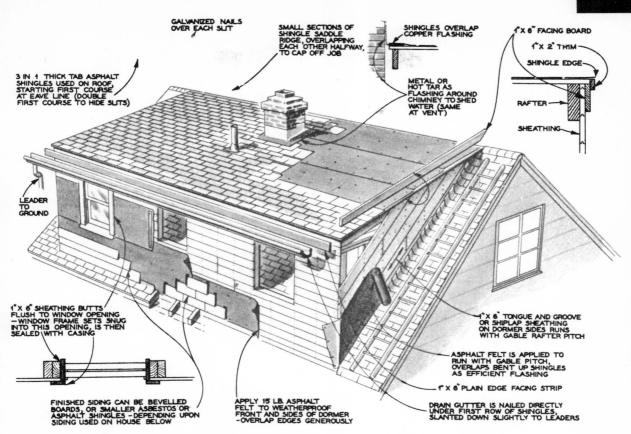

GALVANIZED NAILS OVER EACH SLIT

SMALL SECTIONS OF SHINGLE SADDLE RIDGE, OVERLAPPING EACH OTHER HALFWAY, TO CAP OFF JOB

SHINGLES OVERLAP COPPER FLASHING

1" X 6" FACING BOARD

1" X 2" TRIM

SHINGLE EDGE

3 IN 1 THICK TAB ASPHALT SHINGLES USED ON ROOF, STARTING FIRST COURSE AT EAVE LINE (DOUBLE FIRST COURSE TO HIDE SLITS)

METAL OR HOT TAR AS FLASHING AROUND CHIMNEY TO SHED WATER (SAME AT VENT)

RAFTER

SHEATHING

LEADER TO GROUND

1" X 6" SHEATHING BUTTS FLUSH TO WINDOW OPENING – WINDOW FRAME SETS SNUG INTO THIS OPENING, IS THEN SEALED WITH CASING

1" X 6" TONGUE AND GROOVE OR SHIPLAP SHEATHING ON DORMER SIDES RUNS WITH GABLE RAFTER PITCH

ASPHALT FELT IS APPLIED TO RUN WITH GABLE PITCH, OVERLAPS BENT UP SHINGLES AS EFFICIENT FLASHING

1" X 6" PLAIN EDGE FACING STRIP

FINISHED SIDING CAN BE BEVELLED BOARDS, OR SMALLER ASBESTOS OR ASPHALT SHINGLES – DEPENDING UPON SIDING USED ON HOUSE BELOW

APPLY 15 LB ASPHALT FELT TO WEATHERPROOF FRONT AND SIDES OF DORMER – OVERLAP EDGES GENEROUSLY

DRAIN GUTTER IS NAILED DIRECTLY UNDER FIRST ROW OF SHINGLES, SLANTED DOWN SLIGHTLY TO LEADERS

STEP 5   SHINGLE ROOF, SIDES, INSTALL WINDOWS, FLASHINGS, GUTTERS – THEN REMOVE OLD ROOF INSIDE

before attempting such work or have it done by licensed professionals.

If it is necessary to build your dormer around a chimney, remember that most codes specify a 2-in. gap between the chimney and any framing. So box in the chimney with 2x4s, leaving the required space, and then fill the gap with copper flashing.

Though most front dormers of full length may detract from the architecture of your house, you may add one in addition to the rear dormer and thus nearly double your attic's cubic content. Procedure is basically the same as described here. Build one dormer at a time, however, and do not attempt removing all interior rafters simultaneously. In the case of double dormers, the new attic ceiling joists will extend from one new opposing stud plate to another and form a balanced truss. Be sure adequate bearing walls are erected under these joists.

For space considerations alone, you will find this type of full dormer more advantageous and economical than building twin gable-type dormers which, though they add window area and some space, will still leave completely slanting upstairs ceilings and will not appreciably increase the cubic content of your attic area. •

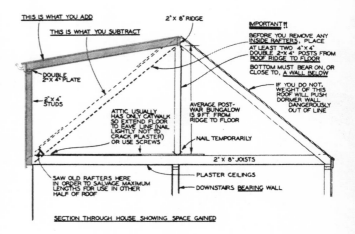

SECTION THROUGH HOUSE SHOWING SPACE GAINED

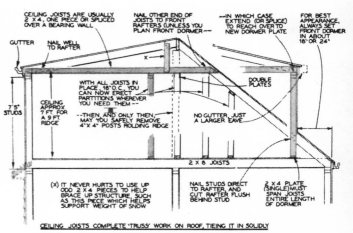

CEILING JOISTS COMPLETE 'TRUSS' WORK ON ROOF, TIEING IT IN SOLIDLY

Ventilate Your Attic

On hot summer nights bring in cool, fresh air for your family's comfort

The first step in installing an attic ventilation fan is to mark the intake louver location in the ceiling, preferably in the center of the house. Above this, in the attic, the fan itself will be mounted.

THINKING of cooling your home? One efficient method and a relatively inexpensive one is to install an exhaust fan that will cool the attic and draw air throughout the house.

On a hot summer day, temperature in the attic can be as high as 130 degrees. Even with normal insulation the upstairs rooms can be 102 degrees and downstairs rooms can be 92. Since walls and ceilings absorb and hold heat, even a cool nighttime temperature will not effectively reduce inside temperatures fast enough for you to sleep comfortably.

A fan in the attic can make considerable difference. The Lau Blower Co. of Dayton, Ohio, conducted tests which discovered that the 130 degree attic temperature could be lowered 27 degrees, with resultant more comfortable temperatures throughout the house.

The fan system can accomplish other things. It keeps inside air fresher and keeps you cooler by increasing perspiration evaporation; the same way a breeze will cool you.

Two factors will decide what fan size you need to provide adequate cooling.

1. The volume of the house and number of air-changes-per-minute desired. One per minute is recommended throughout most of the U. S. If the area measures 24 x 32 x 8 feet, its volume would be 6144 cubic feet (length x width x height). You know the fan must move 6144 c.f.m. (cubic feet per minute). If you desire to cool only certain rooms in the house (the bedroom, for example) choose a fan with a capacity that is 1.2 times the volume of the rooms, since you will always be drawing some air from the other living quarters.

2. Fan location. Best spot is in the center of the house, in the upstairs ceiling if there are two levels. Air flow to fan must not be restricted. Locating the fan close to a wall or in a corner will reduce its capacity. The fan should be installed a distance of its own diameter from the intake grill. This will permit adequate air flow from all sides.

The fan will be most efficient if there are no obstructions within five feet of the fan

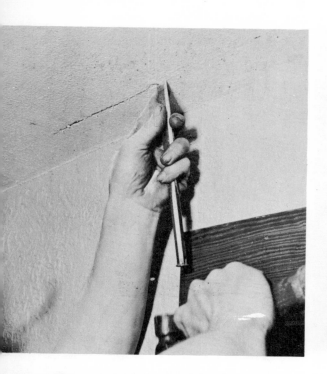

Depending on the size of the intake louver, outline area with a hammer and chisel. You can use this technique either on sheetrock or on plaster.

Clear out the insulation where the fan is to be mounted in the attic. Supporting headers will replace the joist section which must be removed.

Build a platform around fan area for ease of servicing in future. Remove plaster lath by sawing at each end and knock them away from the joists.

After the headers are installed and the opening is cleared away, you can cut off the joist sections. Headers will now support the ceiling load.

outlet. Serious obstructions could even cause the fan motor to burn out.

Provide plenty of exhaust area. Consider the direction of prevailing winds when installing the exhaust grille or openings. Best bet is to have openings on two or more sides of the house to minimize effect of winds.

Here are installation suggestions depending on size and layout of the house.

Single Story Low-Pitched Roof: In ceiling, near as possible to center of house. Install exhaust openings in gable ends or in soffit overhang if house has hip type roof.

House With Attic—No Stairway: Suction box most effective, bringing fan further from the intake louvers and discharging into an unobstructed area of the attic.

Two Story House—Full Attic and Stairway: Suction box over stairway opening to the attic.

Small House With Flat Top: Fan can be installed in a small "penthouse" or in the upper part of a window. Choose window that is located on a side opposite prevailing winds.

Attached Garage: Locate fan at end of garage. Keep garage doors closed, doorway between house and garage open.

General Rule: As warm air rises, best installation of fan is in ceiling or attic wall.

Wherever you put the exhaust grille it should be protected from snow, wind and rain. A porch roof is an excellent place. The exhaust grilles are often placed in the gable ends of the attic. If you install just one, be sure it is in the end away from the prevailing winds. On a flat roof you can install a louvered-wall "penthouse." Louvers can be installed into dormers, or screened openings can be cut into overhanging eaves. Prefabricated louvers are available, so all you need do is cut the opening for them.

The exhaust opening can't be just any size, not for efficient operation anyway. Width and thickness of louvers, size and type of mesh, etc., should be considered since these factors affect the area the exhaust air can move through. Check the accompanying chart for the size opening required for your particular installation.

Certain safety precautions are recommended for the installation of an air exhaust fan.

A frame to support the fan is built of 2x4 stock around the opening and nailed to platform. Size of frame and the opening depend on size of fan.

The fan is now mounted on the platform and centered over the opening; rubber bumpers prevent noisy vibration. Fan shown is the Lau "Rancher."

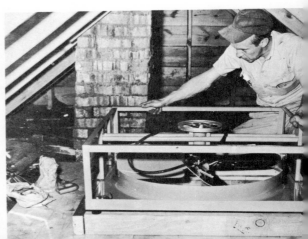

OPENINGS REQUIRED FOR FAN INSTALLATION

FAN SIZE	22″	24″	30″	36″	42″	48″
Full opening (no screen or hardware cloth)	5.5	6	9	12	18	23
Full opening with 16 mesh screen	11	12	18	26	36	46
Full opening with ½″ hardware (cloth)	6.6	7.2	10.8	15.6	21	27
Wood Louvres—no screen or cloth	8	9	13.5	19.5	27	34
Wood Louvres with ½″ hardware (cloth)	9.6	10.8	16.2	23.4	32	41
Wood Louvres with 16 mesh screen	16	18	27	39	54	69
Metal Louvres—no screen or cloth	7.2	7.8	11.7	16.9	23	20
Metal Louvres with ½″ hardware (cloth)	8.6	9.4	14	20.3	28	36
Metal Louvres with 16 mesh screen	14	16	24	33	47	60

Openings are noted in square feet.

1. Adequate size wire should be run in a separate circuit from the main electrical service entrance panel board to the control switch and fan motor.

2. Local codes and ordinances governing electrical installations must be followed. For this reason, it might be wise to have a licensed electrician do the wiring.

3. It is good practice to install a thermostatic switch in the airstream on the suction side of the fan. This will shut off the fan if a fire in the home causes the temperature to get too high. Only a manual reset type should be used.

4. If a suction box is used in the attic with a fixed grille opening in the ceiling, a fusible link should be inserted in the cord that raises and lowers the trap door. If automatic shutters are used in the ceiling opening, neither the fusible link nor the trap door would be required.

5. The fan motor should be equipped with automatic thermal cutouts to prevent the motor from overheating from any cause and to protect it from burning. A motor so equipped is not a fire hazard. Lau fans are so equipped.

6. It is a good idea to locate the manual fan control switch where it won't be mistaken for a light switch. Inside a closet or high on the wall of a hallway, away from a door, are good locations.

Instructions on how to install specific fans are contained in the cartons housing the fans when they leave the factory. The facts stated above should be taken into consideration, before the actual installation begins, so that the correct fan will be installed in the best spot for free, gentle air circulation throughout the house.

Generally speaking, it is proportionately less expensive to install a fan which will ventilate the entire home than it is to install one which will serve adequately for a few specific rooms. Installation costs change very little according to the size of the fan, and the cost of labor is the largest factor in a fan type cooling system.

Regardless of whether or not the entire house is cooled by use of an attic exhaust fan, the long range upkeep is minor and the electricity used is minimal. When the entire home is fan cooled, the operation will pay for itself in comfort over and over again through the hot summer months of many years. •

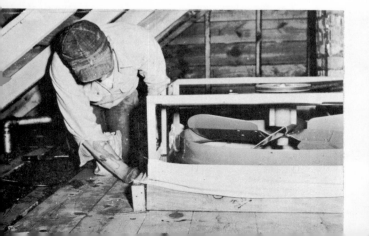

Installations of this type should be on its own electric circuit. Wire can be snaked up through wall at service entrance, then across the attic.

A heavy canvas strip, which is supplied with the fan, is wound around the base of the frame and fastened to prevent air leakage from the sides.

Built-In Attic Closet

FOR this closet, a 24-foot-long side of attic was used. Due to the fact that the opposite wall had to be matched on the outside, construction methods remained the same to a point. However, while the built-in drawer construction dealt with double vertical partitions which formed 4-inch thick pockets the doors could fold into to provide clear passage to the drawers, this was not necessary with the built-in clothes closet.

Single ¾-inch plywood verticals were mounted 9 feet from each end leaving approximately a 6-foot area in the center. This gave the wall a three-part closet which could be nicely divided for the storage of presently used and/or off-season storage.

The metal clothes rack, which is revolutionary, added much to the function and ease of living in this attic. Nylon hooks slide in an extruded gold-anodized aluminum bar, which is mounted with brackets. An additional feature of this new product, a Grant No. 600 clothes rack, has snap-in nylon hooks which can be added or taken off as necessary without having to remove the entire clothes rack first.

This particular attic area had, as shown in the photograph, a duct running across for heating the downstairs. The removal of this duct and the re-routing for the downstairs carrier actually served two purposes. First, it cleared the floor of any obstructions and it lent itself to a floor outlet to heat the attic. The doors were again

Note lineup of doors and their compartmentation. Because of a difference in space, you may need to change this arrangement a bit.

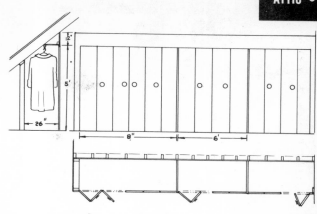

made of ¾-inch Novoply, mounted with No. 2520 Grant folding door hardware. When the entire front was finished, the entire surface was covered with ¼-inch-thick, prefinished Charter walnut paneling.

Due to the fact that there is a long distance between vertical supports, it was necessary to add on to each pair of folding doors a third door, mounted with piano hinge. These doors, of course, are mounted centrally and are not connected with the folding door track. It is, however, necessary to mount door aligners on the inside of the center doors as well as magnetic catches on the top. Because the piano hinged door is not suspended from the folding door channel, the aligner and magnetic catches hold it. ●——*by Bill Baker*

The closet is seen at left with folding doors open beyond planter-room divider of a project that follows. At right, the 24′-long side of the attic that was used for the closet area.

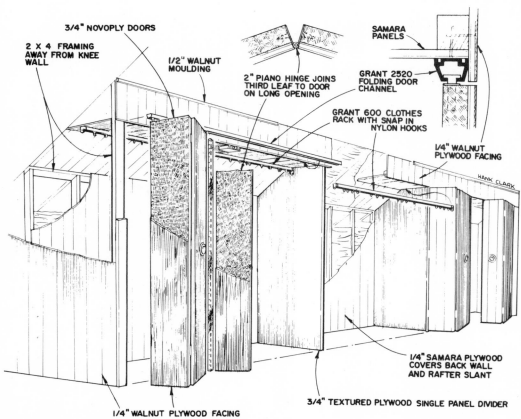

3/4" NOVOPLY DOORS

2 X 4 FRAMING AWAY FROM KNEE WALL

1/2" WALNUT MOULDING

2" PIANO HINGE JOINS THIRD LEAF TO DOOR ON LONG OPENING

SAMARA PANELS

GRANT 2520 FOLDING DOOR CHANNEL

GRANT 600 CLOTHES RACK WITH SNAP IN NYLON HOOKS

1/4" WALNUT PLYWOOD FACING

HANK CLARK

1/4" SAMARA PLYWOOD COVERS BACK WALL AND RAFTER SLANT

3/4" TEXTURED PLYWOOD SINGLE PANEL DIVIDER

1/4" WALNUT PLYWOOD FACING

Disassemble furniture whenever it can be done easily. This makes for simpler handling when finishing.

Attractive Furniture Finishes

by H. W. Kuhn

Be an instant pro by using the right finish where it can perform well

CERTAIN very attractive contemporary decorator furniture finishes are so easy to apply (even for the completely inexperienced, or "all-thumbs") that if you will forget all the reasons you might have for being afraid to try, and actually do it yourself, even on some scrap wood as an experiment, you will join thousands and thousands of others who have discovered that they can quickly, easily produce finished work of such incredible professional appearance that they simply cannot put it into words!

Trick? Yes.

The trick is in selecting certain finishes and using them only where they can perform wonderfully well. And that is exactly what we shall do now.

Complete revision of concept about finishing is the key. Like salvation for the old time sinner, your instant conversion from the evils of superstition, frightening, confusing voodooism, and the unmitigated nonsense of the traditional black magic rites and practices of furniture finishing to the simple truth is our goal. For a basic understanding of the simplicity of these finishes and finishing methods is far more important than a long list of technical formulas, details, as your personal message of salvation and freedom from finishing fear.

Reading is not enough. Do it!

Do it on some unfinished wood pieces, such as a scrap of birch plywood or a small unfinished stool.

Hot chocolate spilled on your new coffee table? Wipe fabric dye on wood—like lamp soot of yore.

Smear wax on the dyed wood. Rub with a scouring pad. That's a genuine antique Stain & Wax finish.

1. Mix up a common fabric dye, such as Rit, but stronger than for tinting cloth. Half a package in an 8 ounce soup can of water, for example. A dark brown tint is walnut, but any will do. Wipe it on the wood with a paper towel. Let it soak about 5 minutes (if you can wait). Wipe it down a little.

2. Use any kind of wax: car, floor, beeswax, candle wax, paraffin wax, or even furniture wax. Smear it right over the stained wood. (It's still damp from water? You don't put wax on wet wood, do you?) Do it!

3. If the wax looks good, it's all done. If the wax looks messy, lumpy, or smeary, let it dry a few minutes until it feels dry to the touch (just like any wax application has to) and then hand rub it with a scouring pad. The soap in the pad won't hurt it. Use the pad wet with water if you wish. Now wipe it off with a paper towel.

4. The final professional touch: Wet a rag with water. Wring it out. Work a little paste wax or liquid wax polish into the wet rag until it feels soft, almost creamy. No lumps of wax on the rag, please. Use this to polish the piece. Just wipe it lightly over the surface to put a very thin, perfectly smooth coating on. Now lightly buff with a dry cloth.

Is salvation in sight? You have just done what great grandmother used to do when, as the original do-it-yourself furniture finisher, she used her head and her kitchen materials instead of a credit card. Country craftsmen did it the same way. Granny didn't use Rit or Tintex, but she used home-made dyes, soot off the oil lamp (black), the juice of beets well boiled (red) and other natural colorants like wine. Sometimes she had oil to use in place of wax.

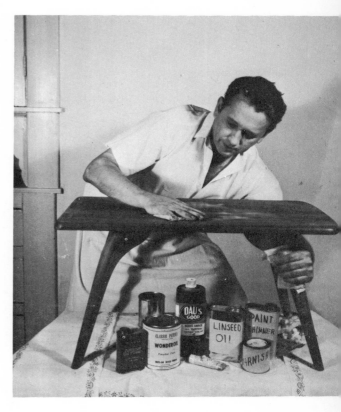

Dump on finishing oil, smear around, let soak in, wipe off excess, dry 2 hours, buff out streaks.

Do it!

1. Stain the wood with Burgundy (red) wine. Dry it—in the sun or under a hair drier for quick action.

2. Wipe cooking oil, salad oil or linseed oil on it. That's an oil finish over an alcohol stain. Ideal for wine-tasting tables. A real *oiled* fashioned finish.

Staining Wood: Wood absorbs liquids

such as water, alcohol, oil. Add coloring matter to such liquids. The liquid carries the color into the wood to stain it.

Oil Stains and Finishes

Household oils are non-drying oils. Finishing oils have to dry for practical use. Boiled linseed oil is the standard furniture finishing oil. "Boiled" means it is formulated to dry much faster than "raw" linseed oil. Available in paint stores.

Because oil colors (artist's or painter's) mix with linseed oil, such colors added to the oil make a stain. Thus, add oil color to oil to stain the wood; usually up to one ounce of oil color per pint of oil. When dry, apply uncolored oil as the "clear finish."

Oil Staining Method: Blend oil colors and linseed oil in a can. Reduce mixture, half & half, with paint thinner. Thinned oil makes a better stain because it penetrates better, dries more rapidly. Vary the amount of paint thinner to suit your own "feel" for the work as you learn through doing. Wipe it on the wood. Let it penetrate to get color intensity desired. Wipe of all excess liquid. Then use a dry cloth to lightly wipe it down a little more. Dry 4 hours minimum (or more) before finishing. Apply a second coat of same color or other color (to alter tone) if desired.

Oil Finishing Method: Use oil as it comes from can, or thin it slightly with paint thinner; three parts oil, one part thinner will do. Vary mixture if you wish as you learn. Slop it on, since it doesn't matter how it goes on. Let soak up to 30 minutes or so. Do not let it dry or get too tacky to manage, especially in hot weather. Add more oil then, if it seems to be soaking in rapidly. Wipe down, removing all excess from surface. Dry 2 hours (or more) and apply a second coat. Let second coat dry 8 hours before additional coatings. After that second, or each subsequent coat, has dried about 2 hours and is no longer tacky, buff with a dry cloth. This does wonders and eliminates messy steel wool rubbing later.

For a final polishing touch, use oil thinned out even more (5 parts thinner, 1 part oil) just like furniture polish. Buff "dry to touch" before allowing it to dry out completely.

Linseed oil is not alcohol stain-proof, and it does water mark, bloom, and ring from wet glasses setting on it. Finishing oils available retail generally are not much better. Only testing can tell you their performance capacity. The clear Antique Oil Finish made by the Minwax people is nationally available, and according to my

(1) Coat cheap fir with thin vinyl paint, dry (2). Wipe thin colored varnish over it (3). Looks like expensive oak (5), not a harsh plain stain (4).

tests (1967) affords good alcohol resistance, and does not water mark, etc.

An alcohol-proof, water-proof, heat-resistant superior finish can be blended easily from off-the-shelf products found in paint stores. Use it in place of oil when desired, and use it just like oil for a clear finish, or in making a stain.

Obtain a bartop or spar varnish that is alcohol and water mark-proof and heat-resistant. Mix about half & half with paint thinner for a clear finish. Add more paint thinner, and color to make a stain.

This thinned varnish can be blended with thinned oil and still provide good protection; two parts of the varnish mix and one part of oil mix, for example. Experimenting will produce your own custom blend most suitable to your creative talents.

Antique Distress Marks: Adding speckles, scratch lines and other imitation age markings, as well as stains, produce the stylish antique distressed finishes. How to do it is discussed further along in this article.

Authentic Hand Rubbing

You just did it. Use no steel wool, rubbing compounds, wet finishing paper. Rubbing an oil or varnish mixture into wood, or over a stain, until it feels dry to the touch, and later buffing it with a dry cloth

Use the "shoe shine" all-over technique to shade turnings when you're wiping color toner or glaze.

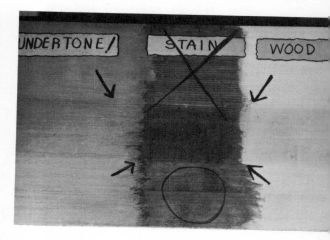

Undertone & color toner subdue harsh contrasts (arrows) and prevent oil stain blotching (circle).

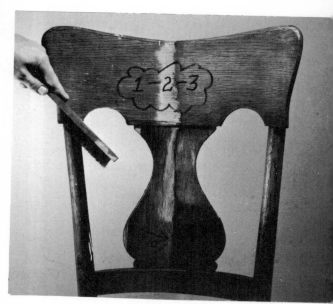

Wire brush removes finish of weathered oak (1). Undertoner (2) & color toner (3) restores lovely light oak finish. Oil stain (below) would ruin it.

Undertone shows grain (arrow) but conceals blemishes (circle) for "natural wood" finished look.

is authentic hand rubbing! Polishing on a thin coat over stain, or a previous coating of oil or finish, or over an undertoner, or undercoater, and letting it dry about an hour before buffing with the dry cloth is also authentic hand rubbing.

Any other method of alleged "hand rubbed finishing" is not the authentic method used by the old masters. You, doing it this way, therefore, produce a better finish than even a professional who uses the difficult, inferior steel wool, etc., scrub down.

Antique Distressed Decorator Styles: Pecan, Avocado, Mediterranean, Provincial

Vinyl acrylic (a "water base") paint dries quickly. When thinned with water, much more than you'd ever do when painting a wall, it becomes a water stain because it soaks into the wood and carries its color with it. It also has a protective finish substance in it that makes it waterproof and paint thinner-resistant when dry. Thus it seals. This means it protects the color from wiping off or smearing when oil or varnishes are applied over it. It also leaves a thin film on the wood (the sealing film) and thus tends to coat *over* the wood a little, not merely penetrate and stain it.

This action provides a very different

To create fine antique distress marks, turn all the kids loose with a rolling pin and enthusiasm.

Brush on thick undercoat to make the brush stroke grooves run the length of surface (not across).

finished effect than a stain and clear finish does. It leads to the beautiful contemporary decorator finishes such as pecan, distressed avocado, antique walnut, Spanish walnut, Mediterranean, distressed provincial, etc. While favored by decorators and furniture manufacturers for its striking beauty, such a finish is, peculiarly, the most "goof-proof" and simple to manage of any finish.

Several decorator styles are done much the same way, but with various color combinations. And, as we'll see, if we use a solid, opaque coat (an undercoater) of unthinned paint in place of the semi-transparent, thinned coating (an undertoner), we produce the "painted antique finishes" like those packaged in the many antique finishing kits.

Do it!

Undertoner

1. Thin out a beige or pastel brown "water base" washable paint (vinyl acrylic is best) with water. About 2 parts paint and 1 part water.

2. Wipe it on unfinished wood, and wipe it down as you proceed. A bold, coarse grain wood gives most interesting results: oak, ash, mahogany, fir. Dry to the touch (perhaps 15-30 minutes).

Color Toner

Mix one ounce (approximately) of burnt umber or raw umber oil color in a toning solution made as follows: ½ pint varnish, ½ pint paint thinner.

3. Wipe the color toner over the dried undertone coat; let soak (it penetrates a little) about 10 minutes. Lightly wipe off most of the excess, using a lint-free cloth pad that is moistened with the color toner but well wrung out. (Place between paper towels and wring it to avoid mess.)

Experiment Creatively: Play with it. Wipe on a little more. Wipe across the grain. Wipe with the direction of the grain. Stipple it. Use a dry paint brush and lightly "dry brush" over it to make decorative effects. Draw little short squiggly lines on it with the color toner. Put little dots of color on it. Let it get tacky and then "dry brush" it, or lightly drag a pad of cheesecloth over it. You'll see before your eyes the antique distressing, glaze, and specking effects that you find on the expensive pieces in the finest stores.

Clear Protective Finish Coat

4. After drying the work about 8 hours, wipe a clear coating over it just as you'd apply furniture polish. Do not rub or scrub, but using a cloth pad lightly moistened with the clear finish gently wipe it over the surface to leave a thin coating on it. About one hour later (when no longer tacky) gently buff with a dry cloth to eliminate erratic gloss streaks and to produce the satiny authentic hand rubbed *feel* and *look*.

Clear Finish Coat Material: Mix a bartop or spar varnish half & half with paint thinner. For the masterful touch, add about a teaspoon of linseed oil to a pint of this mixture.

The Undertone & Color Tone method results in a finish that appears to be a "natural wood" finish — since most of the grain of the wood shows — yet the flaws are concealed, and poor woods turn into handsome pieces.

A somewhat different result is achieved when we coat the wood (or go over an old finish) with an opaque application of paint that is not thinned out. The common "antique kit" provides ready-mixed ma-

SOME ANTIQUE DECORATOR FINISH STYLES

FINISH	UNDERTONE or UNDERCOAT	GLAZE or TONING COLOR
Pecan	beige (yellow, white, burnt umber)	burnt umber or raw umber
Avocado	light avocado (yellow, little black)	dark avocado or raw umber
Antique Olive	light olive (yellow, little black, little white)	darker olive or raw umber or black
Provincial	light brown (raw umber, burnt umber, white)	raw umber
Antique Walnut	medium brown (burnt umber, little white)	burnt umber, black
Mediterranean	same as others, but darker (less white, or add black)	same as others, but processed in finishing for darker tones

Ready-mixed colors from paint dealers, antique kits, eliminate need for color mixing on your part. Modify above basic guide lines by experimenting. Add black, white to basic colors little by little. Mix in a solution, not just pure color. Test combinations before actual use.

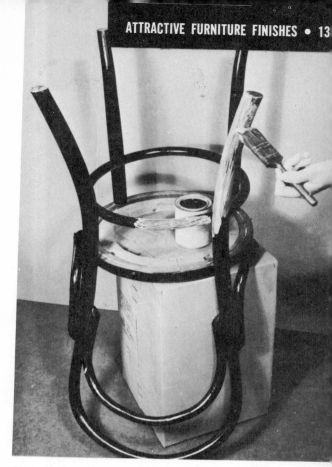

Chair is handled easier by starting upside down. Bold pressure strokes prepare chair for glazing.

Using finger to flick bits of color from brush tip creates a stylish antique decorator finish.

terials for this styling. The opaque coating used is called an undercoat. When dry it is most often glazed, rather than being color toned. But experiment with both ideas.

Undercoater

Select a piece of furniture, preferably a cabinet or table, so badly damaged and beat up it doesn't matter what happens to it, so you can relax and enjoy this experiment.

Materials: Slice of orange, darts, pastry brush, or similar stiff bristle brush, rasp or metal food colander, a tube of burnt umber or raw umber oil color, pint of varnish, quart of paint thinner, pint of Bourbon, rags, paper towels, a quart or so of vinyl acrylic "water base" paint in

In bold antique glazing, glazing solution dries over brush-grooved undercoat. The sandpaper cuts glaze color from high spots, leaves it in grooves.

Cheesecloth glazing. Wipe cloth through glaze. Wrap cloth over cardboard to get to "dead ends."

General rule when sanding: control arm's natural circular motion to avoid cutting across grain.

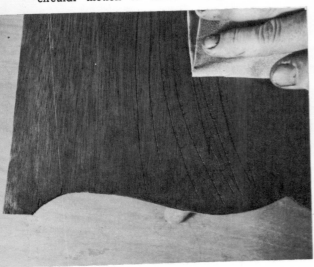

FINISHING FACTS

INTERMIXABLE MATERIALS

Group I: The oil system group, using paint thinner as their solvent. Linseed oil, varnish, oil color, enamel, oil paint, universal tinting color.

Group II: The vinyl system group, using water as their solvent. Vinyl ("water base") paint, artist's water color, poster paint, tempera color, household fabric dye, food color, universal tinting color (when mixed in water paints).

THINNERS, SOLVENTS

Excessive use of thinner reduces or destroys any protective or sealing quality in varnish, oil, vinyl. Test mixtures to learn maximum amounts of thinner practical.

DRYING TIME

Vinyls thinned with water: 10-30 minutes. Varnish, oil finishes, glazes, toners: 1-2 hrs. before dry cloth buffing; 4-8 hrs. before recoating; 2-3 days before harsh use. Damp, cold conditions prevent proper drying; may ruin a finish in process.

VARIATIONS IN WOODS

Soft woods, old wood, absorb more liquid than hard wood. A thin sealer will control penetration in soft woods. Mix a spoonful of varnish into a pint of paint thinner. Apply lightly. Dry about 2-4 hrs. before oil staining.

a beige or pastel brown tone, tin cans, couple marachino cherries, rubber gloves, small pointed tip art brush, rolling pin, bottle of sparkle water, hammer, a nail, ice pick, music to finish by, neighbors to call in for your premiere Finish-In-Party (and laugh when you sit down to fly speck).

Time: Any lazy weekend afternoon on a bright day.

Place: Middle-class America's housing project backyard, or north 4/10ths acre in the country.

The Proper Mood: An *Al Fresco* (whee!) attitude is vitally important, so slam the rolling pin down on the piece to distress it nobly. Kick it. Scratch it with the ice pick. Hammer the nail head into it. Rasp off those sharp corners with the colander. Throw darts at it. (Take out your aggressions on the miserable thing. It's the new game people are learning to play.)

While it is drying, mix up an oil color toner (oil color in thin varnish, remember?). When the painted undercoat feels dry to the touch smear the oil color toner all over it. The undercoat when dry enough can not be rubbed off with paint thinner—unless you bought an inferior type. If so, before color toning over it, you'll now have to seal it with a thin coat of thinned varnish. Just brush it on very lightly so as not to smear the undercoat. Dry about 4 hours, or until when testing with a little paint thinner on a paper towel, you see it is not wiping off.

Let the color toner soak a few minutes, as we learned, and then play with it. Wipe it down gently and you'll see the toning color sticks in the distress marks. Have at it, just as you did in the earlier experiment with an undertone coat.

Antique Speckles

Flies once did all the work, much of it very permanent. But today we can't wait for them to spot the furniture, and we prefer to call the little decorative dots, antique speckling. But by any name they are imitation fly specks. It's fun to do, and brings out the child in us—all eager to demonstrate superior creative ingenuity.

Dip the tip of the pastry brush into the color toner. Wipe off the tip a little. Now finger-flick the brush, so the goop flies in fickle fashion at the furniture. Experimenting with distance, trajectory and the amount of color toner, as well as finger-flick will lead to control of size, distribution and pattern.

When the piece has dried out at least 8 hours (or more in cool damp weather) and when you are sure it is dry (test it with paint thinner), then apply a clear protective coating overall. When this is done, you will have an ANTIQUE DISTRESSED PECAN FINISH. (Or give it any other fancy name that appeals to you.)

Antique Glazing of Painted Undercoats

Toning a color over a painted undercoat is one basic finishing process. Glazing is yet another interesting styling. Antique Kits containing undercoats, glazes and clear finishes have provided an easy source of materials for this type of finish.

Accompanying pictures show the glazing methods much better than words can explain them. Mainly, glazing means to produce fine color lines on the surface rather than a smooth, even toning coat. This is done with cheesecloth which you use to wipe down the glaze coat, or with a brush that is kept wiped "dry" as you work, and with which you stroke over the glaze to drag it into patterns. Doing it will quickly reveal how to do it, and what it looks like in various patterns.

Making A Glaze: It should be thicker

SELECTING FINISHING SUPPLIES

Alcohol proof, stain proof, heat resistant varnish is available as "bar top" or "marine spar" varnishes. Can labels specify these qualities when they exist. Test by letting alcohol, boiling water dry out on a coating (unthinned). Let oven-hot dish completely cool while sitting on a coating.

Vinyl acrylic "water base" paint is water proof and resists paint thinner. Select a national name brand product to be safe. Test. Not alcohol proof.

Varnish & Paint removers: Only the more expensive top grades are worth buying.

Sandpaper: Use only "production finishing papers" made of abrasives other than flint. Aluminum oxide best. Garnet adequate. Grit #150 for coarse work. Grit #220 for final sanding.

Paint thinner: Inexpensive types will do for furniture finishing work.

Antique kits: Both "water base" and oil type undercoats are available from national name brand manufacturers. Purchase undercoats and glazes from open stock to save money. Don't let them kit you if you dont need the other items in the kit.

---

than a toning coat so that it does not flow together or run or drip. It must stick where it is put and remain in place when wiped or brushed to preserve the patterns. Blend the oil color and varnish, but add little if any thinner; when a toning coat, or a too-thin glazing coat has dried out a few minutes over the undercoat of paint and becomes tacky it also can be worked as a glaze.

Toning Over A Glaze: After glazing a painted undercoat, and when the glaze is dry, you can then apply a toning coat also for still greater variations in decorator styling.

Simulated Stains

"Authentic" antique stains add a connoisseur touch to the finishes over and above mere distressing and fly specking. After applying the final protective coating, let it dry only about 4 hours (so it won't be quite alcohol-proof, and will watermark also). Pour some water on it here and there and let it dry out to blemish delicately. Pour a little of the Bourbon on it for a fine old alcohol stain. The orange slice and cherry can be used to stain the undertoner or undercoater before toning or glazing. •

AIR-FILTER replacement can improve an engine's power output dramatically.

Easy Way to Get Ten Extra Horsepower

LIFTER ADJUSTMENT is recommended after tightening head bolts. Paper clip stops oil from squirting out of rocker feed holes.

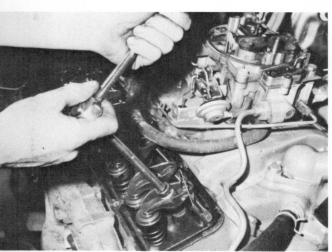

WANT an extra 10 hp from your engine? No, you won't have to shave the cylinder heads or resort to expensive hot-rodding techniques. Chances are, you can pick up at least 10 hp—and often more—with these minor tuning jobs: replace the air filter, change the vacuum advance, wipe off the spark plugs, reroute ignition wires, adjust the timing, tighten the cylinder heads and adjust the valve lifters.

Each job will take two to 30 minutes and the whole list takes no more than two hours.

The simplest job is replacing the air filter. This can improve available horsepower dramatically, especially affecting acceleration and high-speed performance, as well as gas mileage and start-

VACUUM-ADVANCE diaphragm is located in pie-plate housing (fat arrow). To remove, loosen screws and clip (slim arrow).

IGNITION-WIRE arrangement can cause or prevent crossfire. Wires going to plugs firing in sequence should be separated.

ing. On most cars, just unscrew the wing nut on the air-cleaner cover, pull out the dirty filter and install a new one.

If you have a filter made of polyurethane foam, you can clean it in solvent, dunk it in clean engine oil, squeeze out the excess and remount it on the metal frame. Easier still, replace it with a paper element made for your car. It's easier to service and needs service less frequently.

A clogged air filter can restrict air flow so badly that the engine is being

choked most of the time. It loses power, wastes gas and, in severe cases, makes starting difficult.

If your car has over 35,000 mi. on it or is four years old, replacing the distributor's vacuum advance unit should add several horsepower. The diaphragm in this unit advances the ignition timing at part throttle by shifting the position of the breaker point plate. As time goes by this diaphragm loses its airtightness and efficiency. The vacuum advance unit costs from $1.50 to $3 and on many

A TORQUE WRENCH is needed to tighten cylinder head bolts properly. This one reads to 150 ft.-lbs., costs about $10.

TIMING MARKS are way down low on the front of the engine. It's difficult and dangerous to align them with engine running.

cars it can be replaced without pulling out the distributor.

If the vacuum advance is in an awkward position, you can slacken the distributor lock and swing the distributor body into a more convenient position. But first paint a thin line along the distributor body and on the engine with nail polish or touchup paint. When you're finished, the mark will help align the distributor to maintain the timing settings.

The vacuum advance usually is screwed into the distributor body. The diaphragm has an actuating arm that connects to the breaker-point plate, generally by a clip. Just undo the clip, remove the mounting screws and disconnect the vacuum line from the carburetor base. The unit then will come right out.

Merely wiping off the spark plugs and checking the routing of the plug wires can eliminate many mysterious engine ailments.

Wiping off the plug terminals and insulators plus the metal clips on the ignition wires with a dry cloth prevents dirt and moisture from causing short circuits and voltage leaks.

Careful routing of the plug wires will prevent electromagnetic induction, commonly called crossfire. Crossfire can occur when two ignition wires run parallel and close to one another and the two plugs fire one right after the other. It is possible for the electrical impulse to be pulled from one wire to the other. The plug that should spark will fail, while the other one is firing away at the wrong time.

It is a particularly common problem on V8s because each bank has two cylinders that fire in sequence. The firing order will tell you which ones they are.

The thing to do is make sure that the wires to these two plugs are as far apart as possible or else cross each other at right angles. If there are plug wire guides built into the rocker cover, use them to keep the wires in place. If not, buy a set.

Setting ignition timing accurately can mean lots of extra horsepower. The typical weekend mechanic does the job either by ear or with a neon-tube timing light. Both have disadvantages. The timing light involves a tricky procedure that brings head and fingers perilously close to the spinning fan. Playing it by ear can cause engine damage if your ear is bad or the accessories drown out the critical sound you're listening for.

The easiest way to do the job is with the engine not running. The only tool is a test lamp. You can buy one for under $1 or make it from a 12-watt bulb. Merely solder one wire to the base of the bulb and another to the threaded side and attach alligator clips to the other ends of the wires.

First, a little theory: the spark has to be delivered to the plug when the piston is near the top of its stroke. The exact point is measured by the position of the crankshaft, using marks on the drive pulley or crank damper (at the front of the crankshaft) and a reference mark, usually a pointer, on the timing-chain cover. Lining up these marks means that the piston for the No. 1 cylinder is in the right position for the arrival of the spark. Once one cylinder is in time, all the others are.

In order to align these marks, we are going to crank over the engine with the starter until the marks are close to each other and finish the job by hand, using cars it can be replaced without pulling

SPARK PLUGS can collect dirt and moisture, causing voltage leaks and poor spark. Simply wipe clean with dry cloth.

the spark plugs first so you won't be fighting engine compression. It's also a good idea to remove the wire between the distributor cap and the coil so there is no juice flowing through the dangling ignition wires.

You will need the manufacturer's timing specs and if the pulley has several marks, you must find out what lines up with what. Auto-parts stores that serve professional mechanics have specification books and if you patronize them they'll look things like this up for you.

Once the marks are lined up, slacken the distributor lock so the distributor body can be rotated. Now connect one lead of the test lamp to the coil's thin wire terminal. It holds the wire that goes to the distributor body and should be marked CB, D, NEG or with a minus sign. Connect the other test-lamp wire to a metal part of the engine as ground. A cylinder-head bolt is fine.

Turn on the ignition and rotate the distributor body by hand through short arcs, first clockwise and then counterclockwise, until the bulb goes out. Once the bulb is out, slowly turn the distributor body in the opposite direction until it just starts to light. Then tighten the distributor lock.

What you have done is this: the test lamp will light when the points are open and go out when they're closed. You have to set the distributor so that the points are just opening, about to send a spark to No. 1 cylinder in a few thousandths of a second. And you know No. 1 cylinder is in the right position because the timing marks are lined up.

The final jobs on the list, tightening the head bolts and adjusting the valves, go together. When you tighten a cylinder head you reduce loss of compression from the cylinders (and loss of power). Two things are important: uniform tightening of the nuts or bolts and, where possible, readjustment of the valve lifters.

Uniform tightening requires a torque wrench, a tool that indicates—in foot-pounds—the amount of tightening force applied. For $10 you can get a torque wrench that will remain accurate for many years of weekend work. Get a 150-ft.-lb. model.

Head bolts are tightened in an imaginary spiral pattern from the center of the head outward to the ends. You will need the manufacturer's specifications as to the number of foot-pounds of tightening needed. Again, the auto-parts store is the place to go.

Once the head is tightened, the gasket is compressed and there is an effective change in the height of the engine. This changes valve timing a bit and, on cars with adjustable hydraulic valve lifters (Chevrolets and some Fords), you should readjust for maximum performance. Run the engine until fully warmed. Shut it down and pull the rocker cover (one at a time on V8s). You must prevent oil from squirting out of the feed holes in the rockers during idle. You can buy a set of oil stoppers for $3 or bend a large paper clip around the rocker and stick the end into the hole.

With the clips installed, run the engine at slow idle. Using a socket wrench, back off the adjusting nut in the center of the rocker (turn counterclockwise) until the valve just begins to clatter. Next, turn clockwise until the clatter just stops, which indicates that all clearance has been eliminated from the valve train.

Then turn the wrench an additional amount, specified by the manufacturer, to properly position the plunger and lifter. The specifications are given in full and half turns, such as 1½ turns. Check with that friendly parts store before you begin. In fact, be a sport. Buy the air cleaner, vacuum-advance unit and a set of points and plugs—and ask for the pile of specs all at once. Then keep a record of them.

Careful tuning may not bring a corpse back to life but it can add a nice touch of liveliness to a car that just needs a tonic.

If you follow our procedure carefully you'll find our extra-10-hp is a conservative figure. If you don't pick up two or more times that amount of power there probably will be a reason—you've been taking good care of your car all along. •

GIVE YOUR CAR A $40 PAINT JOB!

STAN is a rugged, sandy-haired man whose big hands are rough from years of auto-body work. We were almost afraid to tell him we were planning to paint a car ourselves—we expected him to laugh or at least try to discourage us. He did neither.

"A few years ago I'd have told you to forget it," Stan said, "but with the new fast-drying paints on the market anybody can do a good job." He paused and added, "If he's careful, that is."

Stan is an old friend who has hammered out many a wrinkled fender. He sat down with us for a half hour, outlined all the necessary steps and listed $40 worth of materials we would need. These included one gallon of acrylic lacquer, one gallon of Acry-Seal sealer-primer, two gallons of lacquer thinner, one gallon of degreaser and solvent,

four paint strainers, a spraying mask, two rolls of masking tape, a small can of body putty, a tack cloth, a rubber squeegee, a dozen sheets each of Nos. 220, 320, 400 and 600 sandpaper, three sheets of No. 180 sandpaper, six coarse sanding disks, a tube of sanding-disk adhesive and a week's savings of newspapers and rags. A week later the worn and scuffed Austin-Healey shone like new.

The Austin-Healey is a relatively small sports roadster. If you are painting a large American sedan you will need more paint, lacquer thinner and possibly sandpaper but the rest of the quantities listed should be sufficient.

Here's how it's done.

Before starting the job, get all body damage (dents, tears and holes) re-

REMOVE as much chrome trim as possible.
This eliminates masking and exposes rust.

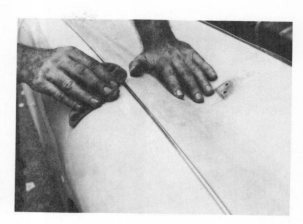

WIPE off entire car with a rag liberally
doused in degreaser solvent to cut road tar.

GRIND all rust spots down to bare metal.
A sanding disk is best for contoured areas.

SAND entire body, using plenty of water
and a squeegee to check for missed spots.

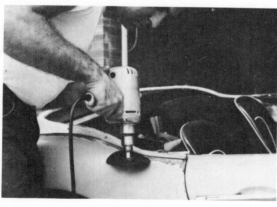

paired. You can do this yourself with one of the inexpensive fiberglass repair kits on the market. Don't worry about minor dimples and rust spots until later.

Remove every part that is not to be painted (side trim, headlight rims, taillights, door molding, grille, handles, mirrors, bumpers, etc.). We removed the hood and trunk lid to work around the edges more easily but this isn't always necessary.

Dechroming takes only a couple of hours if you're lucky but a few frozen hard-to-reach nuts could make it an all-day operation. One hint that will save you time later: keep nuts and bolts and small hardware from each component together in labeled envelopes.

If your old paint is so bad it must be removed, buy a can of non-alkaline paint remover. Spread it on with a large, well-

worn brush and wipe away the paint. Repeat as necessary until most of the paint has been removed.

If the old paint isn't too bad, go on and remove grease, dirt and wax from the body with the degreaser and solvent. This step also is necessary after using paint remover to take off the waxy residue. Pour the degreasing liquid liberally on a clean rag and rub the body briskly. This must be done before sanding the old paint to avoid driving the grime deeper into the finish. From here on avoid touching the car with your hands —the oil in your skin could keep the new paint from sticking.

Do the roughest sanding first. Rust spots (often found below doors and around side trim) must be ground down to bare, shiny metal with a coarse sanding disk or grinding wheel. If you don't

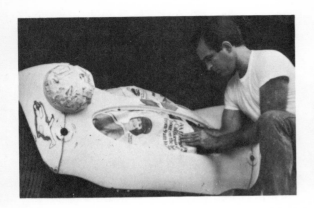

MASK all areas not to be painted. Apply
primer and sand again, repeat as necessary.

AFTER painting, allow an overnight drying
period, then polish with rubbing compound.

own an electric drill or grinder, borrow
or rent one. You'll need it for only a
few minutes, but it will save you hours
of hand-sanding.

After grinding, sand the area with
No. 220 sandpaper until the circular
grinding marks are gone.

Now sand the entire body, first with
No. 220, then No. 320 and finally No.
400 sandpaper. Don't use a sanding
block—it reduces the contact area. Dip
the sandpaper frequently in a pail of
water as you work to clear residue from
the grit and to lubricate the work. Wiping the water from the sanded area with
a rubber squeegee will help you see
spots you may have missed. Sand in
long, horizontal strokes; never cross-
sand.

Tiny nicks in the old paint can be
feather-edged by applying pressure behind the sandpaper with a single finger-
tip. When you have finished, the entire
body should be covered with barely
noticeable lines resembling fine record
grooves. *If your fingers should touch
the body during sanding, apply degreaser to the spot immediately.*

After sanding, wash the entire body
with warm water and a lint-free rag,
wipe with more clean rags and allow to
dry for several hours, preferably overnight.

Next, mask off all areas not to be
painted, such as headlights, window
glass, tires and grille opening. Apply

masking tape along the edge of a newspaper and press carefully along the edge
of the area to be covered. In hard-to-
reach places first apply tape alone and
then tape-edged newspaper.

Before spraying, hose down the garage floor and sweep out the dust. Most
paint-spraying failures result from dust.
A garage is essential—don't try to spray
outdoors. One veteran body man hangs
a chain from a bumper bracket to the
floor to ground the car and prevent
static electricity from attracting dust.
Whether this works is debatable but it
certainly can't hurt.

If you don't own a compressor and
spray gun, you can rent one from a paint
store for a few dollars a day. Be sure to
get a gun with an external-mix nozzle,
one that mixes the paint and air on the
outside. Lacquer tends to clog an in-
ternal-mix nozzle.

Stir in one and a half parts of lacquer
thinner to one part Acry-Seal primer-
sealer and practice your spraying on
some scrap cardboard. Before starting
on the car, wipe the body with a tack
cloth, a rag lightly dampened with solvent that picks up dust.

For large panels, adjust the gun to
deliver a fan-shaped pattern about two
or three in. high and eight or ten in.
wide. For tight areas such as wheels
and door edges use a small, round
pattern the size of a silver dollar. As
you spray from six to ten in. away, the

primer-sealer should go on wet but not so wet that it runs. A spraying mask may feel hot and uncomfortable but it will keep a lot of pigment out of your lungs.

As you move the gun from side to side, always keep it the same distance from the work. Keep the nozzle always perpendicular to the car surface. Don't swing the gun in an arc. And always keep the gun moving. First start your stroke, then press the trigger. After you release the trigger, follow through with the stroke past the edge of the working area.

Spray in horizontal strokes from the top down to avoid brushing against a freshly sprayed area while reaching across the body. Overlap your strokes by a third or more to avoid streaks and unpainted areas.

Allow the car to dry for a half hour, then search for dimples or low spots where you feathered the paint. Level such spots with body putty applied with a squeegee. If the low spots are deep, apply a thin layer of putty, allow to dry for a half hour and cover with another thin layer. Let the putty dry for at least four hours, then *dry sand* with Nos. 180, 220, 320 and 400 sandpaper. Using water at this stage would hurt paint adhesion. Since the putty is softer than steel, use a sanding block to get a smooth surface. Wipe away sanding dust with the tack cloth, reprime the repaired areas and wait another half hour.

Though you can paint over Acry-Seal without sanding first, it is a good idea to go over the entire car lightly with dry No. 400 sandpaper.

Finally you are ready to spray on the paint. By now you should feel more at ease with the spray gun. The priming operation wasn't critical since mistakes are easy to sand down and respray. But with paint, repairs are more difficult.

Stir the paint thoroughly (a piece of coat-hanger wire bent into a squared-off hook and chucked in a power drill makes the job easier). Then filter the paint through a strainer to remove lumps and mix it with an equal volume of lacquer thinner. If you decide not to use acrylic lacquer, check the instructions on the paint can for the proper thinning ratio. Or, check with your paint supplier. Follow his advice to prevent mistakes.

Go over the car once again with a tack cloth and, using the same technique as in priming, apply four or five coats to the entire car. There's no need to wait between coats—by the time you finish one end of the car the other will be dry and ready for more paint.

Wet-sand the entire car lightly with No. 600 sandpaper, wipe thoroughly with clean rags and allow to dry several hours, preferably overnight. Then wipe with a tack cloth and spray on four or five lighter paint coats, using one and a half parts thinner to one part paint. Start with heavy coats and finish with light ones to obtain a finish with maximum gloss.

The next day you can polish the surface with rubbing compound and reinstall the trim and accessories. But wait at least two months before waxing to make sure no moisture is trapped in the paint. •

PROBE badly rusted areas with screwdriver. If the metal gives, first get the area repaired.

TRUNK and hood lids can be removed for sanding and spraying if the edges are rusty.

What you can (and can't) do to your
AUTO AIR CONDITIONER

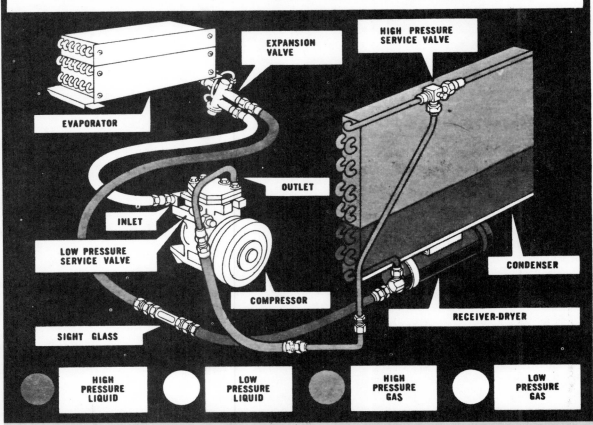

EXPANSION VALVE

HIGH PRESSURE SERVICE VALVE

EVAPORATOR

OUTLET

INLET

LOW PRESSURE SERVICE VALVE

COMPRESSOR

CONDENSER

RECEIVER-DRYER

SIGHT GLASS

HIGH PRESSURE LIQUID

LOW PRESSURE LIQUID

HIGH PRESSURE GAS

LOW PRESSURE GAS

OBTAINING top performance from your auto's air conditioner requires a bit more than driving into a service shop once a year for a $15 refrigerant recharge. Now don't wince at the thought of your laboring over a mass of intricate air conditioning components—we said a *bit more*, didn't we?

Actually, to check out your A/C system, you need only your hands, eyes, a thermometer and about an hour's spare time. That's right—no special tools, no

---

HOW THEY WORK

The compressor changes Freon to a hot gas by increasing its pressure. The condenser is exposed to cool air flow and changes the hot gas to a cool but not cold liquid. The receiver/dryer removes any moisture and stores excess Freon. The expansion valve passes a small amount of liquid to the evaporator.

At this point, the gas pressure drops sharply (due to the suction of the compressor) and causes the liquid to change back into a gas. However, in the process of changing from liquid to gas, the refrigerant draws heat from the evaporator, which, in turn, draws off heat from the passenger compartment and cools it.

---

gauges, not even a wrench is necessary.

In fact, as Freon is a somewhat hazardous gas, under no circumstances should you ever disconnect any unit or hose containing Freon. Nor should you attempt to add more refrigerant. If the following tests show that the system does need some Freon, have it done by an air conditioning specialist.

The cooling source is the compressor, so first make certain there is no slippage between the drive belt and the compressor pulley. (Note that the compressor pulley rotates at all times. When the A/C power switch is turned to On, a magnetic clutch connects the drive pulley to the compressor shaft.)

Since you probably don't have a tension or torsion gauge to check the belt tension, just press down on the belt be-

tween the compressor pulley and the engine's damper pulley. If the belt moves no more than ¼ to ⅜ inch, you can be sure there is no slippage. Be certain to make this check when the belt is *hot* from running. If you have the car's A/C manual, check for the amount of play specified.

Turn the A/C to On and let it run for 15 to 20 minutes. Then place your hand on the hose from the compressor output (where it enters the condenser) and note how hot it feels. Move your hand to the condenser's output hose (generally at the top). It should feel somewhat cooler than the input hose—still hot, but not as hot as the input hose. If the temperatures seem about the same, the condenser isn't cooling the gas properly. The trouble may be caused by dirt clogging the condenser fins, so as a matter of course, clean the condenser every year by scrubbing it vigorously with a stiff brush. Then use a shop vacuum to alternately blow and suck the loosened dirt from the condenser.

Move on to the receiver/dryer and check for clogging by placing your hand on the input hose (the one coming from the condenser) and then the output

COMPRESSOR drive belt must be tight and free of grease to insure good efficiency.

hose (the one going to the expansion valve). Both hoses should feel *equal* in temperature. A clogged filter is generally indicated by an output hose cooler than the input hose. Sorry, but a clogged receiver requires a service shop repair. *Don't try to do it yourself.*

Check the hose at the input to the expansion valve. This usually is located at the firewall in the engine compartment on factory A/Cs or at the evaporator input of add-on models. The hose input to the valve should be hot—if you can feel or get to the valve's output it should be cold. If the hose going in feels cool or if it's hot coming out, your next stop is the service shop.

The output hose from the evaporator to the compressor should be cold. On a cool day you'll even see frost on the metal hose fittings right at the compressor. If the output hose is only *cool*, and not cold, the expansion valve may be ready for replacement or adjustment.

After the initial check-up, belt tightening and condenser cleaning, set the car in the sun with the windows closed and allow the A/C to run for about a half hour. Then check the sight glass (usually part of the receiver or condenser.) If you see bubbles in the sight-glass, the A/C needs additional refrigerant. Note that the bubble check is made *during* operation. It's normal to see bubbles for several minutes after the A/C is turned off.

Next check the cooling efficiency. If yours is a factory installation the car's service manual generally will list the temperature differential that should be measured. An add-on unit generally is rated to drop the inside temperature 15° below the outside air temperature. (Thus if it's 100° outside it's not going to be cooler than 85° inside the car.) If you don't have this information in your factory installation use the 15° test. Position a thermometer over the back of the front seat at about eye level and check that the temperature at this point is 15° below the outside temperature. If you measure less than 15° you might need more refrigerent or a new expansion valve. Have the system checked by an auto A/C *specialist.*

Since air conditioners remove water

A DIRTY radiator will reduce efficiency. Clean with a stiff wire brush and vacuum.

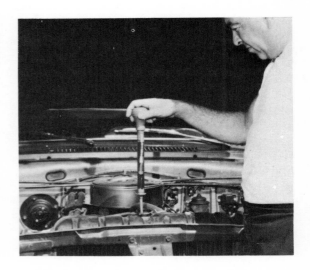

RADIATOR must contain anti-freeze rated at 15° or lower. Check with a hydrometer.

RECEIVER/DRYER isn't clogged if input and output hoses are at same temperature.

(moisture) from the air, make certain the drain holes are open. Otherwise you're likely to get a lap full of water or a block of ice in the evaporator. Add-on models have rubber drain hoses running through holes in the floor. Simply pull up the hoses and check that they aren't clogged with road dirt (which is easily accumulated during the winter months). A few wiggles with a straightened section of coathanger is all it takes to clean the drains. The drain holes for factory installations usually are on, or under, the firewall outside the passenger compartment.

Since the cooling of the condenser is dependent upon sufficient air flow through the condenser and radiator, make certain the radiator is clean. If cleaning is necessary, use a stiff brush and a vacuum. But be careful not to bend and damage the soft metal fins of the radiator. This would prevent cooling air from passing through.

It also is important to have the car's regular cooling system at top efficiency —a hot radiator or engine will reduce the amount of condenser cooling considerably. Make certain the thermostat is working and that the radiator pressure cap is holding at the rated pressure. Also make certain the radiator cap has the correct pressure rating. Cars with factory A/Cs use a cap with a higher pressure rating—never replace it with a standard pressure cap.

Electrical woes are not to be overlooked, either. The extra load of the compressor's electric clutch and the evaporator fan can be as high as 17 amperes.

Thus, factory installed A/Cs usually come as a package with a heavy duty alternator capable of handling the extra current requirements. On the other hand, with an add-on A/C you're stuck with the original generator or alternator—in which case it's possible to exhaust its current handling capacity to the point where there isn't enough juice left to charge a rundown battery. Since just a slight decrease in electrical efficiency can mean insufficient charging current to handle the ignition, A/C and lights, make certain you get all the current the generator or alternator can deliver. Check the generator or alternator belt for excessive play—about ¼ to ⅜ inch in each direction is normal.

With a battery known to be fully charged, check that the combined A/C and bright light current drain does not cause the idiot light or ammeter to show a discharge. If you do get a discharge indication have the voltage regulator checked.

If you have an add-on unit and the car radio is a tube model, the combined drain of the ignition, A/C, brights *and* radio may prove just too much for the charging system—and the charge indicator always will show discharge. One solution is to shut off the radio when the A/C is on. Another is to install a heavy duty generator or alternator. If your car is equipped with a generator that can handle the extra current, you might instead try using an adjustable regulator (one with a knob adjustment that increases the amount of charging current). You can set the regulator to provide extra current needed.

The added load of the A/C compressor on the engine will cause the normal idle speed to decrease. On six cylinder engines the decrease will be 50 to 100 rpm, enough to cause the engine to idle roughly or stall. Simply increase the hot idle adjustment (when the A/C is on) to the rated rpm. If you don't have a tachometer and don't feel like paying a mechanic for a two-second adjustment, simply turn the idle screw very slowly until the roughness just disappears— this will usually restore engine performance. Don't forget to slow the idle speed back to normal come fall.

If your A/C is an add-on model your spring check-up is finished. But if it's a factory job you've got one more step. Most factory installations have the evaporator mounted next to the heater core. Since no heater water is circulated during the summer, the evaporator can freeze the water in the heater—resulting in a ruptured or burst heater. *So never remove the antifreeze from a car with a factory A/C.* In fact, check that the anti-freeze protection during the A/C months is to 15° or lower. •

LOOSEN all the head bolts or nuts in a 10-1 sequence. Follow order of 1-10 to tighten.

A VALVE JOB FOR $20

With a minimum of time and expense, owners of overhead-valve engines can do their own valve jobs. The key: organized labor.

THE mere mention of a valve job seems to be enough to send most motorists into a state of anxiety and apprehension. Aside from the exorbitant expenses involved, there also is an understandable aversion to giving up the buggy for three or four days.

Yet the average Saturday wrench-twirler, by using a straightforward approach, can do a first-rate job in half the time and for a fraction of the normal fee. How? Simply by removing the cylinder heads himself, trotting them down to the nearest automotive machine shop and having the shop complete the job of grinding and reseating the valves, often on a while-you-wait basis. Reverse these steps and your job is completed.

Total cost? Expect to pay a machinist $12 to $18 for reworking a V-6 and about $18 to $24 for a V-8. Add the price of a gasket set ($3 to $9) and your total outlay ranges from $15 to $33, quite a drop from a fee of $70 to $100.

The time involved also is decreased from the mechanic's three or four days to six to 15 hours, usually broken into two sessions. However, by making an appointment with a good machinist, the entire job can be completed in one day.

Why a valve job? Valves control the cycling of each cylinder. Thus, if an exhaust valve is leaking due to carbon build-up or faulty seating power from each combustion cycle will be lost through the exhaust port. Similarly, if the inlet valve is leaking fuel consumption increases greatly without an increase in power output. In this case, flooding, difficulty in starting and knocking usually result. Either way, valves are important and require more atten-

1. DRAIN radiator, disconnect all hoses at intake manifold and swing out of way.

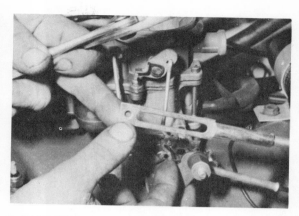

2. REMOVE the throttle linkage, making as few disconnections as possible. Keep notes.

tion than usually is accorded them.

As a rule of thumb, about once a year or every 30,000 miles, pull a valve job. Begin with the following:

• Collect a set of standard wrenches, a screwdriver, torque wrench, scraper and wire brush.

• Dig around for a package of envelopes or small plastic bags, a bunch of tags or labels with tape or wire ties and a pad and pencil.

• Call an automotive machine shop and set an appointment for Saturday afternoon.

• Get a good night's sleep Friday.

Ready? Disconnect the battery cables, drain the cooling system and remove the air cleaner. Disconnect the upper radiator hose and any heater hose that goes into the cylinder head, intake manifold or thermostat housing. Leave the clamps on the hoses so you'll have them at reassembly time.

Now remove the rocker cover(s). Place the nuts or bolts and washers in a bag and label the bag, leaving it in one of the rocker covers.

The next step is to disconnect the throttle linkage from the carburetor. While linkage setups vary, these general guidelines hold for all types of autos:

• Make a sketch of the linkage layout. Even if the arrangement looks simple, by the time you're ready for reassembly you may have forgotten it.

• Disconnect as little as possible. Two or three disconnections will do it

3. DISCONNECT fuel line at carburetor or filter. Swing it out of the way; don't bend.

every time. After a disconnection try to refit pins and clips in the slots or holes from which they came to ease reassembly. If this isn't possible put the bits and pieces and your sketch into a labeled bag.

Disconnect the fuel line at the carburetor or fuel filter, then loosen it at the fuel pump and try to swing it out of the way. If you can't remove the line. Take care not to bend the copper tubing.

Inspect the intake manifold to see whether there's anything else bolted to it (such as a ground strap) or something strung over it (wires, hoses, etc.). To avoid confusion, tag each hose and its connection point as you disconnect.

The intake manifold should be removed with the carburetor left in place. If the ignition coil is mounted on the in-

4. REMOVE bolts holding intake manifold. Compare the size and length of the bolts.

5. COMPLETE any further disconnections and remove the intake manifold carefully.

take manifold just disconnect the wires. Tag each of the two thin wires as you remove them, labeling them with the sign on the coil terminal (usually a plus or minus sign or a letter). Refit the terminal mounting nuts so they don't get lost.

Remove the intake-manifold bolts and swing away anything held to those bolts, such as a throttle-linkage bracket. Then pull off the intake manifold.

The next step usually is generator removal. Even if it is not bolted to the cylinder head it will interfere with head removal on V-8s. You may not have to

pull the generator on a Six so check before you unbolt.

At this point, you have to decide whether to pull the exhaust manifold with the head. This is the usual procedure but it requires disconnecting the exhaust manifold from the exhaust pipe, probably from underneath the car. If this appears difficult unbolt the manifold from the head, pull it away from the head and rethread the nuts or bolts into the head.

Before removing the manifold from the head you probably will have to pull off the spark-plug wires. Otherwise, you can wait until later. Make a layout drawing of the spark plugs, numbering them any way you want so long as you put a number tag on each wire to conform with your drawing.

At this point you're ready to pull the heads. First loosen the bolts or stud nuts, starting with No. 10 as shown in our illustration and proceeding to No. 1. Place them in a labeled bag. On engines with bolts, remove the bolts one at a time and check length. If any are longer than others, make a sketch of bolt locations so you can reinstall them properly.

Remove the rocker assembly. On engines with all rockers in-line on a shaft, don't disturb the rocker adjusting nuts or screws and when you reassemble, valve adjustments will be close.

On engines with non-adjustable rockers, individually mounted or in-line on a shaft, remove and label the shaft or rocker—no settings to disturb.

Now check the highly-popular exception: hydraulic lifters and individually mounted adjustable rockers, used on most Chevy V-8s and some Fords. In this case mark one flat of the rocker's adjusting nut with nail polish and then unscrew it, counting the exact number of turns for each nut. Keep each rocker and nut together in a separate envelope labeled as to exact location on which head. You'll be able to refit them close enough to get the engine running. Final adjustments are explained later.

After the rocker assembly and push-rods have been removed the head should be loose on the block. If not, try to break it loose by prying *the outside* *or body of the head* with a large screwdriver. *Do not insert the screwdriver between head and block.* If there's any real resistance odds are there's a nut or bolt still in place.

After the machine shop is done with the valve part of the job, clean carbon and lead deposits from the combustion chamber, using a wire brush—either hand or electric-drill type. To clean the piston tops, use a scraper with care.

Now you're ready for reassembly, a reversal of disassembly with some important additions.

Scrape all gasket surfaces until clean. Coat both sides of the cylinder-head gasket with a sparing amount of non-hardening sealer and place it on the block. Move the cylinder head into place, then fit the push rods into the lifters at one end and into the rocker seat at the other. Thread in the head bolts and run them down finger tight.

You'll need tightening specifications for the head and rockers. Check your service manual (or ask the machine shop or your auto dealer's service department).

Start by tightening the bolts for the rocker shaft (or the nuts for individually mounted rockers), using a torque wrench on all but adjustable hydraulic arrangements. In this case, turn down each nut the number of turns taken to remove it.

Reversing the removal sequence (start with No. 1, proceed to No. 10) tighten the head bolts slowly, a couple of turns on each bolt at a time in the beginning. This will prevent squashing the lifters or bending the pushrods. Once the head is fully seated use the torque wrench to tighten the head to factory specifications. Tighten the head bolts or nuts in progressive stages. For example, if the setting is 70 ft.-lbs., tighten all bolts first to 25, then 50 and finally 70.

It's primarily straight nuts-and-bolts work from here, reconnecting everything that was disconnected. If you have been careful and made sketches you'll have all parts and know where they go.

Now for the final valve settings on those cars with adjustable lifters. Engines with solid lifters demand a special

6. REMOVE head bolts and rocker assembly. Take out pushrods, unseat head carefully.

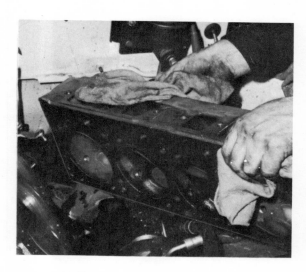

7. REMOVE head and deliver to machinist. Use care not to strike machined surface.

technique. If you don't know how, leave the job to a professional, who should get $2.50 to $4 for the job.

If your engine has adjustable hydraulic lifters, run the engine at a slow idle. Turn the adjusting nut counterclockwise until the valves starts to clatter, then clockwise until the clatter just disappears. Turn an additional 1½ turns on Fords and one additional turn on Chevrolets.

Refit the valve covers and you'll have a valve job done as well as any professional shop could do it—certainly for a lot less money. •

What to do When a Car Won't Start

AN engine that won't start needn't mushroom into lost time, great expense or a migraine headache. In just a few minutes, you usually can isolate the faulty component. Then nine out of ten times you'll find you can correct the problem without even rolling up your shirt sleeves.

The successful procedure lies in analyzing the first symptom—does it or doesn't it crank?

If the engine won't crank—When you turn the key to the *on* position the red ignition light on your dash also should go on, indicating the ignition switch is good and the battery is putting out enough to power the lamp. If the lamp remains off try a short blast on the horn or turn on the lights. There's always the chance that the bulb has burned out.

In the event all these circuits prove inoperative, check the battery and its connections—there should be electrolyte in each of the battery's cells and the cable connectors should be tight. Check the ground connection.

If you're lucky enough to have a hydrometer at hand, use it to check the battery charge. If this is all right, then rumple your suit by peering under the dash and removing the fuse-box cover. While there, you also might look for loose cables. Pull each fuse in turn and hold it to the sunlight or a flashlight to ascertain continuity. If you can identify the ignition-circuit fuse, of course, you need check only that one.

Take one giant step and turn the ignition key to *start* position. You first should hear the starter solenoid fall in with a solid click. If you have an automatic transmission and the engine fails to crank, try starting in both the N and P positions. Jiggle the gear selector a bit—there's a neutral safety switch (for starting only in these two positions) that may have worked loose or failed.

Then if the starter still fails to crank, apply the brakes and attempt to start while moving the selector through the different drive ranges. If maladjusted, the switch may close in one of the drive positions so make this test with caution.

If the engine still fails to crank, touch a battery booster cable momentarily to the battery's positive terminal after connecting the other end to the following points:

General Motors cars—To the solenoid terminal on top of the starter assembly. There are three terminals. The smallest is the proper one for this test.

Chrysler cars—To the solenoid terminal on top of the starter assembly. There are two terminals. Again, the smaller is the right one.

Ford cars—To the starter terminal of the starter relay (the heavy cable from the starter leads directly to the proper relay terminal).

These tests bypass the key-operated starter switch, the neutral safety switch, a relay (on Ford and Chrysler cars) and the interconnecting wiring—all of which make up the starter control circuit.

Thus, if the engine *still* refuses to crank, the starter probably is kaput. Replace it with a new or rebuilt unit after checking the brushes in the original (both are jobs the average weekend mechanic can handle). However, if you happen to discover this while off on

CRANK the engine with coil lead held near a good ground. A strong spark should result.

CHECK the inside of distributor for dust or cracks that mean high-resistance leaks.

a jaunt the only way to get started is to arrange a push.

If the engine cranks—If the starter is cranking in healthy fashion all the foregoing checks are superfluous. Instead, you should begin with these quick but proven tests on the ignition and fuel system:

1. Should the engine start but stall immediately when you release the key it proves that the ignition resistor is defective. This resistor is bypassed during cranking so the engine will start. But once the key is released, current must

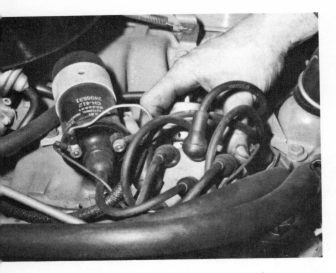

ATTEMPT to move the distributor by hand. If it's loose, ignition timing may be upset.

REMOVE the air filter to check visually that automatic choke opens if engine's hot.

flow through a different circuit, which also includes the resistor. (Note: We're referring to the ignition primary circuit resistor which is put in at the factory, not the radio-suppression type you may have added to the ignition secondary.)

2. Pull the center lead (the one that goes to the coil) from the distributor cap and hold it about a half-in. from electrical ground (any metal part of the engine). Have someone crank the engine for a few seconds. You should see sparks jumping from the end of the wire to ground. If there's no spark move the lead closer to ground. If there's only a

weak spark (probably intermittent) proceed directly to step 4. If no one is around to turn the key to crank the engine you can jump the starter switch by connecting one end of a booster cable to the battery and holding the other end against the starter terminal.

3. A healthy, continuous spark from the coil indicates there's spark going into the distributor cap so check next to see that it's being distributed to the plugs.

Disconnect a few spark-plug wires at the plugs—one at a time. Hold each wire a half-in. from ground and again have the engine cranked. The spark should occur less frequently but should be as robust as the discharge from the coil wire. If it is, the ignition system is good. Proceed to step 7.

If the spark is weak or non-existent, remove the distributor cap and check the inside of the cap carefully (use a flashlight), looking for fine cracks or a dirt film that could provide a leakage path for the spark. Clean or replace the cap as necessary.

Inspect the coil and plug lead inserts in the cap for corrosion which could provide a great deal of resistance and weaken the spark. Clean out any corrosion with a wire brush.

4. No spark or a weak spark from the coil could be caused by a poor coil, improperly gapped points, a defective condenser or a broken or loose connection.

Because it's the most likely item, the point gap should be checked first (with the rubbing block at a peak of the cam). It should be somewhat between .012 and .020-in. (the thickness of one business card or something similar).

Next make a quick check of the ignition primary circuit by turning on the ignition and flicking the breaker points open with a screwdriver. You should see a solid electrical arc at the points, which tells you there is a complete circuit from the ignition switch through the coil to the points.

5. If there is little or no arcing connect a thin jumper from the battery's positive terminal to the coil's primary positive terminal (marked with a plus sign, an S or SW). Try the arcing test again. If it works the problem is a poor

or broken connection at the ignition switch, a junction block, a resistor or the coil itself.

Checking back through the circuit imposes some difficulties for the weekend wrench-twirler. But the jumper wire probably will correct any ignition malfunction and get the car running. Then visit your friendly garage. At least you won't get hit with a towing bill.

If the test produces no results, connect a jumper to the other primary terminal of the coil. With the ignition turned on, scratch the other end of this jumper against a ground. You should see heavy sparking as you scratch. No sparks mean current is not flowing through the coil, which must be open at some internal point. Replace the coil.

6. If this last test is successful, current is flowing through the coil but is not getting to the breaker points. Obviously the lead from the coil to the points is open. Replace it.

7. The sparks not only must be healthy but they must arrive at each cylinder at the proper time. Try to move the distributor body. Don't be bashful about using force. If the distributor moves at all under hand pressure, ignition timing may have been upset by engine vibration.

In checking the fuel system, remember that only in a few cases will a bad carburetor prevent starting. A malfunctioning automatic choke will do it.

The choke should be closed when the engine is cold, open when it's hot. You can check by removing the air filter and looking.

If the choke is in proper position, check for carburetor flooding. If the carb is flooding badly enough to prevent starting you'll smell the raw fuel through a stiff head cold. You might even get the whiff when you're behind the wheel.

More than likely, however, the fuel isn't getting to the carb. A simple check, with the air filter off, is to open the choke manually so you can see into the carburetor air horn. Yank open the throttle and look for a strong spurt of gasoline into the air horn.

If there's only a dribble, chances are the fuel filter is clogged, the fuel line is

CHECK the battery cable terminals. Make sure they are clean and tight at the battery.

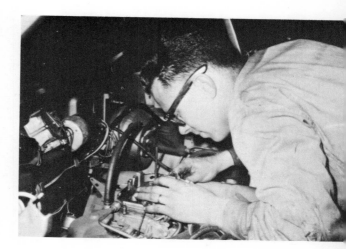

LOOK down carb air horn and yank throttle open to see if fuel is delivered to the carb.

plugged or kinked, or you have a bad fuel pump.

Loosen but don't disconnect the carburetor fuel-line connection at the fuel pump. Crank the engine. If fuel fizzles out the problem is in the line to the carburetor, most likely a clogged filter. If no gasoline comes out the pump is defective.

Under normal conditions it should take less than ten minutes to run the checks we've outlined. For example, if the engine fails to crank, correcting that problem normally will get the car going. Or the engine may crank satisfactorily, permitting you to bypass the series of checks for no cranking. •

Servicing Power Brakes

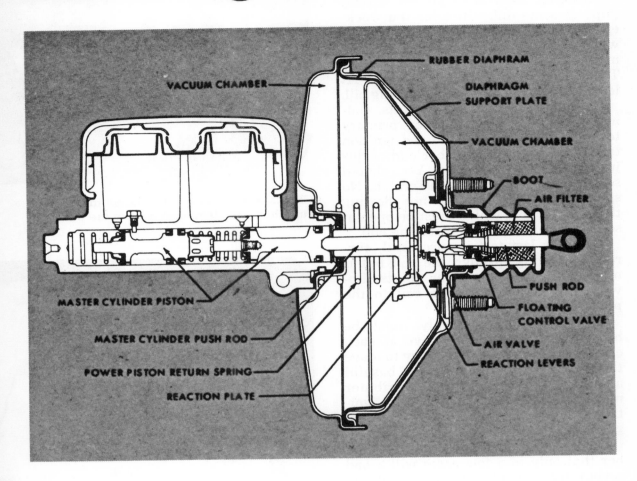

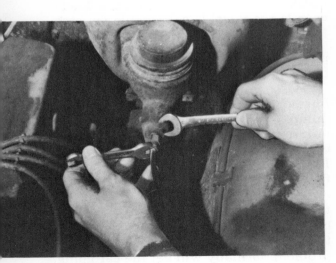

TO BLEED master cylinder remove brake line while someone floors pedal. Cover opening with thumb when brake is released.

POWER accessories are the last thing a weekend mechanic attempts to fix. Although it's good to recognize things you are not equipped to handle, there are many parts of the power steering and braking systems that parallel those in non-power systems.

Many different power brake units are made for passenger cars. All use engine vacuum to boost the braking force supplied by your foot. The units are designed so that, should the power fail, you can stop anyway, although some early models require quite a bit of foot pressure.

When the brake pedal is pushed, a valve in the power unit lets engine intake vacuum suck air out of a chamber on one side of a diaphragm, bellows or

and Power Steering

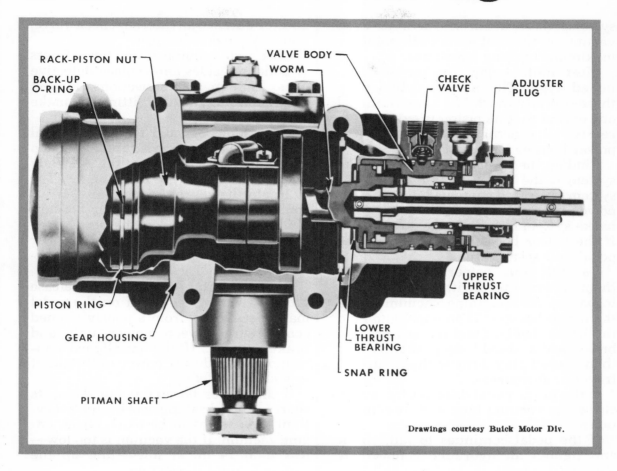

RACK-PISTON NUT

BACK-UP O-RING

VALVE BODY

WORM

CHECK VALVE

ADJUSTER PLUG

PISTON RING

GEAR HOUSING

PITMAN SHAFT

LOWER THRUST BEARING

SNAP RING

UPPER THRUST BEARING

Drawings courtesy Buick Motor Div.

piston. Atmospheric pressure pushing on the other side gives the master cylinder's piston a boost, building up hydraulic pressure in the braking system. You supply a little of the effort and the power booster supplies the rest. Except for the booster unit, the parts of a power brake system are like those of conventional brakes.

A power brake assembly consists of the power booster and a master cylinder. A vacuum hose leads from the intake manifold to the power booster and a hydraulic line (or lines in the case of dual-braking systems) leads to the car's wheel cylinders. Some power brake units have a vacuum reservoir between the power unit and intake manifold. This stores up enough vacuum to make several power-assisted stops without the engine running. All vacuum

EXAMINE power steering cylinder shaft for scoring which causes leaks. Some shafts are covered with protective boots.

systems have a check valve to keep vacuum in the unit at its peak point for maximum braking assistance.

Most units today are the self-contained type. The master cylinder on these is pretty much like a conventional one except that its piston is extended to receive the actuating rod from the power booster unit.

Finding the trouble in a power brake system is the same as for a non-power system until it is narrowed down to the power unit. Always check the regular brake system first, then the power unit. If the power booster fails to work, the pedal will seem hard.

To test your power brakes, apply them several times with the engine off to use up all remaining vacuum inside the power booster. Then apply and hold the brake firmly. Start the engine. The brake pedal should drop slightly but then should stay firm without further travel or sponginess.

If the brake pedal does not fall away, check the vacuum hose and its connections.

If the pedal continues to fall, check and tighten all hydraulic connections and bleed screws. If the pedal still falls when the test is repeated and no fluid leakage is visible, there may be an internal leak in the master cylinder.

If the pedal is spongy, bleed the trapped air out of the hydraulic system.

Release the brake pedal and run the engine a full minute at idle. Then shut it off. After waiting another minute, step on the brake pedal several times. The pedal should become harder each time the brakes are applied. Otherwise there is a vacuum leak.

If the check valve in the power booster system is a separate unit (usually located at the intake manifold), disconnect the vacuum hose from the unit. Cover the hose end with your finger and have someone start the engine to create vacuum. Then shut it off. *Vacuum should hold for at least a minute.* If not, the check valve is defective and should be replaced. If the power

booster unit has an internal check valve, you can't make this test.

Check all vacuum hoses for softness or collapsed sides and replace defective ones. Tighten all connections. Inspect the manifold vacuum fitting to make sure it is clear.

Have someone hold the brake pedal down while the engine is running. Listen for a vacuum leak in the unit. A steady hissing is what you're listening for. Try to locate the source of the noise. If it's coming from inside the power booster, you'll have to abandon the rest of the job to a shop. But you can replace or tighten a leaking vacuum hose or connection yourself.

A power brake that won't release properly when you let off on the pedal may be suffering from a poorly aligned connection between power unit and brake linkage. If the misaligned connection is inside the power unit, take it to a shop for fixing.

If the power booster is not doing its share of the braking work and everything else seems to be okay, check engine vacuum. If the vacuum is too low— less than 14 in. at idle—tune up the engine to raise its vacuum.

Other maintenance tips on power brakes are pretty conventional: Power brakes are more dependent on brake fluid than conventional ones, so use the best. If the unit has an air filter that you can get at, keep it clean. Maintain brake pedal free play the same as for a conventional system. If the brake pedal must be pushed down more than half its total travel distance, the brake linings need adjustment or replacement.

Heavy front ends and wider tires with lower pressures all have increased steering effort in today's cars to the point where power steering is no longer a luxury.

Power steering is really a hydraulic booster arrangement that supplies most of the turning effort when you move the steering wheel. The system consists of an engine-driven pump that supplies hydraulic pressure to the power steering unit. Even if power steering fails, the car can be steered conventionally.

The hydraulic pump is usually belt-driven, but may run off the back of the generator. Using type-A automatic transmission fluid, the pump delivers some 1000 psi. pressure to power unit. A reservoir on pump holds fluid. A filter reservoir keeps the fluid clean.

There isn't much you can do on a power steering system. You can check the fluid level at regular intervals and add type-A transmission fluid if necessary. If the level should get too low, the pump begins sucking air and you may have to bleed the system after topping it off. To do this idle the engine while turning the steering wheel rapidly all the way to one side then the other. Roll the front wheels onto several sheets of newspaper first to prevent scuffing the tires and straining the steering system. If there was much air in the system, you'll have to add more fluid.

Keep watch for fluid leaks on the pavement under the front of your car. Sometimes automatic transmission sealants will stop the leaking for a time. Later you'll need professional repairs.

A leak may simply be from an opening in the gasket between the fluid reservoir and its cover. This lets fluid out until there isn't enough left to make a full turn. The pump growls and you have to provide all the turning effort beyond the emptying point. Replace the gasket, refill with fluid and bleed off trapped air.

To find where fluid is leaking, wipe off all the power steering system parts and turn the steering wheel from side to side several times with the engine idling. Hold the wheel against the lock each way for a short time to build pressure. Then crawl underneath and inspect for leaks. Even if it turns out to be more than you can fix yourself, helping your mechanic to narrow down the trouble should save you money.

Often a leak is in the shaft seal on the pump. Replacing that and overhauling the pump is not very costly. In fact

you can buy a rebuilt pump for $20 to $25 and install it yourself.

If it's a hose that's leaking, a new one costs $6 to $10 complete with end fittings and a tool to install it. Your shop can replace leaky seals in a power cylinder for $8 to $10. A scored piston rod calls for replacement of the entire power cylinder, a $40 to $50 job.

When the trouble is in the control valve or power unit itself, take your car to the shop. Sometimes a simple adjustment is all that's necessary. Other times the unit may need a complete overhaul.

Before putting the blame on power steering, the entire steering system, the suspension and wheel alignment should be checked. Front tire pressure that is too low can also be the source of steering difficulties.

Keep a careful check on the pump belt tension. A belt that's loose will squeal every time the steering meets resistance. Too tight a belt can wear out the pump bearings before their time. See that the belt is not glazed, cracked or worn excessively. If it is, replace it. To do this you may have to remove all the belts. Replace them all too.

On newer cars belt tension must be checked with a belt tension gauge. If you don't have one, take your car to the shop for this part of the checkup. If bad, you can adjust or replace them.

Here are some power steering problems other than leaks which indicate that professional service is needed: (1) Hard or erratic steering. (2) Excessive play or looseness in steering. (3) Noises in pump (slight hissing sound okay). (4) Lack of assist in one or both directions. (5) Steering wheel surges or jerks when turning. (6) Poor return of steering gear to center. (7) Car pulls to one side. (8) Momentary increase in effort when turning wheel fast. (9) Squawk when turning or recovering from turn. (10) No effort required to turn.

Don't tamper with any part of a car still under warranty as "unauthorized repair" may void the entire contract. •

The Band Saw

Pictured is 12-inch Craftsman band saw available at Sears, Roebuck and Co. Motor is ½ hp, 1725 rpm. Attached is vacuum with 3-bushel capacity.

Curved ribs on frame and vanes on the wheels will direct flow of sawdust through exhaust elbow.

Knob at top tightens or relieves the blade tension, which is shown by pointer on the tension scale.

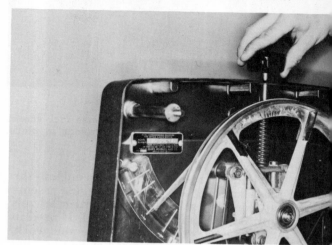

THE band saw, one of the oldest of the woodworking machines, is still basically the same as the one on which William Newberry was granted a patent way back in 1808 in England.

Band saws are now made in many sizes varying from the smallest, such as the little bench models with 9-inch wheels, to the giants used in mills with wheels that are 84 inches and more in diameter. The blades on these large models are as much as 16 inches wide and 50 feet long.

The band mill is used for sawing logs into planks and the band re-saw is used to cut thick stock into thinner boards. A third kind is the band-scroll saw, used for sawing curved or straight work, a combination of both, and on occasion for re-sawing. This third kind is the one illustrated and described in this article. The machine is so named because the cutting blade is actually a narrow, flexible, endless band of steel with teeth on one edge. This blade runs over revolving pulleys or wheels which have rubber tires stretched over their rims.

The size of a conventional band saw is indicated by the diameter of each of its two wheels. For instance, an 18-inch band saw has 18-inch diameter wheels and will cut 18 inches, less the width of the blade guard. In some instances, the size is given as the actual throat opening rather than the wheel size.

Several models of band saws have three, rather than two wheels. This makes possible a much larger throat opening in a smaller, more compact, less expensive machine. A band saw, because it is so well guarded, is one of the safest woodworking

Knob at side adjusts spring tension against the hexagon blade support bar, holds bar where set.

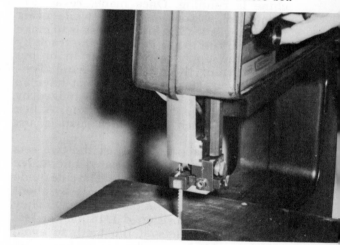

Unlock set screw, turn the knob shown, and blade guides move in or out to set blade for good cut.

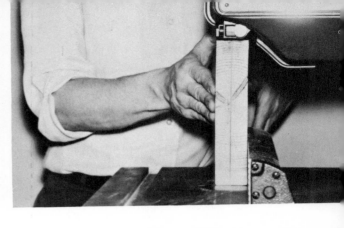

Pick up circular table insert, release lock screw, position lower ball thrust roller, relock in place.

Band saw has normal 6-inch capacity. For a cut of this type, use a rip fence to support heavy stock.

machines to operate. The doors enclose the blade and wheels. The upper guide assembly contains a blade guard which travels with it when raised or lowered. If used in its correct position, just above the work, the blade is always covered except for that part which does the actual cutting.

Adjustments, while not complicated, must be carefully made in the order given and should never be made while the machine is running. Once made, re-adjustments are seldom necessary while using the same blade. The first of these is to make the blade run in the center of the track by tilting the upper wheel either in or out while turning the machine by hand. Tension is next. On saws that do not have an indicator scale, tension may be judged by pressing on the side of the blade. A flex of about ¼-inch in a 6-inch span is just about correct.

The third step is to adjust the two sets of side guides that are located one above and one below the saw table. The side guide pins should each clear the blade by about the thickness of a thin piece of paper. They should also be positioned 1/16 inch or less back of the gullets of the teeth to avoid any injury to them. The blade should not touch the roller guide wheels, usually located just above and back of the side

guards, except when material is being sawed. A clearance of about the thickness of a piece of writing paper should be sufficient. If permitted to continually touch, the back of the blade will become hardened which will hasten its breakage.

The final check on the saw travel is to run the machine by hand. If all seems correct, and provided the doors are closed, a short trial run should be made under power. The table on most saws may be tilted up to an angle of 45 degrees and returned to a right angle to the blade when it is lowered to an adjustable stop screw. It is advisable to check the accuracy of the setting with a square. At least one band saw has a blade which may be tilted 7 degrees forward and 46 degrees backward while the table remains flat. This angle may even be varied while the saw is in motion to make cuts that are impossible on a conventional saw.

Blades for cutting wood on a small band saw include widths from ⅛ to ¾ inch, and from 3 to 7 teeth per inch. If the selection is limited, a ¼ and ⅜-inch size will prove to be satisfactory for most jobs. Tooth styles are the standard and the buttress (skip tooth). The standard is used for regular woodworking operations and

To cross cut 2x6 planks, stand work on edge, then cut across any length. Later, trim angle to size.

Light angle formed after 2x6 plank is cross cut is trimmed to square edge by using a miter gauge.

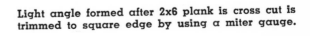

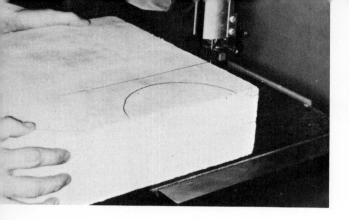

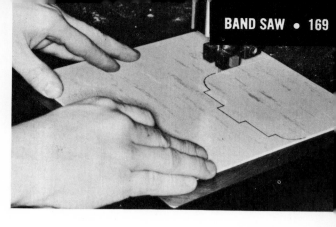

Foam plastics in various thicknesses are easily cut. Vary blades and speeds to test new materials.

Vinyl, rubber, cork, asphalt and other floor tiles are readily shaped to fit door jambs, bad corners.

skip tooth for cutting aluminum or brass, plastic, or any other soft material which may plug up the teeth.

A broken blade may be successfully hard soldered or brazed at home but most people prefer to send these jobs out. Even though new blades are inexpensive and dull ones can be sharpened at little cost, some people like to do the job at home. A simple rig may be made with discs to hold the blade in position as one section at a time is clamped in a small vise for either setting or filing. Teeth are set to alternate sides and are filed straight across as on a ripsaw, using a blunt triangular file with rounded edges.

Blades should be coiled for storage. To do this, hold the blade in a vertical position and with the teeth pointed away, stand on the bottom of the loop. Twisting the blade inwards, you will cause the upper section to bend down toward the lower. Next, place this upper loop inside the lower, move the hands until they cross each other, and three loops will be formed on the floor.

On larger blades where five loops may be desired, one of the three loops formed should be pulled out from the others and twisted as before.

Band saw work is very simple, yet proper technique will result in a saving of time

and material. First, a blade should be selected that is the widest that will do the job. It may help to know that a ¾-inch blade will cut a 1¾-inch radius and a ¼-inch blade will cut one ¾-inch, but also that it is not wise to run quite this small. The complete cut should be thought out in advance to eliminate the necessity of backing out of long stock. Also, a little advance thinking will prevent sawing a piece in the direction that will cause it to run into the column. Similar planning will show the necessity for making the shortest cuts first. Many cuts that do not involve curves may be made by using a miter gauge or a rip fence. Boards may be ripped with their edges square or they may be beveled or chamfered by tilting the blade or table. They may also be re-sawed after first being sawed from both sides on the circular saw.

Many wood joints can be entirely cut on the band saw even though this operation probably can be done more accurately on the circular saw. These joints include end-lap, middle-lap, cross-lap, and slip joints. Parts of others such as tenons and tails of dovetail joints are also possible. When only one curved piece is to be sawed, the outline may be drawn directly on the wood. If this same outline will be duplicated many times,

When cutting paper tubing, be sure to hold the tube securely in a V-block guided by miter gauge.

To cut corrugated paper sheets, form rolls up to 6 inches in diameter and saw to length as shown.

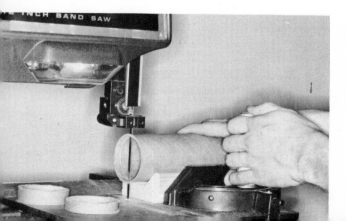

Since metal cutting requires slower peripheral speeds, mount a slow speed converter on saw.

Most ordinary plastics can be cut with ease—sheets, extrusions, moldings, tubing, rounds, etc.

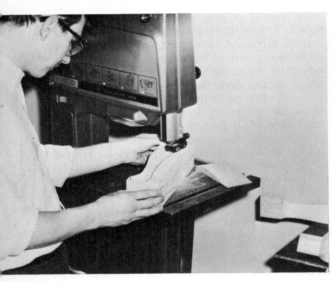

Free form decorative shapes are simple to render on a band saw. Cabriolet furniture legs are easy.

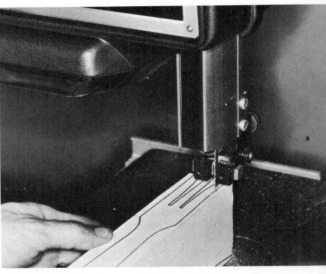

To make a salad fork, use 1½x3x10-inch piece of dressed maple. Draw an outline of the design.

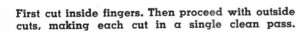

First cut inside fingers. Then proceed with outside cuts, making each cut in a single clean pass.

Place the three pieces back together with masking tape to form original rectangular shape of stock.

a pattern or template should be made of cardboard, hardboard or metal. When two or more pieces are to be sawed to the same shape, work will be more accurate and time will be saved if they are nailed together and sawed as one unit. The nails should, if possible, be in the waste and so located that they will not interfere with the sawing.

Many jigs may be constructed. Some of these make the work easier and some are necessary to perform certain operations. V blocks in various positions may be used to split round stock, to cut triangular pieces, to cut the corners off a square block that is to be turned, or for making diagonal cuts in the end to receive the live center of work to be turned in the lathe.

Circular discs of any predetermined size may be cut accurately by means of a simple jig made of a board clamped to the table. The pivot point is made with a brad driven through the bottom of the board, located at right angles to the blade and at a distance equal to the radius of the circle. If the disc radius is larger than the table, an extension may be made with boards clamped to the table and built up even with its surface. Other jigs include those for doing multiple sawing by using a pattern, for cutting circular arcs or segments, for cutting either parallel or beveled curves and for trimming the ends of glued-up stock, and for cutting tapers or wedges.

The band saw can be used for cutting metal by changing the blade to one suitable for this work. These blades look like and cut like hack saw blades. The same rules apply in their selection. The teeth should not be too fine on heavy work or they will clog, nor should they be too coarse on thin work or they will strip. A good rule to follow is to use a coarse blade whenever possible but always to make certain that at least two teeth are in contact with the stock at all times.

Three styles of sets obtainable are: "every tooth set," which is similar to that on saws used for wood; "regular," has one unset tooth for each pair that is set; and "wavy," where groups of teeth are formed in waves, first to the right and then to the left. If the number of saw blades must be limited, a group of three regular set, one with 14, one with 18 and one with 24 teeth will do most metal cutting jobs in a home shop. Metals are sawed at a slower speed than wood. If the saw is not equipped with a speed control, you can get around this with a set of pulleys used like back gears, or by the use of separate countershaft, or by a drive from the spindle of a metal cutting lathe. •

Now that you have a flat side to support project, proceed with profile cuts. Cuts are 5/16" thick.

Cut one fork, scribe next outline and repeat the process. As piece narrows, use wood push block.

Replace saw blade with band sander and bring each fork to smooth finish. Make matching spoons.

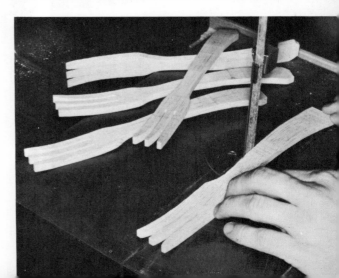

For a liquor cabinet on wheels,
make Bill Baker's compact and convenient

GARDEN BAR CART

Front view of bar cart. Drinking glasses used must be slanted so they slip into, not through, holes.

Side view of bar cart. Entire unit can be made from one piece of plywood, some miscellaneous wood.

BEGIN making your bar cart by tracing the patterns shown in this section. Then cut all the pieces out carefully.

Start assembling as follows: screw "N" onto edge of "Q," holding good side of "N" facing out. Take solid block "A" and insert 4 screws through the inside of "N" and tighten.

Take previous assembly and hold onto inside face of back "O" and flush with top edge, insert two 1½-inch No. 8 flathead screws and tighten.

Turn complete previous assembly upside down, holding flush edges down. Put center shelf "C" onto it with better side down, tight against back, and screw on by starting through the back first and then the other parts.

Turn complete assembly right side up. Set top "B" onto assembly, holding back edge flush with back piece "O," insert 1½-inch No. 8 flathead screws and tighten. Put complete assembly aside.

Take piece "D-1," holding finished side of plywood down, and set piece "D-2" onto it, holding it flush on straight edge and leaving equal margin on the round edge. Nail or screw both pieces tightly together.

Mark ⅜ inch in on long edge (21 inches) of piece "H." Mark one inch in from each end and then in equal spaces for 5 screws. Bore holes for 1½-inch No. 8 flathead screws and countersink on unfinished side of plywood.

Plant previous piece onto straight edge of assembly "D-1" and "D-2," holding it flush with outside edge of smaller circle "D-2" and let it reach to the bottom surface of bottom circle. Insert 1½-inch No. 8 flathead screws and tighten.

Take complete previous assembly, hold it onto bottom surface of center shelf "C" making sure that all front edges of the round portion extend equally. This can be done by nailing a 1x2-inch strip 26 inches long onto front edge (round portion) of both top and center shelf and using that as a guide for the lower front shelf assembly. Insert 1½-inch No. 8 flathead screws through holes of shelf "C" into piece "H," making sure that "H" will be recessed one inch on each end and tighten. Now line up and square up lower front shelf assembly. Hold it in place and put nail through temporary 1x2-inch guide so that all pieces will stay in place for further assembly.

Turn assembly upside down. Put bottom "K" of cabinet on assembly by propping it up with same guide and holding flush with bottom edge of back "O". Insert 1½-inch No. 8 flathead screws through back into bottom and tighten. This completes the first part of the assembly.

Now cut 10 pieces, 1 inch thick x 3½ inches wide x 7¼ inches long out of solid wood. Dado out both edges and back of each piece. Cut two pieces 1 inch thick x 3¾ inches wide x 7¼ inches long out of solid wood. Dado out one edge and back of each piece; however, on these two pieces, the side that you dado out will be opposite on each piece. On one piece you will plough out from the front of the panel, while on the other piece dado out from the back as you did on one side of each of the previous 10 pieces. Now bevel both front edges of all 12 pieces. The dados or cutouts will be $\frac{3}{16}$ of an inch deep x 1½ inches wide and in the back of each panel ¼ inch deep x 2 inches wide. Mark on all 12 panels, ⅜ inch from each end for two screws. Bore holes, countersink surface for 1½-inch No. 8 flathead screws.

Cut two pieces, 1 inch thick x 3½ inches wide x 16 inches long out of solid wood. Also cut two pieces 1 inch thick x 4 inches wide x 16 inches long out of solid wood. Dado out and bevel edge on all four pieces. On these four pieces, the dados or cutouts will be ½ x ½ inch.

Mark ⅜ inch from bottom of each piece and bore two holes through each piece on this line. Countersink on surface for 1½-inch No. 8 flathead screws.

Mounting Panels

Mount each pair of panels onto cabinet, holding them flush with bottom surface of cabinet bottom and snug against bottom surface of center shelf and flush with the surface of piece "H." Bore two holes for each panel through center shelf and countersink for 1½-inch No. 8 flathead screws. Insert screws and tighten.

Set first short panel approximately in center of round section onto bottom and lower front shelf reinforcement, again holding it snug against lower front shelf and flush with bottom of cabinet. Tack on with two finishing nails to hold piece in place. Now start inserting all the panels to both sides, tacking them on temporarily with finishing nails. After they are all properly fitted in place, insert 1½-inch No. 8 flathead screws through all holes.

Cut two pieces "U," 1 inch thick x 3 inches wide x 24¾ inches long out of solid wood. Bore two holes ⅜ inch from bottom edge of each piece and countersink for 1½-inch No. 8 flathead screws. Insert each piece on back corner of each side of cabinet, holding them flush on bottom and flush with cabinet back and snug against cabinet top and inside of notch of center shelf. Insert two screws on the bottom and two screws through the top and bore additional holes to go into back

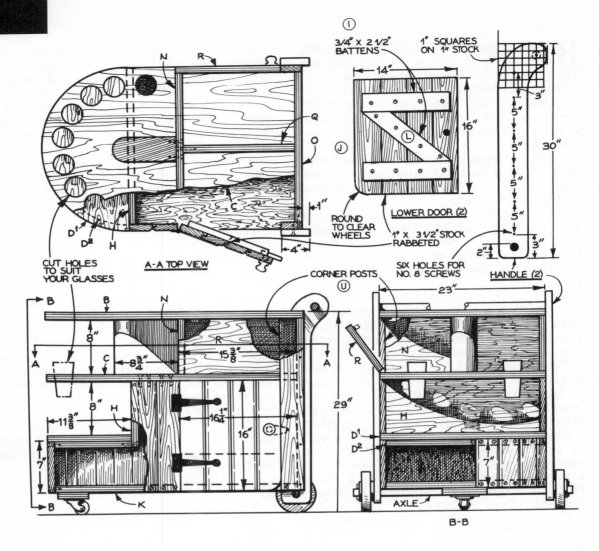

and center shelf and countersink for 1½-inch No. 8 flathead screws.

Fit doors "R" in both top spaces on each side, holding a ¾-inch piano hinge underneath and a piece of cardboard on one side on top. Door edge must be flush with vertical partition "N." Mount piano hinges, doors and touch latch.

Mount handles and wheel supports onto each side of cabinet, holding them flush with inside edge of piece "U" and let bottom one-inch dowel hole just clear. First mount one handle by inserting screws and tightening. Cut one-inch dowel 24 inches long. Sand smooth and insert into hole of fastened handle. Now insert into hole of loose handle and fasten same with screws. Insert one one-inch No. 8 flathead screw through handles into dowel.

Make complete wheel assembly. For the wheels use 1½-inch solid wood and for the little side wheels use ½-inch solid wood. Before putting wheel assembly into handle and wheel support, cut one inch dowel 31½ inches long. Bore one hole six inches from each end through dowel and

countersink for 1½-inch No. 8 flathead screws. Sand six inches of dowel from each end well. Rub large amount of paraffin onto sanded ends. Now insert dowel through bottom holes of handle and wheel support, leaving equal amounts extended on each side.

Once wheels are finished, mount small ½-inch washer-like wheel solidly onto large wheels using glue and finishing nails. Bore a $1\frac{1}{16}$-inch hole through center of complete wheels. Put paraffin inside hole in wheels and on top of small washer-like wheel which faces cabinet. Put wheels on and bore ¼-inch hole on dowel extending beyond wheel. Insert a ¼-inch thick dowel two inches long in axle to hold wheels in place. Insert two 1½-inch No. 8 flathead screws through axle where holes are and fasten against cabinet bottom.

Bore holes and countersink for 1½-inch No. 8 flathead screws. On bottom surface of cabinet bottom in exact center of round portion one inch in from outside edge, mount piece "E" with glue and screws. Now mount a rubber caster onto block.

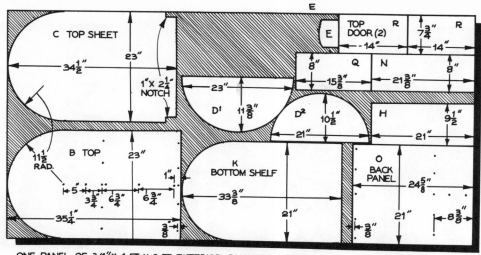

ONE PANEL OF 3/4" X 4 FT. X 8 FT. EXTERIOR PLYWOOD YIELDS ALL MAJOR COMPONENTS

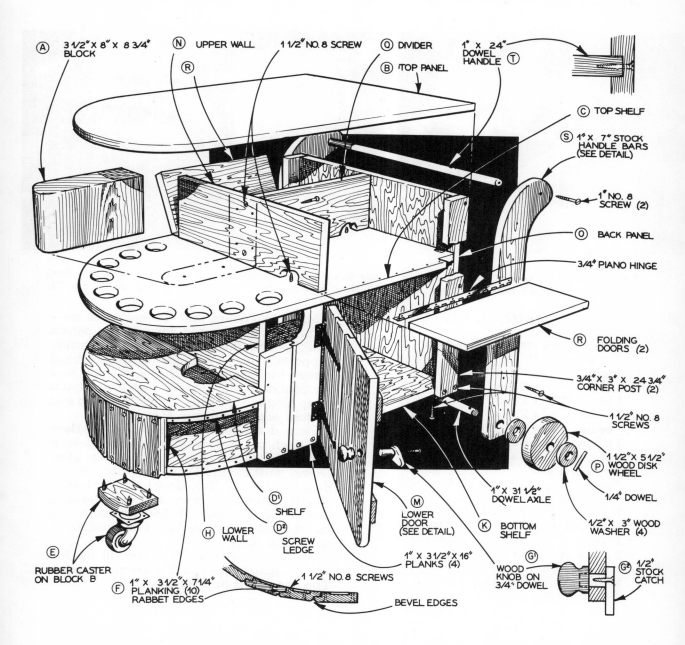

(Left to right) After cutting all pieces, bore holes through shell "C" according to size of glasses to be used. Attach back reinforcing strips "U" to back "O." Assemble "Q" and "N" partitions to block "A."

Fasten assembly "Q-N-A" to back "O" in upside down postion on level surface to keep all edges flush. Still in upside down position, attach shelf "C." Now turn assembly right side up and attach top "B."

MATERIAL LIST

1 sheet ¾" plywood, 4' x 8' (outdoor waterproof)
3 boards, 1" x 4" x 8'
1 board, 1" x 8" x 3'
1 board, 1½" x 6" x 12"
1 board, ½" x 3" x 12"
1 board, ¾" x 2½" x 8'
2 hardwood dowels, 1" x 3'
2 pair, ornamental strap hinges, 6" with screws
2 pieces, ¾" piano hinge, 14" long, with ½" screws
1 gross flathead screws, 1½" #8
4 flathead screws, 1" #8   2 touch latches
1 length, ¼" dowel   1 rubber caster
2 pieces, 10" length brass chain, plus 4 pieces ¾"
#6 roundhead screws and washers
Waterproof glue

Make two doors, one *reverse*. Use one-inch thick solid wood for outside panels and ¾-inch thick solid wood for inside supports. Use 1½-inch No. 8 flathead screws for assembling. Bore a ¾-inch hole for doorknob. Put two six-inch ornamental strap hinges 3¼ inches center from top and bottom edges of doors. Mount doors.

Turn doorknob out of solid wood. Bore a ¾-inch hole half way in. Insert a ¾-inch hardwood dowel into knob using glue. Dowel must extend 1⅛ inches. Cut out two door latches ("G-2"). Bore holes for 1-inch No. 8 flathead screws and countersink. Sand extended part of dowel smooth and insert through hole in door. Glue and screw latch into place.

Sand all edges and surfaces using No. 2/0 sandpaper (preferably Garnet paper). The bar cart is now finished.

Assemble pieces "D-1" and "D-2," holding edges flush at back. Turn assembly upside down and use guide strips for spacing and support as 'H" and "D-1" and "D-2" are mounted. Then attach bottom piece "K."

Handle and wheel supports are mounted, holding them flush with front edge of back reinforcing strips "U." Then attach side panels, lower panels, and upper doors. Next step: construction of lower doors.

Outside face of lower door gets ornamental hinges door knob, catch. As lower door is mounted, cart is on level surface so door is flush with bottom of cart. Last job: attach caster on mounting block of front bottom.

Build a Stone Fireplace

An economic double hearth for family outdoor cooking and entertainment

YOU CAN SPELL the beginning and end of many serious fireplace-building projects with just one word: foundation. Unless your structure is to be small, lightweight, on well-drained, frost-free ground, the foundation of your fireplace is as important as all the above-ground structure.

To play it safe we used a reinforced concrete slab. This seemed to offer the layman the best possible and lowest cost foundation that would give the least amount of trouble in the greatest number of climates.

In the selected site, measure off an area with at least a 1-inch border further out than the fireplace base will be on all sides. In the fireplace herein illustrated, the base was 46″ x 46″ so the measured area was no less than 48″ x 48″. At each corner drive a long stake deep into the transcribed area just outside, to hold the form solidly. Using boards of 6-inch width (or more if you like), construct the form for the foundation slab. Take special care in insuring the levelness of the top edges of your form.

Dig the foundation hole to a depth of 19 inches below ground level. Pitch in the direction of the terrain slope to allow drainage in the natural direction. Then fill the first 8 inches with fist-sized rocks. Fill the next 9 inches with smaller stones, cinders or gravel. In most areas it is possible to find stones to fulfill these requirements.

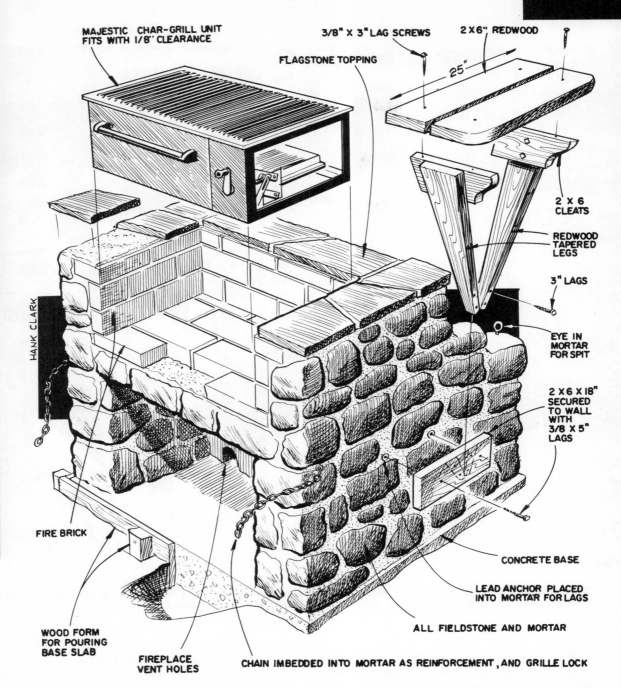

MAJESTIC CHAR-GRILL UNIT FITS WITH 1/8" CLEARANCE

FLAGSTONE TOPPING

3/8" X 3" LAG SCREWS

2 X 6" REDWOOD

25"

2 X 6 CLEATS

REDWOOD TAPERED LEGS

3" LAGS

EYE IN MORTAR FOR SPIT

2 X 6 X 18" SECURED TO WALL WITH 3/8 X 5" LAGS

HANK CLARK

FIRE BRICK

CONCRETE BASE

LEAD ANCHOR PLACED INTO MORTAR FOR LAGS

WOOD FORM FOR POURING BASE SLAB

FIREPLACE VENT HOLES

ALL FIELDSTONE AND MORTAR

CHAIN IMBEDDED INTO MORTAR AS REINFORCEMENT, AND GRILLE LOCK

The last 2 inches are filled with construction sand. Water thoroughly to force sand down among the rocks and stones. Do this several times to force the sand down into the crevices and cavities. Now fill the form to within 5 inches of the top with more sand and tamp down solidly until well packed. This should bring you up to within 1 inch of the lower edge of the 6-inch wood frame for your concrete.

Before mixing the cement and filling the form to make the slab, here are a few facts about concrete: concrete is a mixture consisting of a water and cement paste which binds fine and coarse materials, called aggregate, into a rocklike mass. Unless all the aggregates are completely covered with water and cement paste, you will not get a strong concrete. The cement and aggregates are put in a mixing container and water is added as the mixture is turned over. Mixing is continued until the water and cement paste have completely soaked and covered all materials. Be sure to use both clean aggregates and clean water.

To test your mix, take a handful of the mixture, mold it into a ball; if it holds the shape without running or crumpling, you have a good consistency. Crystallization of the cement should start within 45 minutes. Try to make use of your mixture before this time elapses.

Measure and stake out an area 48 inches square. Dig a hole 24 inches deep and fill the first 8 inches with large rocks. The next 9 inches are filled with smaller stones or coarse gravel and then wet down.

Now put some dirt and rock around the outside of the form to strengthen it and to absorb any seepage, and fill the form to within 3 inches of the top. Onto this lay a 4' x 4' piece of galvanized fence wire, for reinforcement, as flat as possible. Then fill to the top of the form. It is best not to eliminate this step, since such reinforcing will double the strength of the slab. Now smooth the slab with a piece of scrap lumber. After "floating" (about 10 to 15 minutes) level with a long 2 x 4, using the smoothest, straightest edge. Be certain this level is longer than the width of your form. Level with a back-and-forth, side-to-side motion. A few hours after the concrete has set, sweep the top of the slab to remove any glaze left from the leveling process.

Cover the slab with wet burlap sacks during the curing period—about a week. Keep bags damp all the time for the best curing and strongest slab. This dampness aids uniform drying. Complete curing takes about 28 days. For the builder this amounts to no fire in the new fireplace for at least a month, and it should be kept dampened for about three weeks. The last week allows slow drying out of the whole structure. A week is sufficient before beginning the stone structure, however.

In buying mortar for the above-ground construction, ask your building supplier to give you a mortar mix designed especially for this type of construction. This contains a lime additive that is recommended for all types of above-ground binding. Use this mortar for the top of your first course of rock, on up. On the bottom, next to the slab, mix your mortar using the same cement as used on the base slab.

To start the base, keeping the form intact if working on the slab before a week has passed, lay a strip of mortar about 15" wide and 1½" thick along the left side of the slab. Be sure the slab has been wet down first and sprinkled lightly with dry cement powder. Then lay a strip of chicken wire, about 4' square, over the newly laid mortar. Pin down the loose end with a rock and lay the first corner stone on top of the chicken wire and mortar bed; work down into the mortar. Lay ½ inch of mortar over the exposed wire around the base of the corner stone and trowel mortar up against the stone, filling all spaces to prevent water seepage, which, when frozen, would crack the structure. Wash the next rock and place it up against the first. Fill in again with mortar and continue to lay stones, maintaining straight line construction.

Once the left wall is finished, begin the right-hand wall in the same manner. Keep about 1 inch in from the edge of the slab. As each wall reaches a height of 19 inches, level it with mortar 1½ inches thick.

The chicken wire covering the base slab will serve to tie the opposite walls together, since cement will be laid over the slab between the two walls. Wet slab before covering with cement and sprinkle with cement powder dampened by a mist from the garden hose. Float cement smooth,

being sure it is snug against the bases of the two walls. When set up, brush lightly to remove the glaze. Allow a minimum of two days, keeping the new work damp with bags or damp straw, for the structure to become firm and strong. During the drying time, build a strong, durable wooden platform to fit between the walls and come up level with the tops of the walls. This must be strong enough to sustain the weight of the mortar and bricks that will form the crossover between and on top of the walls. It will be removed at the completion of the job, of course.

Lay a strip of mortar across the leading edge of the platform, once in place, and imbed the center section of a ten-foot chain in the mortar. This will reinforce the arch and, once again, help to tie the whole fireplace together. Cover the chain with mortar and lay small stones across the top of the arch, on top of the chain. Mortar is then laid over the top and in between the stones, as shown in the photos, to form the leading edge of the fireplace.

The wooden platform should be about 25" deep. Sufficient mortar is mixed to fill in between the two fireplace walls across the top of the platform. First lay newspaper across the top of the wood platform. This is to prevent the mortar from adhering to the wood. Mist spray the leading edge and the tops of the two walls. Sprinkle lightly with cement powder and spray again, being sure to dampen the powder without wetting it so it runs. Immediately fill the tops

After adding 2 inches of sand, pour 3 inches of concrete, lay fence wire, and add last 3 inches.

After floating with a small board, use a smooth 2x4, 4½ feet long to do the final leveling step.

When slab has cured for one week, lay chicken wire over slab and use mortar to bind the first course.

Build wall up 19 inches high, lay 1½ inches of mortar on top. Level and float, then begin right-hand wall.

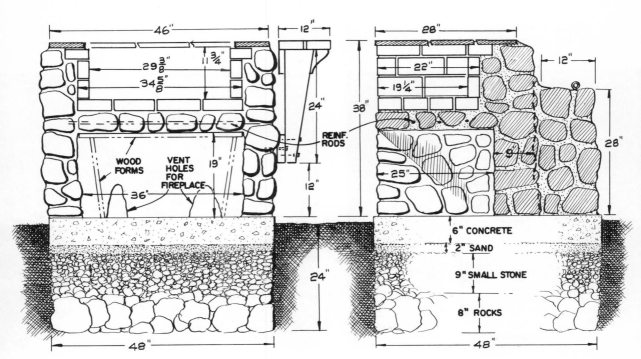

46"

12"

28"

12"

29 3/8"

11 3/4"

34 5/8"

22"

19 1/4"

24"

38"

REINF. RODS

WOOD FORMS

VENT HOLES FOR FIREPLACE

19"

9"

28"

25"

36"

6" CONCRETE

2" SAND

9" SMALL STONE

8" ROCKS

24"

48"

48"

Embed the center section of a 10-foot chain across the front of the fireplace in 1½ inches of mortar. This chain will reinforce and bind the structure together.

of side walls, the leading edge stones and the platform with mortar. Lay 22-inch high, 5-foot long length of border fencing (about 16 gauge, 5-inch mesh, galvanized) to extend beyond the edges of the walls. Push fencing down into the mortar until it tends to stay embedded. Add about 1½ inches more mortar on top of this. Wait about five minutes and float it level. In another 10 minutes float again with a flat board and check the levelness of the whole top. It is important that the whole top be perfectly level.

Place a rock at the right side, wedged into the wire, and on the left as well, to help keep the fencing pulled down into the mortar. Rocks can be removed in about two days when mortar has set. A straight, flat board is temporarily, but very firmly, set on edge across the back of the structure to serve as a guide for firebrick top surface and rear alignment.

Before laying, wash each brick. Firebrick is used exclusively for this part of the operation. First course consists of five bricks laid as shown, about 1½ inches back from the front edge of the fireplace. The first course goes all the way across the structure to within 1 inch of the left and right outside edges of fireplace walls. As each brick is laid in the mortar, put pressure on it and wiggle it a little to create a suction between the brick and the mortar. This also causes the cement-water paste to work up into the pores of the brick and do a better bonding job. Take care to

set the bricks firmly, in a straight line, and level all the way across. Leave about ⅛ inch to ¼ inch all around each brick for mortar. Work mortar down between bricks to a depth of about 1 inch from the top.

Start the second course about 2 inches in from the right end and use four firebricks. Start a third course about 2 inches in from right end of second course and use four bricks. Start fourth course in line with the first course and use four bricks. The fifth course starts 2 inches in from the right end of the fourth course and uses four bricks. This is the floor of your firebox. If there is any pitch at all, a very slight pitch to the front is permissible to aid drainage. Too much will cause the need of extra shimming when the firebox is put in place. *Note:* After regular mortar is forced down between bricks to about 1 inch from the tops of the bricks, mix 50% fireclay with 50% cement powder with a bit of water and fill in the cracks completely. Level off.

A Majestic Masonry Char-Grill was used as the actual grill unit. This is a well-constructed, heavy-duty unit with vented pull-down front doors. Unit has a heavy metal firepan which can be easily lifted out and emptied of ashes. The crank arrangement permits a raising or lowering of the entire firepan. You can vary the intensity of your heat by moving your coals up closer to the grill or farther down from the grill surface. This is an extremely simple means of offering a wide range of heat control.

After laying firebrick as shown in above photo, work mortar down into the spaces between the bricks to 1 inch from top. Fill with fireclay and cement mixture for last inch.

Right-hand photo shows how a 5-foot piece of galvanized wire fencing is laid into mortar on top of the temporary wooden platform between the walls. This doubles strength of slab.

Self-tapping flat head screws were used to form a raised triangle to keep hot pans off the wood.

Lag bolts are tightened while level is used. If necessary, use wood shims to make corrections.

Rear of fireplace is for open wood burning and cooking that requires no special heat control.

In installing any kind of metal in a fireplace you must be sure to allow for metal parts expanding and contracting. The simplest way of allowing sufficient room for this is to cut pieces of corrugated cardboard to the size of the sides and back of the masonry unit you are going to install. Attached to the grill unit the cardboard will act as an adequate spacer, when the unit is placed on top of the firebrick base. Now the sides and back of the firebrick encasement can be installed. Note the drawings for the placement of these bricks. They lie on their sides, not as was done on the base. Mortar is applied to the outer edges of the bricks, leaving the side nearest the metal grill free for a later filling in of the mortar and fireclay mixture. The unit is left in while all construction goes on around it. The fireclay mixture is the last to go in, naturally, after the unit has been removed, for final touchup.

Before cementing up the sides, the overlap of wire fence is cut off with a hack saw as close to the side wall as possible. To show how the rear of the partly completed fireplace should look, this fireplace was finished up to a point where it would be possible to see all of the major steps of construction: *First*, the last course of fire brick will be laid on its side (3rd course up); the two courses laid on edge are shown. Note how firebrick makes a lining inside the outer fireplace wall. *Second*, the firebrick, after being mist sprayed and salted with a straight cement is stuccoed with mortar. More mortar is added as rocks are laid tightly against this section to form the firebrick lining all around. *Third*, the lower portion of the rear fireplace has been started. The center portion of this was started with very large, heavy rocks. This center portion may be joined to the bottom of the firebox area. Note the draft holes at left and right corners of rear fireplace. Rear lower area is built up and joined to the side walls of the fireplace. Also note how mortar was spread over the sides and back to help tie both sides of the structure together.

Excess wire fencing was hooked together and set into the mortar around the corner. This was covered with two inches of mortar all around the side. Then the left side was constructed on top of it.

The top is built up to a height of approximately 37 inches; width runs to 46 inches and depth is 28 inches. The top course of firebrick was laid a half inch back from the lower firebrick wall to allow for easy removal of the cover when the grill is in use. Properly dampened firebrick was then covered with a one-inch layer of mortar, and colorful flagstones were set in place. The spaces between the flagstones were cemented and the whole top was checked and leveled.

The last step involves going over the entire structure with a water and cement powder mixture called grout, filling in cracks, smoothing corners and generally bringing the appearance up to par. Then, after a sufficient drying time, brush the stone with a stiff brush, or use muriatic acid, to remove excess cement.

Before finishing off the rear of the fireplace, set 2 eye bolts in the mortar about 2 inches in from the inside edge of the rear wall. Coil a piece of coat hanger around the base of the bolt. Then the whole piece is put in with mortar, troweled smooth and allowed to set. This arrangement will hold a spit or a rod to hold a kettle.

The redwood table is made from 1¾-inch planking 5½ inches wide by 10 inches long. Vertical supports are 24 inches long.

Cut the base plate first from 2 x 6 stock eighteen inches long. Fasten it to the fireplace with 5-inch lag bolts through previously set lead slugs. Some shaping may be necessary to fit the stone contours. Fasten two 24-inch tapered supports to base plate after drilling ⅜-inch holes to accept 3-inch lag bolts. Shape 2 x 6 cleats with a jig saw and fasten them to vertical supports as shown in drawing. Now place table top planks, 25 inches long, onto the cleats and drill for lags. Glue should be used between all wood parts for greater strength and weatherproof durability. Cut top boards to shape and fasten them in place using a level and wood shims to keep even. Fasten down and add two self tapping screws to the top, forming a triangle with lags and allowing a ¼-inch clearance between the wood and the screw tops for possible hot metal pan placement.

Flagstones finish off the fireplace rear and the small shelf on the left side of the rear fireplace. Any leftover firebrick can be used on the floor of the rear fireplace also and the lower facings in the rear are cemented with a 50% fireclay and 50% cement mixture to protect the firewall.

The Char-Grill unit is intended for charcoal burning, giving the advantages of controlled heat. The rear fireplace is perfect for logs and less formalized back-yard cookery. The two make up all that is needed for outdoor cooking and entertaining, yet the cost is equivalent to that of just one fireplace. It all adds up to a true bargain for your outdoor pleasure and that of your family. ● —— *Emil E. Brodbeck.*

Most meals prepared in a kitchen can be cooked on this grill. Intensity of heat is varied by moving the coals closer to the grill. On other side is fireplace for logs and more usual type of outdoor cooking.

Large enough for four people seated comfortably, this lightweight, fold-away is the ideal summer companion for a charcoal grill and a pile of hamburgers. It can be tucked away into the trunk of a car, too.

Folding Picnic Table

An easy-to-make outdoor table for the suburban family, designed for the patio or small back yard, and as convenient to store away as a card table

FOR those whose tastes and desires run to the great outdoors but who are hampered by a small area which is anything but suitable for the large cumbersome standard picnic table, this folding one with its unique attached seats and drop leaf extensions goes a long way toward solving the problem. Made from durable pine or cedar and finished in the natural or colored paint this type of table can be moved about with little effort, and when completely folded up can readily be stored in an unused corner of the patio or back yard, or even in the garage.

Fully extended, the area of the top allows four people to sit comfortably and with no danger of getting one's elbow in the neighbor's salad; if unexpected guests drop in, a couple of chairs placed at either end enlarges the serviceability of the project. A unique method of supporting the table extensions is a feature of the table; when the extensions are locked, and held in place, there they stay and eliminate hazards of the soup or salad gracing some dress or trousers. Should the craftsman desire to make the project even more portable, the legs can be shortened and casters added.

Since most of the work is done on the leg assemblies of the table and seats, it is well to get this done first, and best results are obtained in this respect by first making a full-scale layout of the leg assemblies on a separate sheet of material such as Masonite or thin plywood. This will enable the craftsman, by using a protractor or T-bevel, to determine the correct angle of cutting for the individual legs for the table and seats.

After marking to the correct sizes given in the plans, cut one end of all twelve legs, and, by the use of a stop, cut them to the correct sizes desired. As noted in the plans, the top rails of both the table and seats are set in a dado and cut into the upper end of the legs. The cutting of these dadoes is the next step. When these dadoes and those for the bottom rails have been cut, the rails are then attached to the legs. This is where the full-sized layout comes in since it enables the craftsman to assemble the parts accurately and identically. The top rails are secured in positions with glue and two 1¼-inch RH No. 10 steel wood screws driven in from each of the two faces; the bottom rails in much the same

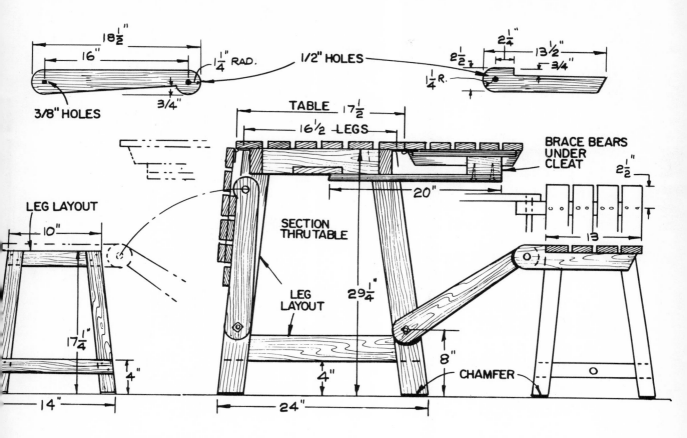

manner except that the screws are entered only through the front.

Side or spacer rails are attached at the top section of the table leg assemblies by means of two ⅜-inch dowels in either end. Between these two spacer rails and in the center between the two legs assemblies two rail supports are attached as shown in the plans, and, on the bottom face of these rails is attached the extension support. Use 2½-inch finishing nails and glue to attach these three items to one another.

Since a feature of the project is the spaced-slat table and seats, it is well to prepare all the slats necessary for these components at the same time. The plans show that, for the table proper, six slats are required—two of them being 3 inches wide and the remaining four being 2¼ inches in width; for each of the two leafs or extensions five slats 2¼ inches wide are needed, and for each of the two seats four slats 2¼ inches wide are used; making a total of:

13 slats ¾″ x 2¼″ x 40″
2 slats ¾″ x 3″ x 40″
10 slats ¾″ x 2¼″ x 35½″.

All of the 2¼-inch slats used in the top have three holes bored and countersunk: one in the center and one 2¾ inches from either end; the two 3-inch slats have, in addition to the two holes bored near the ends, three others spaced equidistant between these two and 1 inch from the inner face.

The slats for the extension have three holes bored and countersunk: one also in the center and one 5 inches from either end.

The slats for the seats have three holes bored and countersunk: one in the center and one 2½ inches from either end.

All the above holes are $\frac{5}{32}$ and are countersunk.

Remove the sharp edges from the top surfaces of the slats with a hand plane chamfering $\frac{1}{16}$ inch; sand the ends and chamfer them on the sander. Prepare also the reinforcing cleats under the extensions, and the seat brackets. In the latter item, bore the ¾-inch hole before attaching slats.

The attachment of the slats to the table framework, the seat brackets, and the extension cleats is a relatively simple operation and can be carried out with the required results by making constant use of the square and a spacing strip. In the case of the table frame, this latter has al-

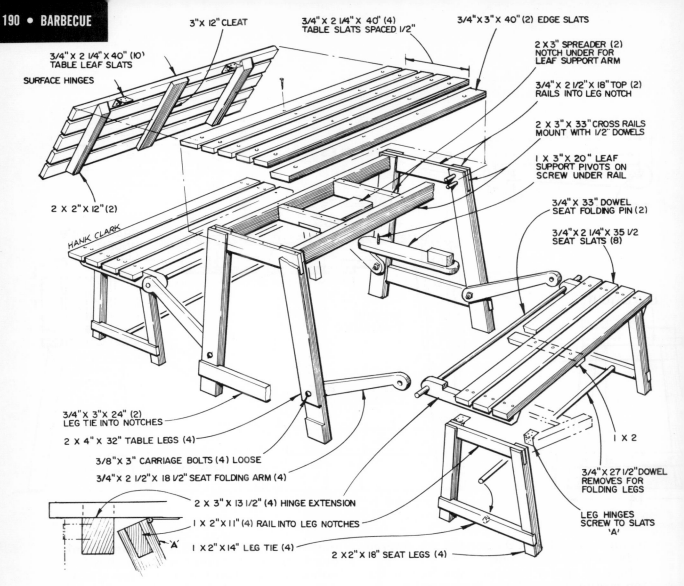

3"x 12" CLEAT

3/4" x 2 1/4" x 40" (4) TABLE SLATS SPACED 1/2"

3/4"x 3"x 40" (2) EDGE SLATS

2 X 3" SPREADER (2) NOTCH UNDER FOR LEAF SUPPORT ARM

3/4" X 2 1/2" X 18" TOP (2) RAILS INTO LEG NOTCH

3/4" X 2 1/4" X 40" (10) TABLE LEAF SLATS

SURFACE HINGES

2 X 3" X 33" CROSS RAILS MOUNT WITH 1/2" DOWELS

1 X 3" X 20" LEAF SUPPORT PIVOTS ON SCREW UNDER RAIL

3/4" X 33" DOWEL SEAT FOLDING PIN (2)

2 X 2" X 12" (2)

3/4" X 2 1/4" X 35 1/2 SEAT SLATS (8)

HANK CLARK

3/4" X 3" X 24" (2) LEG TIE INTO NOTCHES

2 X 4" X 32" TABLE LEGS (4)

3/8" X 3" CARRIAGE BOLTS (4) LOOSE

3/4" X 2 1/2" X 18 1/2" SEAT FOLDING ARM (4)

2 X 3" X 13 1/2" (4) HINGE EXTENSION

1 X 2" X 11" (4) RAIL INTO LEG NOTCHES

'A'

1 X 2" X 14" LEG TIE (4)

2 X 2" X 18" SEAT LEGS (4)

1 X 2

3/4" X 27 1/2" DOWEL REMOVES FOR FOLDING LEGS

LEG HINGES SCREW TO SLATS 'A'

The legs fold toward the center of the bench, leaving the bench unit free to swing in easily.

The side leaf drops down over the folded seat to hold it securely. Other side works the same.

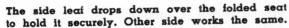

MATERIALS NEEDED

PINE OR CEDAR

2 pieces 1½'' x 3½'' x 32'' (Table Legs)
2 pieces ¾'' x 2¼'' x 18'' (Top Rails)
4 pieces ¾'' x 2½'' x 24'' (Bottom Rails)
2 pieces 1½'' x 2¼'' x 33'' (Cross Rails)
2 pieces 1½'' x 2¼'' x 12½''
  (Rail Spreaders)
2 pieces ¾'' x 3'' x 40'' (Top Slats)
4 pieces ¾'' x 2¼'' x 40'' (Top Slats)
4 pieces 1½'' x 1½'' x 18'' (Seat Legs)
4 pieces ¾'' x 1¾'' x 11'' (Top Rails)
4 pieces ¾'' x 1¾'' x 14'' (Bottom Rails)
2 pieces ¾'' x 1¾'' x 9''
  (Cleats under Slats)
4 pieces 1½'' x 2½'' x 13½''
  (Hinge Extensions)
2 pieces ¾'' x 2½'' x 12''
  (Center Leaf Cleat)
8 pieces ¾'' x 2¼'' x 35½'' (Seat Slats)
4 pieces 1½'' x 1¾'' x 12''
  (Outer Leaf Cleat)
10 pieces ¾'' x 2¼'' x 40'' (Leaf Slats)
4 pieces ¾'' as per plans (Seat Arms)
2 pieces ¾'' x 2½'' x 19½''
  (Leaf Support)

OTHER MATERIALS

2, ¾'' x 33¼'' Dowels
2, ¾'' x 27½'' Dowels
6 pr. 1½'' x 1½'' Surface Hinges
4, ⅜'' x 3'' Carriage Bolts, Nuts,
  Flat Washers
50, 1½'' #10 FH Steel Screws
30, 1¼'' #10 FH Steel Screws

It's easy to build and difficult to break, all of which makes it a necessary item for yardbirds.

ready been squared up when the side rails were attached to the leg assemblies. The one point to remember is the spacing.

The plans indicate that the first slat has an overhang of 2 inches; when this slat has been attached and the overhang checked, it is a simple matter to proceed with the remainder. Similar measurements are given in relation to the seats and extensions.

The plans indicate the manner in which the extension support is attached to the underside of the side rails. Use a 2½-inch No. 10 RH steel screw for this, inserting between the extension support and the edge of the rail a ¼-inch steel flat washer.

For storage, provision is made for the leg assemblies of the seats to fold up under the seats, and this is done by the attachment, to each of the leg assemblies, of a pair of hinges. When in use, and to prevent the leg assemblies from folding in, a length of ¾-inch dowel fits snugly into a hole bored on the inside of the bottom rail of each leg assembly.

In order to make a snug fit and so prevent sloppiness, the ¾-inch dowel at the front of each seat, which passes through the seat bracket, is glued and bradded in place; the end of this dowel protruding ⅝ inch past the outer surface of the bracket.

The extensions or leaves are attached to the outer slats of the table by means of three surface hinges applied underneath, and the extension held in a horizontal position by swinging the support on its swivel screw and bringing the projection directly under the center cleat.

Attachment of the seats to the table legs is done by means of two outer members for each seat—called the seat folding extensions. As the plans indicate, these have a ⅜-inch hole bored in one end and a ¾-inch hole, bored to a depth of ⅝ inch in the other end, and bored in such a manner as to make these members in pairs. Two ⅜ x 3-inch carriage bolts with flat washers between the two members, and flat and lock washers under the nuts, hold these members to the legs. At the other end, projecting ¾-inch dowel is inserted in the ¾-inch hole bored for that purpose, and prevented from slipping off by insertion of a 1¼-inch RH screw.

Folding of the unit begins with the seats. Remove ¾-inch dowel spacer, and fold in and under the two leg assemblies. Lift up the front face of the seat and lodge it against the leg. Hold the extension up a little, swing the support back out of the way and against the side rails, and allow the extension to assume a position vertical to the top. •——*by C. L. Widdicombe*

Improvised Barbecues

Wheelbarrows, oil drums and kettles are easily converted into grills for outdoor cooking

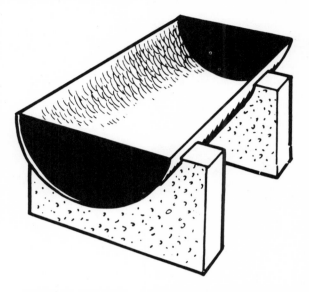

SMART, SIMPLE, functional, this home-made portable grill is merely a piece of sheet metal and three lengths of half-inch steel pipe. Cut "piece of pie" out of circle, rivet joint, weld or rivet to legs.

A BIG OIL DRUM, split lengthwise and mounted on concrete piers makes a good grill with large cooking area. Fill bottom of cavity with sand to raise fire and to prevent bottom from burning out.

HUGE KETTLE once used for boiling maple syrup is suspended from a post-and-arm of 4x4. Mount post firmly in concrete. Pave area around the kettle. Fill part way with earth. Cooks from any side.

A LARGE-SIZE BELL TILE is a ready-made outdoor grill. Mount it in a circular slab of concrete so it won't tip. Fill it with sand or earth so fire will be about 8 inches down. Use charcoal.